19-22
26-35
147-160

Praise for *The 1960s*

"Brian Ward has crafted a cool, clever, and incisive Sixties reader. Expertly introduced, the documents range from the Monkees' 'Pleasant Valley Sunday' to Ronald Reagan's career-making 1964 speech on behalf of Barry Goldwater. Pedagogically sophisticated and thought-provoking, this reader gives instructors an invaluable tool as it gives students a wide-ranging tour of Sixties politics and culture."

> David Farber, Temple University, author of *The Age of Great Dreams: America in the 1960s* and *Taken Hostage: The Iran Hostage Crisis and America's First Encounter with Radical Islam*

"With his thoughtful introduction and excellent selection of documents, Brian Ward has done an outstanding job of bringing to life the complexities and contradictions of the era."

> Kevin M. Kruse, Princeton University, author of *White Flight: Atlanta and the Making of Modern Conservatism* and coeditor (with Thomas Sugrue) of *The New Suburban History*

"In this collection of documents, Brian Ward recaptures much of the variety, vitality, and energy of the 1960s. Many of the documents Ward selects are iconic: Eisenhower's 'Farewell Address,' King's 'I Have a Dream,' and Rachel Carson from *Silent Spring*. Others are more surprising though equally telling, ranging from *Billboard*'s record charts to Country Joe's 'I Feel Like I'm Fixin'-to-Die Rag,' and the Redstockings 'Manifesto.' Taken together they bring back the sometimes raucous, mostly contentious, but never dull era we call the '60s. Ward's fine and incisive introduction puts the discordant parts into a coherent context."

> Mark Lytle, Bard College, author of *America's Uncivil Wars: The Sixties Era from Elvis to the Fall of Richard Nixon* and *The Gentle Subversive: Rachel Carson, Silent Spring, and the Rise of the Environmental Movement*

"This brilliant collage of political and cultural documents brings the 1960s back to life as presidents, activists, musicians, and social critics from the left and right offer competing visions of national purpose and American identity. An extraordinary teaching resource."

> Matthew .... ;an, author of *The Sile* .... *the* .... *uth*

Uncovering the Past: Documentary Readers in American History
Series Editors: Steven Lawson and Nancy Hewitt

The books in this series introduce students in American history courses to two important dimensions of historical analysis. They enable students to engage actively in historical interpretation, and they further students' understanding of the interplay between social and political forces in historical developments.

Consisting of primary sources and an introductory essay, these readers are aimed at the major courses in the American history curriculum, as outlined further below. Each book in the series will be approximately 225–50 pages, including a 25–30 page introduction addressing key issues and questions about the subject under consideration, a discussion of sources and methodology, and a bibliography of suggested secondary readings.

Published

Paul G. E. Clemens
The Colonial Era: A Documentary Reader

Sean Patrick Adams
The Early American Republic: A Documentary Reader

Stanley Harrold
The Civil War and Reconstruction: A Documentary Reader

Steven Mintz
African American Voices: A Documentary Reader, 1619–1877

Robert P. Ingalls and David K. Johnson
The United States Since 1945: A Documentary Reader

Camilla Townsend
American Indian History: A Documentary Reader

Steven Mintz
Mexican American Voices: A Documentary Reader

Brian Ward
The 1960s: A Documentary Reader

Nancy Rosenbloom
Women in Modern America, 1880–Present: A Documentary Reader

In preparation

Jeremi Suri
American Foreign Relations Since 1898: A Documentary Reader

The 1960s

A Documentary Reader

Edited by
Brian Ward

WILEY-BLACKWELL

A John Wiley & Sons, Ltd., Publication

This edition first published 2010
© 2010 Blackwell Publishing Ltd except for editorial material and organization © 2010 Brian Ward

Blackwell Publishing was acquired by John Wiley & Sons in February 2007. Blackwell's publishing program has been merged with Wiley's global Scientific, Technical, and Medical business to form Wiley-Blackwell.

Registered Office
John Wiley & Sons Ltd, The Atrium, Southern Gate, Chichester, West Sussex, PO19 8SQ, United Kingdom

Editorial Offices
350 Main Street, Malden, MA 02148-5020, USA
9600 Garsington Road, Oxford, OX4 2DQ, UK
The Atrium, Southern Gate, Chichester, West Sussex, PO19 8SQ, UK

For details of our global editorial offices, for customer services, and for information about how to apply for permission to reuse the copyright material in this book please see our website at www.wiley.com/wiley-blackwell.

The right of Brian Ward to be identified as the author of the editorial material in this work has been asserted in accordance with the Copyright, Designs and Patents Act 1988.

Wiley also publishes its books in a variety of electronic formats. Some content that appears in print may not be available in electronic books.

Designations used by companies to distinguish their products are often claimed as trademarks. All brand names and product names used in this book are trade names, service marks, trademarks or registered trademarks of their respective owners. The publisher is not associated with any product or vendor mentioned in this book. This publication is designed to provide accurate and authoritative information in regard to the subject matter covered. It is sold on the understanding that the publisher is not engaged in rendering professional services. If professional advice or other expert assistance is required, the services of a competent professional should be sought.

Library of Congress Cataloging-in-Publication Data
The 1960s : a documentary reader / [compiled by] Brian Ward.
    p. cm. — (Uncovering the past)
  Includes bibliographical references and index.
  ISBN 978-1-4051-6329-3 (hardcover : alk. paper) – ISBN 978-1-4051-6330-9 (pbk. : alk. paper)
  1. United States–History–1961-1969–Sources. 2. United States–Politics and government–1961-1963–Sources. 3. United States–Politics and government–1963-1969–Sources. 4. United States–Social conditions–1960-1980–Sources. I. Ward, Brian, 1961-
  E838.3.A155 2010
  973.92–dc22
                                                      2009020189

A catalogue record for this book is available from the British Library

Set in 10/12.5pt Sabon by SPi Publisher Services, Pondicherry, India
Printed in the USA by Sheridan Books, Inc.

02 2014

Contents

Series Editors' Preface

Primary sources have become an essential component in the teaching of history to undergraduates. They engage students in the process of historical interpretation and analysis and help them understand that facts do not speak for themselves. Rather, students see how historians construct narratives that recreate the past. Most students assume that the pursuit of knowledge is a solitary endeavor; yet historians constantly interact with their peers, building upon previous research and arguing among themselves over the interpretation of documents and their larger meaning. The documentary readers in this series highlight the value of this collaborative creative process and encourage students to participate in it.

Each book in the series introduces students in American history courses to two important dimensions of historical analysis. They enable students to engage actively in historical interpretation, and they further students' understanding of the interplay among social, cultural, economic, and political forces in historical developments. In pursuit of these goals, the documents in each text embrace a broad range of sources, including such items as illustrations of material artifacts, letters and diaries, sermons, maps, photographs, song lyrics, selections from fiction and memoirs, legal statutes, court decisions, presidential orders, speeches, and political cartoons.

Each volume in the series is edited by a specialist in the field who is concerned with undergraduate teaching. The goal is not to offer a comprehensive selection of material but to provide items that reflect major themes and debates; that illustrate significant social, cultural, political, and economic dimensions of an era or subject; and that inform, intrigue and inspire undergraduate students. The editor of each volume has written an introduction that discusses the central questions that have occupied historians in this field and the ways historians have used primary sources to answer them. In addition, each introductory essay contains an explanation of the kinds of materials available to investigate a particular subject, the methods by which scholars analyze them, and the considerations that go into interpreting them. Each source selection is introduced by a short head note that gives students the necessary information and a context for understanding the document. Also, each section of the volume includes questions to guide student reading and stimulate classroom discussion.

Brian Ward's *The 1960s* is a documentary history that looks at this transformative period in US history from a fresh perspective. In an exciting departure, Ward refashions the decade of the 1960 into the "long sixties," an era that begins in the mid-1950s and extends into the early 1970s. He does this convincingly by focusing on the major themes that distinguish this era. These readings document economic abundance alongside the growing awareness of poverty, the heightening of the Cold War and the impact of Vietnam, movements for racial, gender, and sexual equality, challenges to mainstream culture, and breakthroughs in science and technology. While this book offers evidence of the triumph of political liberalism, at the same time it is especially valuable in recognizing the development of political conservatism, the New Right, which would come to dominate American politics for the next forty years. Divided into twelve chapters, this volume offers a wide range of documents including presidential speeches, court decisions, excerpts from path-breaking books, advertisements, song lyrics, film dialogue, cartoons, and proclamations and manifestos from protest groups, all of which allow readers to taste the flavor of the period as well as digest its substance. Ward concludes the book with a selection of documents reflecting on the important legacies of the long 1960s. *The 1960s* reshapes our view of this era and provides students with the sources to understand it in all of its complexities. In addition, the book provides a valuable list of sources to guide students in pursuing their own research projects.

Steven F. Lawson and Nancy A. Hewitt, Series Editors

Acknowledgments

Compiling, editing, and writing about the primary sources in this book has been an exacting but illuminating challenge. I have learned a lot from the experience and extend grateful thanks to Steven Lawson and Nancy Hewitt for inviting me to contribute to their fine series; to Peter Coveney at Wiley-Blackwell for agreeing that this was a good idea; and to his colleagues Deirdre Ilkson and Galen Smith for being so attentive and helpful throughout the production process. The anonymous reviewers' reports on the proposal and the draft manuscript, along with judicious comments from Steven and Nancy, were extremely valuable in helping to establish the scope of the book and identifying the kinds of material that would be most useful to students and teachers alike. Of course, I take full responsibility for the choice of texts and for the interpretative material contained in a book which, as a consequence, remains conspicuously devoid of any Jackson Browne lyrics. Marple Public Library, Mellors coffee bar, and the Stock Dove pub in Romiley provided congenial settings for much of my research and writing – although thanks to the patience, love, and support of Jenny and Katie Ward, home wasn't too shabby a place to work either! The book is dedicated to Katie, who had the last of a long succession of third birthday parties on the day it was completed: may she grow up to live in a world where tie-dying is never again considered cool, but where the best hopes and dreams of the 1960s finally come to pass.

Brian Ward, August 2008

Introduction

Few decades in American history have achieved the iconic status of the 1960s. Images and storylines from the decade pervade American popular culture and social memory while the legacies of the decade, real and imagined, continue to shape domestic political debates and foreign policy calculations.

Yet widespread agreement that the 1960s constitute a pivotal period in modern US history does not mean that there has been a similar consensus among historians about how best to characterize the decade, measure its main accomplishments and failures, or even define its relationship to previous eras and subsequent developments in the US and beyond. Perhaps this is not surprising. There is something rather arbitrary about assigning special characteristics to any decade – which is, after all, merely a ten-year unit of time commencing with a year that happens to end in zero. To analyze the 1960s as some kind of discrete, unified entity risks hauling it out of the flow of history, simplifying its complexities and leaving it isolated without traceable lineage or legacy.

As the selection of texts and images in this Reader demonstrate, different kinds of evidence, drawn from different kinds of sources and interpreted from different ideological and methodological perspectives, can yield a dizzying array of competing visions of the 1960s. Consequently it has become commonplace, but no less true for that, for historians to stress that the 1960s was a time of many cross-currents, paradoxes, and contradictions. It was an era when the peace-and-love ethos of Haight-Ashbury, the hippies, and Woodstock co-existed with the murderous mayhem of the Manson Family slayings, Vietnam, political assassinations, urban riots, Hell's Angels, and Altamont; when unparalleled economic growth, prosperity, and rampant consumerism contrasted with abject poverty and serious critiques of the social, ethical, and psychological costs of free enterprise capitalism; when tremendous progress in science and technology took place alongside reckless disregard for the environment; when genuine advances in civil and political rights for marginalized groups such as African Americans, women, and homosexuals took place despite fierce opposition from, not thanks to the support of, many Americans; when a grassroots commitment to traditional values clustered around Christianity, patriotism, the family, home, hard work, sobriety, and law and order gained enormous traction notwithstanding the headlines grabbed by the counterculture, the New Left, and various social movements that appeared to question many of those institutions and values; and when the apparent ascendancy of a post-New Deal liberal consensus committed to the idea that the federal government should take a leading role in trying to improve the lives of all American citizens masked a growing disaffection with "big government" and a rejection of the kind of ambitious social reforms associated with President Lyndon Johnson's Great Society.

Given these tensions and ambiguities it is no coincidence that histories and memoirs of the 1960s frequently bear titles evoking the turbulent, fraught nature of the decade or suggesting the collapse of the kind of social and political consensus that seemed to characterize much of American life during the decade or so after World War II. John Blum's *Years of Discord* (1991), David Chalmers's *And the Crooked Places Made Straight* (1991), Peter Collier and David Horowitz's, *Destructive Generation: Second Thoughts about the Sixties* (2nd edn, 2002); Alice Echols's, *Shaky Ground* (2002); Todd Gitlin's *The Sixties: Years of Hope, Days of Rage* (1993); Maurice Isserman and Michael Kazin, *America Divided: The Civil War of the 1960s* (3rd edn, 2006), and Mark Lytle's *America's Uncivil Wars* (2006) all, to a greater or lesser extent, emphasize conflict and struggle, rupture, dislocation, and instability as key aspects of a decade that historian Allan Matusow has suggested saw the "unraveling of America." Such titles also hint at the battle among historians, politicians, cultural commentators, religious leaders, and various kinds of creative artists for control over the meaning of a decade that continues to resist easy generalizations. Indeed, Gerald DeGroot's *The Sixties Unplugged* (2008), a transnational study of the 1960s that is generally skeptical about its positive accomplishments, is aptly subtitled *A Kaleidoscopic History of a Disorderly Decade*.

The kaleidoscope is a good image to keep in mind when thinking about the primary sources in this Reader. The complex patterns visible inside a kaleidoscope are made up from hundreds of shards of colored glass reflected in a movable mirror; any given pattern remains fixed in place only until the kaleidoscope is shaken or the mirror turned, whereupon a new pattern emerges. The 1960s are a bit like that: the slightest shift in the perspective of the observer or a change in the shards of evidence under scrutiny can radically alter the appearance of the decade, generating very different assessments of its most significant features, lessons, and legacies. Compare, for example, the diagnosis of America's national ills and prescription for recovery offered by the Young Americans for Freedom (YAF) in their Sharon Statement of 1960 with those presented by the Students for a Democratic Society (SDS) in their Port Huron Statement a couple of years later. Or compare Dan Quayle's "Murphy Brown" speech, in which George H.W. Bush's vice-president blamed the moral laxity and legislative failures of the 1960s for many of the social problems of the 1990s, with Stephen Holden's review of two feature films set in a clichéd Hollywood version of the 1960s, in which Holden insists that the earnest pursuit of social justice and personal liberation were not frivolous or narcissistic distractions, but among the most inspirational bequests of the 1960s to subsequent generations.

While the primary materials contained in this Reader cannot possibly cover every aspect of the 1960s that merit serious attention, cumulatively they do help to explain why the decade continues to spawn such divergent readings and heated debate. Part of the problem historians face here is simply the glut of evidence. Historians of the 1960s are often overwhelmed by the sheer surfeit of data, much of it contradictory but almost all of it – even from the most biased, inaccurate, or discredited sources – potentially useful in understanding the era. And not only is this evidence voluminous, it is also extremely varied in form as well as content, requiring any historian hoping to understand the decade as a whole to embrace a wide range of analytical approaches. Of course, many historians specialize in certain aspects of the decade, focusing on topics that we might think of primarily as either political, or social, or cultural history, or else focusing on particular groups, locales, or issues. These narrower specialist works, some of which are listed in the guide to Further Reading at the end of the book, are vital in constructing a more nuanced understanding of the decade as a whole, serving as the building blocks for more general overviews.

Still, all historians sifting through the mountains of oral, aural, visual, and documentary evidence from the 1960s need to apply a guarded variant on Marshall McLuhan's famous dictum that "the medium is the message" by paying close attention to the *kinds* of sources they have at their disposal, as well as to their literal content. In a series of influential 1960s books including *The Gutenberg Galaxy* (1962) and *Understanding Media* (1964), media and communications scholar McLuhan argued that the means by which any society and its sub-groups communicate (by gesture, orally, through the printed word, electronically) was inextricably linked to the psychological imperatives and social structures of those groups. Therefore, McLuhan concluded, it is as important to study the nature of those media as the substance of the messages they carry in order to comprehend the core characteristics of any society. To appreciate the full historical significances of the texts and images in this Reader, it is not enough to consider just the content, the "factual" details or explicit analysis contained in each of the selections; it also requires attention to the venues where those selections initially appeared, the circumstances of their production, the audiences for which they were intended, and the kinds of media used to disseminate them. To give but one example, the development of the counterculture was closely related to the ease with which fliers, posters, and newsletters could be mimeographed quickly and cheaply, as well as to the presence of other media such as radio, particularly FM radio, and the ubiquitous single and long-playing records that provided its soundtrack.

While hardly exhausting the different kinds of evidence generated during the 1960s, the Reader samples widely in terms of both form and content. Some of the extracts may be quite familiar, forming part of an accepted canon of key 1960s documents the construction of which is itself an interesting historical phenomenon. Other selections are more obscure. Some of the shorter texts appear in their entirety; others have been edited for relevance, clarity, and brevity. Individually, each of the selections provides a valuable perspective on one or more aspect of the decade; collectively they constitute a mosaic of primary sources covering most of the era's dominant issues. There is material from the "high politics" of electoral campaigns and official government sources, including presidential papers, congressional acts, reports, and hearings, and Supreme Court rulings from what was a period of vigorous judicial activism. In an era haunted by the specter of conspiracies and the realities of covert government operations at home and abroad, there are also classified memos and secretly recorded conversations that shed new light on official policy decisions and public pronouncements. From beyond the world of traditional politics, there are manifestos, position statements, fiery polemics, and carefully argued critiques from some of the individuals and organizations at the heart of the decade's extraordinarily vibrant grassroots political, cultural, and social activity. There is also reportage from mainstream news outlets like *Time* and the *Los Angeles Times*, as well as from alternative sources of news and opinion like *Ramparts* and *The Village Voice*, since both kinds of media offer insights into the zeitgeist of the era and the preoccupations of different constituencies within American society. So, too, do the advertisements that simultaneously reflected the assumptions and shaped the aspirations of their target demographics in an era of rampant consumerism.

The final major mode of evidence in the Reader is participant-observer testimony. Whether expressed in private correspondence, public speeches, various kinds of interviews or memoirs, or channeled into the visual arts, music, or creative writing, the personal reflections of those who actually participated in the making of the 1960s offer unique, if rarely unproblematic, views of the era's key themes and events; they provide access to emotional and psychological dimensions of the era that other kinds of primary sources simply do not reveal. Ultimately, of course, it is only by reviewing these different kinds of evidence together, by evaluating the significance of the form and the content of each source in the context of other available evidence, that historians can really begin to get to grips with the intricacies of such a volatile decade.

While the sheer volume and diversity of evidence seems to mock any attempt to impose narrative or interpretive coherence on the 1960s, historians have gamely tried to do just that. Most would at least concede that the most significant events and themes of the decade – like most of the selections in this Reader – can be interpreted within the context of one or more of the following five frameworks: first, the Cold War and America's sense of a global responsibility to protect democracy and US economic interests abroad, as well as freedom from communist subversion at home; second, a series of ongoing and intersecting struggles to define the boundaries of US citizenship and the nature of its rights and responsibilities; third, the impressive and sustained, if by no means even, economic growth which brought with it both the triumph of consumerism and an unusually expansive brand of social and economic liberalism that in turn stimulated an intense conservative backlash; fourth, the demographics of the "baby boom" era that saw a dramatic rise in the absolute and proportionate numbers of young people in the country; and fifth, dramatic technological and scientific advances that affected every area of American life, public and private, at work and at play.

In their quest to impose some kind of interpretative order on the 1960s, historians have often mixed attention to these broad themes with their traditional interest in matters of chronology and periodization. While the answer may seem self-evident, they have also devoted a lot of attention to the question of when "the 1960s" actually started and ended. Because history never pauses to check the date on the calendar, most have long since given up trying to squeeze the decade into a rigid, ten-year framework. Instead, they now tend to write of "a long 1960s" that situates the decade in the broader sweep of post-World War II events. David Farber (ed.), *The Sixties: From Memory to History* (1994), Douglas Miller, *On Our Own* (1996), and Mark Lytle, *America's Uncivil Wars*, for example, offer more elastic chronologies that emphasize how many of the themes typically associated with the 1960s had roots and prequels in the 1950s, just as some of those themes were not played out fully until the mid-1970s or even later. Some of those storylines, such as the struggles for peace, racial justice, gender equality, the eradication of poverty in the world's richest nation, and a national commitment to a responsible environmental policy are still ongoing.

The chronological scope of this Reader, with selections drawn from the 1950s to the twenty-first century, acknowledges the analytical usefulness of the idea of a "long 1960s." Not only does it help us to identify continuities and connections with previous and later periods in American history, but it also promises to make us more sensitive to those things about the 1960s that really were distinctive. In a variation of a paradox at the heart of much historical enquiry, the texts and images collected in this Reader suggest a "long 1960s" marked by both continuity – much more continuity than many contemporaries and some of its earliest historians appreciated – and change, some of it very rapid, significant, and enduring, some of it rather more transitory and ephemeral.

Some historians, often following the recollections of participant-observers, have endorsed the idea of a succession of very different 1960s. Certainly, the kinds of judgments made about the decade often depend on which facet or phase of the 1960s is under review. And those distinctions often map onto a general sense that there was a "good" early 1960s typi-fied by optimism, peaceful protests to secure legitimate social, political, and economic opportunities for all US citizens, expanded protection for basic individual freedoms and collective rights, rising prosperity, and consensus politics, which sometime around 1966 or 1967 gave way to a "bad" 1960s of disillusionment, lawlessness, militant pursuit of un-deserved minority entitlements, moral disintegration, growing distrust of the federal government, and intense ideological factionalism in the political arena.

There are variants on this commonly accepted narrative progression in many scholarly accounts of the decade. For example, in his excellent *Decade of Nightmares: The End of the Sixties and the Making of Seventies America* (2006), Philip Jenkins argues that the modern conservative ascend-ancy in American politics and culture was secured during the period be-tween 1975 and 1986 by groups and individuals, interests and ideologies associated with the New Right that were very self-consciously opposed to the perceived failings and excesses of the 1960s. But which 1960s were those conservatives responding to and which 1960s is Jenkins writing about? For him and for them, the pertinent 1960s really began in November 1963 with the assassination of John Kennedy and ended with the fall of Richard Nixon in 1974.

Yet this Dallas-to-Watergate chronology excludes from the "real" 1960s the sit-ins and freedom rides that kick-started a genuinely mass movement for African-American civil rights in the South, as well as the March on Washington and Martin Luther King's "I Have a Dream" speech; Kennedy's election and embrace of the space race; Cold War flashpoints like the Bay of Pigs invasion and the Cuban Missile Crisis, as well as increased US involvement in Vietnam; the introduction of the oral contraceptive pill; important Supreme Court decisions relaxing obscenity laws and striking down state-mandated school prayer; the emergence of YAF and SDS as youthful standard bearers for the New Right and New Left respectively; and the publication of highly influential works of social criticism like Rachel Carson's *Silent Spring* (1962), Betty Friedan's *The Feminine Mystique* (1963), and Michael Harrington's *The Other America* (1962). It also ignores signature early 1960s creative works like Joseph Heller's *Catch-22* (1961), Ken Kesey's *One Flew Over the Cuckoo's Nest* (1962) and Thomas Pynchon's *V.* (1963), Stanley Kubrick's Cold War satire *Dr. Strangelove*, Andy Warhol's first solo pop-art exhibition, the emergence of the black-owned Motown Records as a major force in popular music, and Bob Dylan's first brace of albums. Jenkins is doubtless correct that it was the later "bad" 1960s that intensified the "conservative backlash" and ensured the political success of the New Right. Yet, as many of the texts in this Reader relating to the 1950s and early 1960s suggest, it seems more perverse than productive to isolate the latter part of the decade when so many of the themes, events, trends, organizations, personalities, and legal frameworks that shaped the entire period were established well before Kennedy's assassination.

The difficulties inherent in trying to sort out a persuasive chronological framework for the 1960s are also apparent in Mark Lytle's *America's Uncivil Wars* – perhaps the most judicious overview of the era yet written. Lytle offers a particularly elaborate scheme, sub-dividing the "long 1960s" into three distinct phases: an era of "consensus politics" running from 1954 until Kennedy's death; the years from 1964 to 1968 when he argues that most of the critical themes associated with the 1960s coalesced; and an era of "essentialist politics" extending from 1969 until Nixon's resignation in August 1974 and marked by the intensification of radical antiwar, environmental, and identitarian protest movements and the ruthless repression of such dissent by the federal government. Again, while it is tempting to think in such terms in an effort to impose narrative coherence on a surfeit of evidence there is something overly schematic about this kind of formulation, as Lytle himself appreciates. The very effort to parse the history of the decade – even the long decade – in this way risks privileging change over the continuity evident in many areas of American life across the different phases of the long 1960s. It tends to prioritize moments of dramatic rupture, of which there were several, to be sure, but in doing so can obscure slower processes of evolutionary change which were also at work. And it can undervalue the persistence of deep social, political, economic, and ideological structures that remained fundamentally unchanged by the upheavals of the 1960s.

Having lamented the difficulties faced by historians dealing with the 1960s, it would be foolish to hazard any kind of comprehensive overview of the decade in this Introduction. It may, however, be useful to offer observations on a number of historical and historiographical themes that help to contextualize the primary sources in the Reader.

It is striking that both Lytle and Jenkins agree that the assassination of President Kennedy marked a decisive watershed in the 1960s. They are hardly alone. Kennedy's murder was, according to novelist Don DeLillo in *Libra* (1988), the "seven seconds that broke the back of the American Century," a shocking blow to the nation's optimism about its historic destiny and unimpeachable virtue. Similarly, *American Graffiti*, film-maker George Lucas's nostalgic 1973 evocation of small-town teenaged life in the early 1960s, replete with an all-American, pre-Beatles rock and roll soundtrack and depictions of scampish rather than revolutionary defiance of authority, prefigures DeLillo's idea that the assassination represented a seismic shift in American history: it was the beginning of the end of the "good 1960s." "Where were you in '62?" asked the advertising for *American Graffiti*, suggesting – as did the film itself – that 1962 was the final year of innocence and promise before a whole generation was consumed, like Kennedy, by the corrupt and cynical world they hoped to redeem.

The mystique of Kennedy and "Camelot," as his White House circle was quickly dubbed, continues to exert a powerful influence on popular perceptions of the 1960s. While historians have been divided on how to assess a presidency that was cut short after just 1,000 days with relatively few tangible achievements to its name, Kennedy does seem to have personified and helped galvanize something of the youthful spirit of the age. More problematic, however, is the way in which many accounts have used the transition from the avuncular, golf-playing President Dwight D. Eisenhower to the youthful and flamboyant Kennedy as a simplistic metaphor for the contrast between the cultural vibrancy, bold social experimentation, and widespread popular engagement in the major political issues of the day associated with the 1960s and the stolid cultural, social, and political conservatism attributed to the 1950s. In such accounts, Eisenhower, with his impeccable military credentials and steadfast commitment to civic duty, fiscal responsibility, limited government, states rights, and traditional morality, represented a steady hand on the tiller of state, guiding it on a path determined largely by Cold War security concerns and the needs of big business. Kennedy by contrast, appeared to offer a daring challenge to Americans to join him in a collective effort to steer a revitalized nation towards an exciting New Frontier, whether at home, abroad or in outer space. "The torch has been passed to a new generation of Americans," Kennedy announced in his stirring Inaugural Address.

In a literal sense, Kennedy was absolutely right. By 1965, 41 percent of the population was under 20 years of age: a demographic shift that affected almost every aspect of the decade's history. Young people were everywhere: mobilizing against the draft or actually bearing the physical and emotional burden of fighting in Vietnam where the average age of combatants was 19; campaigning for civil rights; making and buying rock, folk, and soul music; experimenting with drugs and sex; tuning in and dropping out, but also getting educated in unprecedented numbers; spearheading new innovations in fashion, art, and culture; challenging conventional family and religious values; and exploring new avenues of spirituality. Even the conservative backlash against the perceived social and political excesses of the 1960s was in some regards an effort to halt attacks on adult authority by the young. Generational changes do not explain everything about the 1960s, of course, but baby-boomers were seldom too far from the centre of the decade's leading stories.

And yet, as close reading of some of the evidence in the Reader attests, the transition from the aged Ike to the youthful JFK, like that from the nominally conservative, sober, and ascetic 1950s to a liberal, hopped-up, and innovative 1960s, was neither as dramatic, nor as unequivocal as once believed. Eisenhower's 1961 Farewell Address, the epitome of corporate-sponsored, country club Republicanism, railed against the increasingly tight and unregulated connections between major US industries and the military establishment in America. Very similar sentiments would later appear in SDS's Port Huron Statement and become a cornerstone of New Left politics for much of the decade. By the mid-to-late 1960s, as America became ever more mired in Vietnam, peace campaigners, countercultural commentators, environmentalists, and social activists of all stripes echoed Ike's warnings about the damaging influence of the powerful military-industrial complex on US domestic politics and foreign policy.

There were many other examples of this kind of continuity from the 1950s to the 1960s in the White House. Although he could count the creation of the Peace Corps as one of his most enduring accomplishments, Kennedy was just as hawkish as Eisenhower when it came to countering perceived communist threats to US power and influence around the globe. This was amply demonstrated by his support for the disastrous 1961 Bay of Pigs invasion designed to liberate Cuba from the control of Fidel Castro's communist government. Moreover, first Kennedy then his successor Lyndon Johnson broadly accepted Eisenhower's "Domino Theory" regarding the dangers of a "state-by-state" spread of communism to justify increased US involvement in Southeast Asia. The broad assumptions and conduct of American foreign policy in the 1960s changed relatively little from the 1950s and were dominated by an emphasis on the need to "contain" the Soviet threat and a belief in the importance of maintaining a powerful nuclear deterrent to communist aggression. Fears about "the bomb" provided a grim, apocalyptic backdrop to the entire decade.

Kennedy was initially no more willing than Eisenhower to put the full power and prestige of his administration behind the African American campaign for basic civil and voting rights – a campaign which had itself gained momentum in the 1950s with Supreme Court decisions such as the 1954 *Brown* ruling that declared segregated schools unconstitutional, and the spread of mass black nonviolent protests such as the Montgomery Bus Boycott. In the end, it was not Kennedy but Lyndon Johnson, a son of the segregated South, who finally responded to the cumulative effect of years of protest and petition by African Americans and their allies and committed the full force of the federal government to comprehensive civil and voting rights legislation. The Civil Rights Act of 1964 and the Voting Rights Act of 1965 changed the course of America's racial and political history.

It was also Johnson whose vigorous executive leadership extended the "Imperial Presidency" and liberalism of his idol Franklin Delano Roosevelt to fashion the era's most important legislative achievements and preside over the apogee of national faith in the capacity of the federal government to cure the nation's most important social and economic ills. Yet, Johnson, the most towering political figure of his time, whose own contradictions encapsulated many of the perils and prospects of the 1960s, also condemned America to the expensive and bloody stalemate of the Vietnam War rather than, as his secretly recorded conversation with Georgia senator Richard Russell reveals, lose face or jeopardize his own political power. And, as conservative critics such as Ronald Reagan and members of YAF frequently pointed out, LBJ and his Democratic colleagues oversaw the expansion of a gargantuan, often unwieldy, intrusive, and profligate federal bureaucracy that many felt undermined traditional American values of self-reliance, individualism, private enterprise, competitiveness, and family stability by using taxpayers' hard-earned money to offer welfare "hand-outs" to the undeserving and indolent.

Johnson declined to run again for the presidency in 1968, his credibility undermined and his spirit broken by Vietnam: "that bitch of a war," he later admitted, "killed the lady I really loved – the Great Society." His successor, Republican Richard Nixon, claimed the White House by appealing to a "Silent Majority" who were disillusioned with Johnson's brand of liberalism and traumatized by what appeared to be an apocalyptic breakdown of traditional moral values, law and order, and respect for authority. Nixon's victory was a triumph for the rapidly emerging New Right – an amorphous yet potent coalition of evangelical Christians and secular conservatives. In particular, it reflected the effectiveness of the GOP's "southern strategy" which exploited the national Democratic Party's close identification with support for the rights of African Americans, women, and other disadvantaged groups to consolidate Republican influence among white voters in a region that was once solidly Democrat.

Race and the anxieties about the loss of white privileges, exploited so well on a national as well as a regional stage by politicians like Alabama's segregationist icon George Wallace, explained much of this shift of southern white voter allegiances to the GOP. But it did not explain it all. An economic boom in the Sunbelt South gathered pace during the 1960s, especially after the demise of legally sanctioned Jim Crow which had been expensive to maintain and a huge deterrent to outside investors. Fueled primarily by petro-chemicals, modernized agribusiness, new computer technologies, tourism, and lavish military expenditure, the boom brought new migrants and new wealth to what was once the nation's poorest region. As a result, some people simply felt that the Republican Party, with its mantra of lower taxes and a firm rhetorical – if seldom realized – commitment to reducing federal bureaucracy, expenditures, and intrusiveness in the day-to-day lives of regular citizens and local community affairs, now served their economic interests better than the Democratic Party. By the time Richard Nixon was re-elected in 1972, crushing liberal Democratic candidate George McGovern, much of the country seemed to think the same way.

And yet Nixon did not immediately seek to dismantle the major legislative accomplishments of Great Society liberalism. Critical "war on poverty" programs like Medicare, Medicaid, expanded social security, and Aid to Families with Dependent Children remained in place. Although Nixon oversaw the dismantling of the Office of Economic Opportunity in 1973, most of its functions continued through other federal agencies. Nixon actually extended government support for certain Affirmative Action policies that had their roots in the Kennedy and Johnson years. He created both the Occupational Safety and Health Administration and the Environmental Protection Agency and even proposed comprehensive welfare reform that would have guaranteed a minimum wage for American workers, only to have the measure defeated by a Democrat-dominated Senate.

It was not really until the "Reagan Revolution" of the 1980s that the core federal programs of the Great Society, along with many of the collective, class-action protections of group rights won during the 1960s and early 1970s, came under sustained attack. Ronald Reagan rode to the presidency with the support of the nation's evangelical Christians and libertarians, triumphantly declaring "Morning in America" after the long night of liberal excess and preaching a gospel of smaller government, individual and communal self-reliance, moral re-armament, and the kinds of old-fashioned family and faith-based values that conservatives felt the liberalism of the 1960s had threatened to destroy. It was a compelling ideological cocktail that he had been refining ever since he emerged as a significant national political presence with his speech nominating Barry Goldwater for the presidency at the 1964 Republican Convention.

Sources relating to party and presidential politics in the 1960s naturally offer a very distinctive and limited perspective on the decade's events. Nevertheless, they reveal a history of conflict between sincere and spirited, if sometimes naïvely conceived and poorly executed, attempts at innovative social reform and equally determined, principled, and resourceful efforts to affirm traditional values that was mirrored at all levels of America's social, cultural, and political life. Similarly, the messy overlap between the four presidential administrations and their policies makes it difficult to draw absolute distinctions between them, encapsulating as they did a mix of continuity and change that was just as apparent in the realm of social mores and practices as it was in high politics.

If the 1960s was, in the reductive terms and banner headlines much beloved of the media and Hollywood, a time of unbridled sex, drugs, and rock and roll, many of the documents collected in Chapter 1 remind us that some people – especially young people – had actually been having sex, taking drugs, and even listening to rock and roll music for some time before the dawn of the decade. Often portrayed nostalgically as a golden era of family stability and sexual restraint, the 1950s actually witnessed a teenage birth rate unmatched in the US before or since: many of those births were to unwed mothers who contributed to an 80 percent increase in the number of out-of-wedlock babies placed for adoption between 1944 and 1955. Nora Johnson's investigation into "Sex and the College Girl" underscores the later verdict of historians like Beth Bailey, Alan Petigny, and Stephanie Coontz that there was a significant shift in American sexual behavior and attitudes underway by the 1950s which the mass media and general public simply failed to comprehend.

When it came, this belated popular awareness was closely linked to the introduction of widely available oral contraception. One of the most important scientific developments of the decade, the pill had enormous social ramifications. As nervously reflected in a 1966 US News & World Report investigation, the pill became a convenient lightning rod for anxieties about declining morals and new gender roles. Most significantly, it conferred new power on women by reducing the threat of unplanned pregnancy, thereby giving them much greater control over their bodies and the consequences of their sexual behavior. Other contextual factors also helped to shape the social impact of the pill and what enthusiasts embraced and critics condemned – usually with equal vehemence, exaggeration, and hyperbole – as an era of "free love" and sexual liberation. The relaxation of obscenity laws and the concomitant rise of explicit sexuality in literature, art, music, advertising, and the mass media; expanded co-ed arrangements at colleges; demographic shifts which meant that there were simply many more young, sexually active people around; greater access to automobiles – always a prospective site of clandestine sexual activity; the popularity of sexology which brought to light a previously unacknowledged range of human sexual needs, desires, and practices; developments in Freudian and neo-Freudian psychology which sought to avoid the debilitating neuroses caused by sexual repression; the rise of the women's liberation movement and the trends towards later marriage and childbirth which themselves reflected greater educational and career opportunities for many women – all these factors combined with the pill to change sexual behavior among many American women in the 1960s.

The "sexual revolution" did not impact all women equally or in the same manner, but few were left unaffected by it. New ideas of what was sexually acceptable informed significant developments in female art and culture from the "confessional" poetry of Sylvia Plath and Anne Sexton to rock star Janis Joplin's unashamedly predatory persona. They also underwrote the idea that "the personal is political" providing a link between the politics of female sexuality, reproduction rights, and the struggle for gender equality. For many feminists, as for the gay rights movement which moved above ground after the 1969 Stonewall Riot in New York, the quest for sexual freedom and a non-exploitative erotic politics was inextricably linked to the struggle for full civil rights and equal educational and economic opportunities.

Despite these signs of sexual liberation, conventional gender roles with men as breadwinners and women as primarily housekeepers and mothers continued to dominate the American social and cultural landscape throughout the 1960s. Indeed, in the Cold War, the integrity of the traditional, God-fearing, nuclear, two-headed family was depicted as every bit as vital to the internal security of the nation as the nuclear missiles which promised to keep America safe from external threats. These idealized patriarchal family arrangements were never as ubiquitous or inflexible as contemporary popular culture and political rhetoric suggested, particularly in communities where poverty or cultural factors altered the gender dynamics within the household. Nevertheless, expectations and assumptions about "correct" gender roles and the "proper" structure of the American family continued to exert considerable, if not always predictable, social, political, and psychological influence. Paradoxically, these familial and sexual norms prompted both feminist challenges to oppressive patriarchal structures from groups like the National Organization for Women and the more radical Redstockings, and the kind of conservative mobilizations associated with Phyllis Schafly that championed the moral correctness and social benefits of traditional male-headed nuclear families.

Prevailing orthodoxies about gender also exerted enormous influence on ideas about manhood and the proper performance of masculinity in America. For many men in the 1950s and 1960s, John Wayne's brave, no-nonsense, stoic film characters – rarely encumbered by the emotional baggage or sexual distractions brought by women – remained exemplary models of independent, self-reliant manhood. Meanwhile, by 1963 Hugh Hefner boasted sales of nearly 1.9 million copies each month for his flagship publication *Playboy*. The vast majority – 75 percent – were bought openly at the news-stand, suggesting a relative absence of stigma about adult men buying the magazine. Notwithstanding a legitimate reputation for carrying some very important interviews and current affairs articles, the enormous success of *Playboy* rested on catering to adult male sexual fantasies that were deemed broadly acceptable as long as they were channeled into Hefner's mix of continental chic, locker-room humor, and resolutely heterosexual voyeurism. Given its casual objectification of women – all pneumatic breasts and carefully airbrushed visages – and complete avoidance of gay or bi-sexuality, it is hard to cast Hefner and *Playboy* as an especially progressive let alone liberating phenomenon. And yet Heffner did offer persistent and well-funded challenge to legal and customary restrictions on freedom of sexual expression in art, film, literature, and music. When he won a succession of courtroom battles against accusations of obscenity this fed into a more permissive judicial climate in areas of sexuality and reproductive rights.

For many people, the increased sexual permissiveness associated with the pill and *Playboy* was nothing to celebrate, but merely evidence of the corruption of core American values by moral relativists and cultural radicals. In 1969, 68 percent of Americans still maintained that it was wrong for a man and a woman to have sex before marriage while a survey the previous year discovered that 78 percent of Americans believed that life "in terms of morals" was getting worse. If the 1960s was doubtless an era of accelerated and expanded sexual awareness for many men and women, there was always a strong counter-movement dedicated to reversing the permissive trend in popular culture, in the mass media, and in the activities of the young, deviant, hairy, and unwashed. Such people would often gravitate towards the New Right, where traditional family values, deference to properly constituted – invariably male – authority and unquestioning patriotism often fused with a religious commitment to moral probity.

As several of the texts and images in this Reader suggest, nowhere was the battle over the "correct" structure of the household, appropriate gender roles, and the place of the young fought more keenly than in the suburbs. The 'burbs were themselves a powerful symbol of the material abundance that, although unevenly spread, shaped much of American life, politics, and culture in the 1960s. During the decade, the official poverty rate fell from over 22 percent to 12 percent of the population, while the national economy grew every single month between 1961 and 1969 – a period of sustained expansion unprecedented in American history at that time. Many Americans used that prosperity and the 75 million cars that were on the road by 1965 to flee the congestion of old city centers for a more peaceful life in the suburbs.

Capital and class were not the only factors at work in the process of suburbanization, however. During the 1950s, a net total of 3.6 million whites had moved to the suburbs while a net total of 4.5 million non-whites moved into the dozen largest cities in the nation. By 1960, the US was already predominantly suburban-dwelling, yet only 5 percent of African Americans lived in such locations. Despite the creation of the Department of Housing and Urban Development in 1965 and a succession of Great Society programs designed to alleviate chronic interlocking inner-city problems of poverty, poor schools, inadequate health care and social services, dwindling demand for unskilled and semi-skilled labor in an era of deindustrialization, discriminatory housing practices, and escalating crime rates, the urban situation became steadily worse. By the end of the decade, particularly after the race riots of the mid-to-late 1960s, the predominantly white flight to the suburbs was accompanied by the encrustation of an urban underclass comprised primarily of blacks and Hispanics.

If the urban crisis deepened during the 1960s, all was not necessarily well out on America's "Crabgrass Frontier" where the young and women, in particular, exhibited creeping disillusionment. Betty Friedan's *The Feminine Mystique*, for example, was largely based on her response to male-defined expectations of suburban housewives in popular magazines and advertisements. Members of the New Left and the counterculture regularly lambasted what they saw as the sterility, conformity, sexism, and racial exclusivity associated with suburban living, seeing it as a symbol of the way that modern consumer society substituted superficial signs of physical comfort and crass materialism for true spiritual satisfaction, self-expression, and a healthy social conscience.

Condemnations of middle-class conformity also provided staple fare for members of the folk and later progressive rock music scenes, as in Malvina Reynold's "Little Boxes" or even Joni Mitchell's "Woodstock." Mitchell's paean to the 1969 high-point of the counterculture's "Aquarian dream" of love, peace, and spiritual rejuvenation turned on a common rejection of the material trappings and claustrophobia of suburban and urban living in order to get "back to the garden" – a romantic, almost Edenic vision of plain, honest, rural, or small-town living. During the 1960s, this kind of pastoral nostalgia for the land, romanticized as a natural antidote to both the economic decay and racial conflagrations of the inner cities and the artificiality of suburbia, seeped into various corners of American politics and culture. It helped secure support for environmental protection measures such as the 1964 Wilderness Act; it led Bob Dylan to abandon the urban speed-freak rock poetry of his mid-1960s albums *Highway 61 Revisited* and *Blonde on Blonde* for the stripped-down music made privately (though massively bootlegged) with The Band in the basement of a rural retreat in upstate New York and on the bare-bones countrified albums *John Wesley Harding* and *Nashville Skyline*; it led scholars to write influential American Studies texts like Leo Marx's *Machine in the Garden* (1964) which lamented the loss of some kind of national innocence that was frequently framed in terms of shift from a small town, agrarian to an urban, industrial nation; and it led the Diggers, one of the most radical, if also among the most disorganized, of the San Francisco "hippy" collectives in its rejection of individual property rights, to abandon Haight-Ashbury for communal living in the hills of Northern California.

Predictably, while hippies dreamed and occasionally acted on their bucolic dreams, on the land itself things were far from idyllic. The number of farms in America declined by nearly a million during the decade from

3.71 million in 1959 to 2.73 million in 1969, although the size and efficiency of the remaining ones, if not their eco-friendliness, increased. Meanwhile the plight of many rural laborers was grim. Appalling conditions among grape farm workers in California prompted César Chávez and Delores Huerta of the United Farm Workers to organize a major protest, including a national boycott of non-union grapes and lettuce, to secure union recognition and decent contracts for a largely Mexican American workforce. In a decade when the fortunes of organized labor generally declined, with membership levels among non-agricultural workers falling from 31.4 percent to 27.4 percent, the strike was a rare if limited victory that helped elevate Chávez and Huerta to prominence in the wider battle for Chicano rights.

Rejection of the trappings of urban and suburban living was not surprising coming from people closely associated with the counterculture or the New Left. However, it is probably even more revealing, not to say ironic, that in 1967 the Monkees, initially a wholly prefabricated pop group, should also record a jaunty jibe at "status symbol land" in "Pleasant Valley Sunday." But then capitalism, commerce, and the counterculture were always closely connected, with advertising executives only too eager to appropriate youthful images and psychedelic effects to sell their products. This commodification of the counterculture was not always a case of avaricious commercial interests co-opting and repackaging grassroots ideas for mass consumption. As the extraordinary commercial success of Stewart Brand's guide to self-sufficiency, *Whole Earth Catalog* (1968), demonstrated, the counterculture spawned its own entrepreneurial spirit and often sought to commandeer, rather than destroy, the apparatus of corporate America. Even the most acerbic critiques of the dominant culture and rampant consumerism, even the most dramatic gestures of defiance to the mainstream, were often conceived with the mass media and commercial possibilities of one sort or another in mind. Certainly, there was a performative aspect to the decade which helps to explain some of its dramatic impact and enduring fascination, as well as determining the kinds of sources historians have had at their disposal.

The 1960s was, quite literally, a most spectacular decade. To a hitherto unprecedented extent, critical social, cultural, and political phenomena such as the civil rights struggle, the Vietnam War and the Peace Movement, the battle for the rights of women, gays, and various other disadvantaged groups in America, even riots and the assassinations of presidents and candidates, were played out in the full glare of television cameras, before radio microphones, and under the scrutiny of eager journalists and photographers. Even the most radical, disaffected activists invariably coveted and tried to control this publicity for their own ends. The Yippies!' rejection of war-mongering mainstream politics, culminating in their protests at the 1968 Chicago Democratic Party Convention and the violence it provoked from the Chicago police, was an exercise in high-risk street theater, as was the 1969 occupation of Alcatraz Island by Native Americans. So, too, was the early civil rights movement, with its ability to dramatize the clash of good and evil, justice and injustice in the South through the use of non-violent direct-action protests that prompted white violence and thus ensured media attention. Black Power militants also catered to the demands of the news cycle and the editorial room. The Black Panther Party was especially skilled in the politics of revolutionary style, attracting a great deal of media attention – little of it favorable – with their paramilitary couture and conspicuous carbines. Similarly, when sprinters Tommie Smith and John Carlos thrust black gloved hands into the air at the 1968 Mexico Olympics 200-meter medal ceremony, their gesture of support for black and human rights was seen live on television across the globe and captured forever on moving and still film.

Conservative voices in America railed against falling moral standards in the mass media and popular culture in general, but they were especially agitated by the time and space that was devoted to individuals and organizations who deliberately courted sensationalism as they challenged traditional structures of power and authority. Richard Nixon's vice-president Spiro Agnew was among those who regularly blasted the sensation-hungry media for encouraging, rather than merely reporting, the dramatic public protests and pseudo-events that seemed to have replaced conventional politics as a means to air individual and collective grievances. Whatever the merits of Agnew's denunciations of a liberal media conspiracy in America, thanks to those media the spectacular public events of the 1960s have left behind their own kinds of visual and aural evidence – the contemporary news footage, photo-journalism, radio broadcasts, even the television shows, feature films, and recordings that augment the more traditional documentary sources in this Reader.

Chapter 1   Into the 1960s

1. Jack Gould, Elvis Presley on the Ed Sullivan Show, 1956

When Elvis Presley burst into mass American consciousness in 1956 with a series of best-selling records, an exhilarating live show, and several highly controversial appearances on network television, much of adult America recoiled in disgust and disbelief. Some were alarmed by Presley's lower-class southern origins; others saw the unwanted specter of race-mixing in his uninhibited fusion of black rhythm and blues and gospel influences with the nominally white sounds of country and pop. However, for most opponents of Presley and rock and roll more generally, it was Presley's perceived sexual threat that was most troubling. For many guardians of traditional standards, including the New York Times' *eminent television critic Jack Gould, the popularity of Presley's cacophonous and lewd rock and roll, coupled with his flamboyant, hyper-sexual performance style were indicative of declining moral values among the nation's youth – a trend that was exacerbated by the mass media and music industries as they relentlessly pursued a highly lucrative new youth market with little regard for taste or decency.*

While Gould chastised the entertainment industry for giving a platform to Presley and assumed that his popularity would quickly wane, huge numbers of teenaged Americans hailed the arrival of a new icon and embraced rock and roll music as performed by a whole raft of black and white acts such as Little Richard, Chuck Berry, and Buddy Holly as the sound of their generation. Increasingly, young Americans would use music to express their dissent not only from the musical culture of their parents, but also from some of the core values of mainstream society.

Television broadcasters cannot be asked to solve life's problems. But they can be expected to display adult leadership and responsibility in areas where they do have some significant influence. This they have hardly done in the case of Elvis Presley, entertainer and phenomenon.

Last Sunday on the Ed Sullivan show Mr. Presley made another of his appearances and attracted a record audience. In some ways it was perhaps the most unpleasant of his recent three performances.

Mr. Presley initially disturbed adult viewers – and instantly became a martyr in the eyes of his teen-age following – for his striptease behavior on last spring's Milton Berle program. Then with Steve Allen he was much more sedate. On the Sullivan program he injected movements of the tongue and indulged in wordless singing that were singularly distasteful.

At least some parents are puzzled or confused by Presley's almost hypnotic power; others are concerned; perhaps most are a shade disgusted and content to permit the Presley fad to play itself out.

Neither criticism of Presley nor of the teen-agers who admire him is particularly to the point. Presley has fallen into a fortune with a routine that in one form or another has always existed on the fringe of show business; in his gyrating figure and suggestive gestures the teen-agers have found something that for the moment seems exciting or important.

Void

Quite possibly Presley just happened to move in where society has failed the teen-ager. Certainly, modern youngsters have been subjected to a great deal of censure and perhaps too little understanding. Greater in their numbers than ever before, they may have found in Presley a rallying point, a nationally prominent figure who seems to be on their side. And, just as surely, there are limitless teen-agers who cannot put up with the boy, either vocally or calisthenically.

Family counselors have wisely noted that ours is still a culture in a stage of frantic and tense transition. With even 16-year-olds capable of commanding $20 or $30 a week in their spare time, with access to automobiles at an early age, with communications media of all kinds exposing them to new thoughts very early in life, theirs indeed is a high degree of independence. Inevitably it has been accompanied by a lessening of parental control.

Small wonder, therefore, that the teen-ager is susceptible to overstimulation from the outside. He is at the age when an awareness of sex is both thoroughly natural and normal, when latent rebellion is to be expected.

But what is new and a little discouraging is the willingness and indeed eagerness of reputable business men to exploit those critical factors beyond all reasonable grounds.

Television surely is not the only culprit. Exposé magazines, which once were more or less bootleg items, are now carried openly on the best news-stands. The music-publishing business – as *Variety* most courageously has pointed out – has all but disgraced itself with some of the "rock 'n' roll" songs it has issued. Some of the finest recording companies have been willing to go right along with the trend too.

Distinctive

Of all these businesses, however, television is in a unique position. First and foremost, it has access directly to the home and its wares are free. Second, the broadcasters are not only addressing themselves to the teen-agers but, much more importantly, also to the lower age groups. When Presley executes his bumps and grinds, it must be remembered by the Columbia Broadcasting System that even the 12–year-old's curiosity may be oversti-mulated. It is on this score that the adult viewer has every right to expect sympathetic understanding and cooperation from a broadcaster.

A perennial weakness in the executive echelons of the networks is their opportunistic rationalization of television's function. The industry lives fundamentally by the code of giving the public what it wants. This is not the place to argue the artistic foolishness of such a standard; in the case of situation comedies and other escapist diversions it is relatively unimportant.

But when this code is applied to teen-agers just becoming conscious of life's processes, not only is it manifestly without validity but it also is perilous. Catering to the interests of the younger generation is one of television's main jobs; because those interests do not always coincide with parental tastes should not deter the broadcasters. But selfish exploitation and commercialized overstimulation of youth's physical impulses is cer-tainly a gross national disservice.

Sensible

The issue is not one of censorship, which solves nothing; it is one of common sense. It is no impingement on the medium's artistic freedom to ask the broadcaster merely to exercise good sense and display responsibility. It is no blue-nosed suppression of the proper way of depicting life in the theatre to expect stage manners somewhat above the level of the carnival sideshow.

In the long run, perhaps Presley will do everyone a favor by pointing up the need for earlier sex education so that neither his successors nor TV can capitalize on the idea that his type of routine is somehow highly tempting yet forbidden fruit. But that takes time, and meanwhile the broadcasters at least can employ a measure of mature and helpful thoughtfulness in not contributing further to the exploitation of the teen-ager.

With congested schools, early dating, the appeals of the car, military service, acceptance by the right crowd, sex and the normal parental pressures, the teen-ager has all the problems he needs.

Mercenary

To resort to the world's oldest theatrical come-on just to make a fast buck from such a sensitive individual is cheap and tawdry stuff. At least Presley is honest in what he is doing. That the teen-ager sometimes finds it difficult to feel respect for the moralizing older generation may of itself be an encouraging sign of his intelligence. If the profiteering hypocrite is above reproach and Presley isn't, today's youngsters might well ask what God do adults worship.

2. Martin Luther King, Jr., "Our Struggle," 1956

The African American freedom struggle occupied a preeminent place in the culture and politics of the 1960s. However, the dramatic events of the 1960s represented just the latest phase in a centuries-long battle for racial justice in America that quickened in the decade or so after World War II. Attuned to the possibilities created by America's Cold War desire to promote its democratic credentials abroad, African Americans intensified their demands for full citizenship rights at home. When it became apparent that an obdurate white South had little intention of abandoning its commitment to white supremacy by actually complying with federal court rulings such as the Brown *decision that declared segregated schools unconstitutional, African Americans and their allies turned to direct-action tactics to protest the continuing denial of black rights.*

The most significant of this new wave of mass demonstrations was the year-long Montgomery Bus Boycott. Sparked on December 1, 1955 by the

arrest of Mrs. Rosa Parks, who refused to obey a white driver's order to move
to the back of a segregated bus, the campaign was founded on a
well-established network of activists and the organizational power of the city's
black churches. One clergyman, Martin Luther King, Jr., was chosen to head
the Montgomery Improvement Association, an organization of organizations
that coordinated the protest. Although King lacked experience as a movement
leader and initially had no overarching philosophy of social change, under the
tutelage of visiting activists such as Bayard Rustin he came to appreciate both
the practical efficacy and moral appeal of nonviolent direct-action tactics.

"Our Struggle" was originally drafted by Rustin and appeared in the
second issue of Liberation, *a new journal edited by Rustin and other radical*
pacifists. The article focused on the details of the boycott and on the
psychological changes evident among African Americans that made such
mobilizations not just possible, but inevitable. In a theme that would be
repeated by just about every black leader of the 1960s, Rustin and King
announced the emergence of a "new Negro" who was no longer willing to
settle for second-class status.

The segregation of Negroes, with its inevitable discrimination, has thrived on elements of inferiority present in the masses of both white and Negro people. Through forced separation from our African culture, through slavery, poverty, and deprivation, many black men lost self-respect.

In their relations with Negroes, white people discovered that they had rejected the very center of their own ethical professions. They could not face the triumph of their lesser instincts and simultaneously have peace within. And so, to gain it, they rationalized – insisting that the unfortunate Negro, being less than human, deserved and even enjoyed second class status.

They argued that his inferior social, economic and political position was good for him. He was incapable of advancing beyond a fixed position and would therefore be happier if encouraged not to attempt the impossible. He is subjugated by a superior people with an advanced way of life. The "master race" will be able to civilize him to a limited degree, if only he will be true to his inferior nature and stay in his place.

White men soon came to forget that the Southern social culture and all its institutions had been organized to perpetuate this rationalization. They observed a caste system and quickly were conditioned to believe that its social results, which they had created, actually reflected the Negro's innate and true nature.

In time many Negroes lost faith in themselves and came to believe that perhaps they really were what they had been told they were – something less than men. So long as they were prepared to accept this role, racial peace could be maintained. It was an uneasy peace in which the Negro was forced to accept patiently injustice, insult, injury and exploitation.

Gradually the Negro masses in the South began to re-evaluate themselves – a process that was to change the nature of the Negro community and doom the social patterns of the South. We discovered that we had never really smothered our self-respect and that we could not be at one with ourselves without asserting it. From this point on, the South's terrible peace was rapidly undermined by the Negro's new and courageous thinking and his ever-increasing readiness to organize and to act. Conflict and violence were coming to the surface as the white South desperately clung to its old patterns. The extreme tension in race relations in the South today is explained in part by the revolutionary change in the Negro's evaluation of himself and of his destiny and by his determination to struggle for justice. We Negroes have replaced self-pity with self-respect and self-depreciation with dignity.

When Mrs. Rosa Parks, the quiet seamstress whose arrest precipitated the non-violent protest in Montgomery, was asked why she had refused to move to the rear of a bus, she said: "It was a matter of dignity; I could not have faced myself and my people if I had moved."

The New Negro

Many of the Negroes who joined the protest did not expect it to succeed. When asked why, they usually gave one of three answers: "I didn't expect Negroes to stick to it," or, "I never thought we Negroes had the nerve," or, "I thought the pressure from the white folks would kill it before it got started."

In other words, our non-violent protest in Montgomery is important because it is demonstrating to the Negro, North and South, that many of the stereotypes he has held about himself and other Negroes are not valid. Montgomery has broken the spell and is ushering in concrete manifestations of the thinking and action of the new Negro.

We now know that:

We can stick together. In Montgomery, 42,000 of us have refused to ride the city's segregated busses since December 5. Some walk as many as fourteen miles a day.

Our leaders do not have to sell out. Many of us have been indicted, arrested, and "mugged." Every Monday and Thursday night we stand before the Negro population at the prayer meetings and repeat: "It is an honor to face jail for a just cause."

Threats and violence do not necessarily intimidate those who are sufficiently aroused and non-violent. The bombing of two of our homes has made us more resolute. When a handbill was circulated at a White Citizens Council meeting stating that Negroes should be "abolished" by "guns, bows and arrows, sling shots and knives," we responded with even greater determination.

Our church is becoming militant. Twenty-four ministers were arrested in Montgomery. Each has said publicly that he stands prepared to be arrested again. Even upper-class Negroes who reject the "come to Jesus" gospel are now convinced that the church has no alternative but to provide the non-violent dynamics for social change in the midst of conflict. The $30,000 used for the car pool, which transports over 20,000 Negro workers, school children and housewives, has been raised in the churches. The churches have become the dispatch centers where the people gather to wait for rides.

We believe in ourselves. In Montgomery we walk in a new way. We hold our heads in a new way. Even the Negro reporters who converged on Montgomery have a new attitude. One tired reporter, asked at a luncheon in Birmingham to say a few words about Montgomery, stood up, thought for a moment, and uttered one sentence: "Montgomery has made me proud to be a Negro."

Economics is part of our struggle. We are aware that Montgomery's white businessmen have tried to "talk sense" to the bus company and the city commissioners. We have observed that small Negro shops are thriving as Negroes find it inconvenient to walk downtown to the white stores. We have been getting more polite treatment in the white shops since the protest began. We have a new respect for the proper use of our dollar.

We have discovered a new and powerful weapon—non-violent resistance. Although law is an important factor in bringing about social change, there are certain conditions in which the very effort to adhere to new legal decisions creates tension and provokes violence. We had hoped to see demonstrated a method that would enable us to continue our struggle while coping with the violence it aroused. Now we see the answer: face violence if necessary, but refuse to return violence. If we respect those who oppose us, they may achieve a new understanding of the human relations involved.

We now know that the Southern Negro has come of age, politically and morally. Montgomery has demonstrated that we will not run from the struggle, and will support the battle for equality. The attitude of many young Negroes a few years ago was reflected in the common expression, "I'd rather be a lamp post in Harlem than Governor of Alabama." Now the idea expressed in our churches, schools, pool rooms, restaurants and homes is: "Brother, stay here and fight non-violently. 'Cause if you don't let them make you mad, you can win." The official slogan of the Montgomery Improvement Association is "Justice without Violence" . . .

We Southern Negroes believe that it is essential to defend the right of equality now. From this position we will not and cannot retreat. Fortunately, we are increasingly aware that we must not try to defend our position by methods that contradict the aim of brotherhood. We in Montgomery believe that the only way to press on is by adopting the philosophy and practice of non-violent resistance.

This method permits a struggle to go on with dignity and without the need to retreat. It is a method that can absorb the violence that is inevitable in social change whenever deep-seated prejudices are challenged.

If, in pressing for justice and equality in Montgomery, we discover that those who reject equality are prepared to use violence, we must not despair, retreat, or fear. Before they make this crucial decision, they must remember: whatever they do, we will not use violence in return. We hope we can act in the struggle in such a way that they will see the error of their approach and will come to respect us. Then we can all live together in peace and equality . . .

We do not wish to triumph over the white community. That would only result in transferring those now on the bottom to the top. But, if we can live up to non-violence in thought and deed, there will emerge an interracial society based on freedom for all.

Source: *Liberation*, April 1956, pp. 3–6. Copyright 1956 Dr. Martin Luther King, Jr.; copyright renewed 1986 Coretta Scott King.

3. Nora Johnson, "Sex and the College Girl," 1957

In this article Smith College alumnus Nora Johnson uses the story of "Susie" and her boyfriend "Joe" to capture the complex and often confusing rituals surrounding appropriate sexual activity for young heterosexual middle-class women in the 1950s. During the postwar era, traditional patterns of female and male expectations regarding sex and gender roles more generally remained largely intact, with marriage and children the primary ambition for most American women. The sexual – and sexist – "double standard" was certainly alive and well: most young men and women continued to distinguish between "good" girls who remained chaste until marriage and "bad" girls who did not, although pre-marital sexual experimentation by men rarely carried any such stigma. And yet, as Johnson's article reveals, these norms were already coming under strain from a variety of powerful social and cultural forces, including the expansion of opportunities for women in higher education. The article wryly observes how many young women forged an often frustrating compromise with their bodies, consciences, and boyfriends by adhering to elaborate codes of acceptable sexual activity short of full intercourse; others reserved intercourse only for those to whom they were "pinned" or engaged; others simply decided that there was nothing immoral or shameful about sex and moved towards the kind of sexual freedom that would be an important, if often caricatured and exaggerated, part of the "sexual revolution" of the 1960s.

Ever since Gertrude Stein made her remark about the Lost Generation, every decade has wanted to find a tag, a concise explanation of its own behavior. In our complicated world, any simplification of the events around us is welcome and, in fact, almost necessary. We need to feel our place in history; it helps in our constant search for self-identity. But while the Beatniks travel about the country on the backs of trucks, the rest of us are going to college and then plunging – with puzzling eagerness – into marriage and parenthood. While the Beatniks are avoiding any signs of culture or intellect, we are struggling to adapt what we have to the essentially nonintellectual function of early parenthood. We are deadly serious in our pursuits and, I am afraid, non-adventurous in our actions. We have a compulsion to plan our lives, to take into account all possible adversities and to guard against them. We prefer not to consider the fact that human destinies are subject to amazingly ephemeral influences and that often our most rewarding experiences come about by pure chance. This sort of thinking seems risky to us, and we are not a generation to take risks. Perhaps history will prove that we are a buffer generation, standing by silently while our children, brought up by demand-feeding and demand-everything, kick over the traces and do startling things, with none of our predilection for playing it safe....

Since so many of us are going to college, a great many of our decisions about our lives have been and are being made on the campuses, and our behavior in college is inevitably in for some comment. Two criticisms rise above the rest: people in college are promiscuous, for one thing, and, for another, they are getting married and having children too early. These are interesting observations because they contradict each other. The phenomena of pinning, going steady, and being monogamous-minded do not suggest sexual promiscuity. Quite the contrary – they are symptoms of our inclination to play it safe...

Susie has, on the whole, kept her chastity. She is no demimondaine, and she wants to be reasonably intact on her wedding night. She had an unfortunate experience at Dartmouth, when she and her date were both in their cups, but she barely remembers anything about it and hasn't seen the boy since. She has also done some heavy petting with boys she didn't care about, because she reasoned that it wouldn't matter what they thought of her. She has been in love twice (three times, if you count Joe), once in high school and once in freshman year with the most divine Yale senior, whom she let do practically anything (except have intercourse) and who disappeared for no reason after two months of torrid dating. It still hurts her to think about that.

She has kept Joe fairly well at arm's length, giving in a little at a time, because she wanted him to respect her. He didn't really excite her sexually, but probably he would if they had some privacy. Nothing was less romantic than the front porch of the house, or Joe's room at the fraternity with his roommate running back and forth from the shower, or in the back of someone's car with only fifteen minutes till she had to be in. Anyway, it might be just as well.

Susie and Joe have decided that they will sleep together when it is feasible, since by now Joe knows she is a nice girl and it's all right. But they will be very careful. Susie, like all her friends, has a deep-rooted fear of pregnancy, which explains their caution about having affairs. They have heard that no kind of birth control is really infallible. And, today, shotgun weddings are looked down upon and illegal abortions sound appalling. It simply isn't worth the worry. She will sleep with Joe, if they become engaged, because he wants to, and if she becomes pregnant, they can get married sooner. But they will do everything possible to prevent it.

Obviously, Susie is hardly in love with Joe in the way one might hope. But she is sincerely fond of him, she feels comfortable with him, and, in some unexplained way, when she is with him life seems much simpler. The decision about her life keeps her awake at night, but when she is with Joe things make more sense. The prospect of marrying Joe gradually becomes more attractive . . .

If Susie becomes engaged, she can, in a way, stop trying so hard. She can let go. For college (though it may not sound it from this account) hasn't been easy. Her liberal education has had the definite effect of making her question herself and some of her lifelong ideas for the first time, sometimes shatteringly. She has learned to think, not in the proportions of genius, but intelligently, about herself and her place in the world. She realizes, disturbingly, that a great many things are required of her, and sometimes she can't help wondering about the years beyond the casserole and playpen. The beginnings of maturity are taking place in her.

The Eastern women's colleges (and I can speak with authority only about Smith) subtly emanate, over a period of four years, a concept of the ideal

American woman, who is nothing short of fantastic. She must be a successful wife, mother, community contributor, and possibly career woman, all at once. Besides this, she must be attractive, charming, gracious, and good-humored; talk intelligently about her husband's job, but not try to horn in on it; keep her home looking like a page out of House Beautiful; and be efficient, but not intimidatingly so. While she is managing all this, she must be relaxed and happy, find time to read, paint, and listen to music, think philosophical thoughts, be the keeper of culture in the home, and raise her husband's sights above the television set. For it is part and parcel of the concept of liberal education to better human beings, to make them more thoughtful and understanding, to broaden their interests. Liberal education is a trust. It is not to be lightly thrown aside at graduation, but it is to be used every day, forever.

These are all the things that a liberally educated girl must do, and there has been in her background a curious lack of definition of the things she must not do. Parents who have lived in the Jazz Age can not very well forbid adventurousness, nor can they take a very stalwart attitude about sex. Even if they do, their daughters rarely listen. What or what not to do about sex is, these days, relative. It all depends. This is not to say that there are no longer any moral standards; certainly there are – the fact that sex still causes guilt and worry proves it. But moral generalizations seem remote and unreal, something our grandparents believed in.

Today girls are expected to judge each situation for itself, a far more demanding task. A man recently told me that he had found girls rather inept at this, since taking a square view of a new relationship at the beginning, before sex has entered it, requires more maturity and insight than most college girls have. He said he had found such girls inconsistent in their attitude toward him – sexual sirens at first (when they wanted to attract him), promising everything, then becoming more and more aloof and more and more anxious to discuss the relationship step by step, when logically their behavior should be quite reversed; he had thought that as they got to know and like him they would be more relaxed about sex.

The fact is that, lacking a solid background of Christian ethics, most girls have only a couple of vague rules of thumb to go by, which they cling to beyond all sense and reason. And these, interestingly enough, contradict each other. One is that anything is all right if you're in love (romantic, from movies and certain fiction – the American dream of love) and the other is that a girl must be respected, particularly by the man she wants to marry (ethical, left over from grandma). Since these are extremely shaky and require the girl's knowing whether or not there is a chance of love in the relationship, sex, to her, requires constant corroborative discussion while she tries to plumb the depths of a man's intentions. Actions alone are not trustworthy. After all, a prostitute can arouse a man as well as (and probably better than) a "nice" girl. But if a man loves her for herself, and not just her body, he will augment his wandering hands with a few well-placed words of love. Clinging to her two contradictory principles, she tries to be a sexual demon and Miss Priss at tea at the same time; she tries not to see what strange companions love and propriety are.

On the other side of the coin, men do little to clarify the situation. Some, at least, are simple-minded about it. They divide girls into two categories, bad and good: the bad ones have obvious functions, and the good ones are to be married; but good ones, once pinned or engaged (and the official definition of being pinned is "being engaged to be engaged") must loosen up immediately or run the risk of being considered cold or hypocritical. This would require the girl to be an angel of civilized and understanding behavior at first, pacifying her man by a gentle pat on the knee at just the right time and keeping him at bay and yet interested – in a way both tactful and loving (the teen-age magazines devote a lot of space to this technique and recommend warding off unwise passes by asking about the latest football scores), and then, once the pin has been handed over, to shed her clothes and hop into bed with impassioned abandon.

Even more complicated to deal with is the intellectual-amoral type of man, who has affairs as a matter of course and doesn't (or says he doesn't) think less of a girl for sleeping with him. He is full of highly complicated arguments on the subject, which have to do with empiricism, epicureanism, live today, for tomorrow will bring the mushroom cloud, learning about life, and the dangers of self-repression, all of which are whipped out with frightening speed and conviction while he is undoing the third button on his girl's blouse. ...

A girl, then, by the end of college is saddled with enough theories, arguments pro and con, expectations, and conflicting opinions to keep her busy for years. She is in the habit of analyzing everything, wondering why she does things, and trying to lay a pattern for her life. Her education, which has laid such a glittering array of goals before her as an educated American woman, has also taught her to be extremely suspicious of the winds of chance. She has been told that she is a valuable commodity, that only efficiency will allow her to utilize all her possibilities, and that to get on in this risky and nerve-racking world she must keep what a disillusioned male friend of mine calls "the safety catch." There must always be something held in reserve, a part of her that she will give to no one, not even her husband. It is her belief in herself, modern version, and the determination to protect that belief. It is the vision of possibility which remains long after she is mature enough to accept the eventual, gradual limitation of the things that will happen to her in life. It is the dream of the things she never did. . . .

Source: *The Atlantic*, November 1957.

4. *Time*, "The Roots of Home," 1960

Suburbs began to emerge on the periphery of America's cities during the second half of the nineteenth century and flourished with the development of streetcars and other mass transit systems around the turn of the early twentieth century. However, it was in the post-World War II era, with the rapid expansion of America's middle-income families and a similarly impressive escalation in car ownership, that they became a dominant factor in the political, social, economic, and cultural life of the country. Serving as a conspicuous site of middle-class affluence and as an important stimulus to the booming economy of the late 1950s and early 1960s, the suburbs, as this Time *cover story explained, became almost synonymous with the idea of the American Dream: a place where traditional values associated with hard work, good citizenship, and the centrality of family, school, and religion were celebrated, and where leisure, recreation, and consumerism – the spoils of abundance – could flourish in communities of generally like-minded, predominantly white, Americans. And yet, the suburbs were not without their internal tensions, nor beyond criticism, even from suburbanites themselves. While recognizing that suburban living remained a coveted symbol of material progress and social status for many Americans, the* Time *report foreshadowed some of the critiques of suburbia as the centre of vacuous consumerism, superficial community, cultural conformity, and stultifying gender norms that would become even more prominent during the 1960s.*

For better or for worse, Suburbia in the 1960s is the U.S.'s grassroots. In Suburbia live one-third of the nation, roughly 60 million people who represent every patch of democracy's hand-stitched quilt, every economic layer, every laboring and professional pursuit in the country. Suburbia is the nation's broadening young middle class, staking out its claim across the landscape, prospecting on a trial-and-error basis for the good way of life for itself and for the children that it produces with such rapidity. It is, as Social Scientist Max Lerner (*America as a Civilization*) has put it, "the focus of most of the forces that are remaking American life today."

If Suburbia's avid social honeybees buzz from address to address in search of sweet status, Suburbia is at the same time the home of the talented and distinguished Americans who write the nation's books, paint its paintings, run its corporations and set the patterns. If its legions sometimes march into frantic activity with rigorous unison, they march for such causes as better schools, churches and charities, which are the building blocks of a nation's character. If Suburbia's ardent pursuit of life at backyard barbecues, block parties and committee meetings offends pious city-bred sociologists, its self-conscious strivings to find a better way for men, women and children to live together must impress the same observers.

Suburbia is a particular kind of American phenomenon, and its roots lie in a particular kind of American heritage. In a casual, ill-planned way it is the meeting ground between the growing, thriving city and the authentic U.S. legend of smalltown life. Says Sociologist Alvin Scaff, who lives in Los Angeles' suburban Claremont: "If you live in the city, you may be a good citizen and interest yourself in a school-board election, but it is seldom meaningful in human terms. In a suburb, the chances are you know the man who is running for the school board, and you vote for or against him with more understanding." Says Don C. Peters, president of Pittsburgh's Mellon-Stuart Co. (construction) and chairman of the board of supervisors of suburban Pine Township: "The American suburb is the last outpost of democracy, the only level left on which the individual citizen can make his wishes felt, directly and immediately. I think there's something idealistic about the search for a home in the suburbs. Call it a return to the soil. It's something that calls most people some time in their lives." ...

The key figure in all Suburbia, the thread that weaves between family and community – the keeper of the suburban dream – is the suburban housewife. In the absence of her commuting, city-working husband, she is first of all the manager of home and brood, and beyond that a sort of aproned activist with a penchant for keeping the neighborhood and community kettle whistling. With children on her mind and under her foot, she is breakfast getter ("You can't have ice cream for breakfast because I say you can't"); laundress, house cleaner, dishwasher, shopper, gardener, encyclopedia, arbitrator of children's disputes, policeman ("Tommy, didn't your mother ever tell you that it's not nice to go into people's houses and open their refrigerators?").

If she is not pregnant, she wonders if she is. She takes her peanut-butter sandwich lunch while standing, thinks she looks a fright, watches her weight (periodically), jabbers over the short-distance telephone with the next-door neighbor. She runs a worn track to the front door, buys more Girl Scout cookies and raffle tickets than she thinks she should, cringes from the suburban locust – the door-to-door salesman who peddles everything from storm windows to potato chips, fire-alarm systems to vacuum cleaners, diaper sendee to magazine subscriptions. She keeps the checkbook, frets for the day that her husband's next raise will top the flood of monthly bills (it never will) – a tide that never seems to rise as high in the city as it does in the suburbs.

She wonders if her husband will send her flowers (on no special occasion), shoos the children next door to play at the neighbor's house for a change, paints her face for her husband's return before she wrestles with dinner. Spotted through her day are blessed moments of relief or dark thoughts of escape . . .

In Suburbia's pedocracy huge emphasis is placed on activities for the young (Washington's suburban Montgomery County, Md. – pop. 358,000 – spends about $34 million a year on youth programs). The suburban housewife might well be a can-opener cook, but she must have an appointment book and a driver's license and must be able to steer a menagerie of leggy youngsters through the streets with the coolness of a driver at the Sebring trials; the suburban sprawl and the near absence of public transportation generally mean that any destination is just beyond sensible walking distance. Most children gauge walking distance at two blocks. If the theory of evolution is still working, it may well one day transform the suburban housewife's right foot into a flared paddle, grooved for easy traction on the gas pedal and brake.

As her children grow less dependent on her, Suburbia's housewife fills her newfound time with a dizzying assortment of extracurricular projects that thrust her full steam into community life. Beyond the home-centered dinner parties, Kaffeeklatsches and card parties, there is a directory-sized world of organizations devised for husbands as well as for wives (but it is the wife who keeps things organized). In New Jersey's Levittown, a projected 16,000 – unit replica of the Long Island original, energetic suburbanites can sign up for at least 35 different organizations from the Volunteer Fire Department to the Great Books Club, and the Lords and Ladies Dance Club, not to mention the proliferating list of adult-education courses that keep the public school lights glowing into the night. "We have a wonderful adult-education program," says Suburbanite (Levittown, L.I.) Muriel Kane (two children), "where women can learn how to fix their own plumbing and everything." . . .

Since Suburbia was conceived for children (and vice versa), the Suburban housewife is the chief jungle fighter for school expansion and reform. Beyond that the path leads easily to the thickets of local politics. Only recently, after the Montgomery County manager whacked $11 million from the 1961 school budget, the county council was invaded by an indignant posse of 1,000 P.T.A. members. The council scrambled to retreat, not only restored the cuts, but added a few projects of its own for good measure. The tax rate jumped 5¢ per $100 valuation as a result, but there was scarcely a whimper ...

The suburbanite has been prodded, poked, gouged, sniffed and tweaked by armies of sociologists and swarms of cityside cynics, but in reality he is his own best critic. Organized suburban living is a relatively new invention, and already some of its victims are wondering if it has too much organization and too little living. The pressure of activity and participation in the model suburb of Lakewood, for example, can be harrowing. The town's recreation league boasts no boys' baseball teams (2,000 players), 36 men's softball teams, ten housewives' softball teams. In season, the leagues play 75 boys' and 30 men's basketball teams, 77 football teams, all coached by volunteers, while other activities range through drama, dance and charm classes, bowling, dog-training classes, "Slim 'n' Trim" groups, roller skating, photography, woodcraft, and lessons in how to ice a cake. Says Joy Hudson, 35, mother of three children: "There is a problem of getting too busy. Some weeks my husband is home only two nights a week. My little boy often says, 'Anybody going to be home tonight?'" Suburbia, echoed Exurbanite Adlai Stevenson (Libertyville, Ill.) recently, is producing "a strange half-life of divided families and Sunday fathers." ...

In those suburbs where families, income, education and interest are homogenized, suburbanites sometimes wonder whether their children are cocooned from the rest of the world. "A child out here sees virtually no sign of wealth and no sign of poverty," says Suburbanite Alan Rosenthal (Washington's Rock Creek Palisades). "It gives him a tendency to think that everyone else lives just the way he does." Suburbanite-Author Robert Paul ("Where Did You Go?" "Out." "What Did You Do?" "Nothing.") Smith (New York City's Scarsdale), complains that Scarsdale is "just like a Deanna Durbin movie: all clean and unreal. Hell, I went to school in Mount Vernon, N.Y., with the furnace man's son – you don't get that here." ...

And what of the grownups themselves? For some, the suburban euphoria often translates itself into the suburban caricature. The neighborhood race for bigger and better plastic swimming pools, cars and power mowers is still being run in some suburbs, and in still others, the chief warm-weather occupation is neighbor watching (Does she hang her laundry outside to dry? Does he leave his trash barrels on the curb after they have been emptied?). In Long Island's staid, old Garden City, observes Hofstra Assistant Sociology Professor William Dobriner, "they don't care whether you believe in God, but you'd better cut your grass." In close-by Levittown, a poll of householders some time ago showed that the No. 1 topic on people's minds was the complaint that too many dogs were running unleashed on the lawns. Topic No. 2 was the threat of world Communism....

Suburbia's clergymen tend to be most keenly aware of Suburbia's disappointments and Suburbia's promise. "Many people," complains Kansas City Rabbi Samuel Mayerberg, "mistake activity for usefulness." Says Dr. Donald S. Ewing, minister of Wayland's Trinitarian Congregational Church near Boston: "Suburbia is gossipy. So many of the people are on approximately the same level economically and socially. They're scrambling for success. They tend to be new in the community and they're unstable and insecure. When they see someone else fail, in work or in a family relationship, they themselves feel a rung higher, and this is a great reason for gossip. I think socially we're flying apart – we don't meet heart to heart any more, we meet at cocktail parties in a superficial way. We value smartness rather than depth, shine rather than spirit. But I think people are sick of it; they want to get out of it."

In Chicago's suburban Elk Grove Village, busy Lutheran Minister Martin E. Marty, who writes for the *Christian Century*, and who devotes much of his time to patching up corroding marriages, sighs wearily: "We've all learned that Hell is portable. I think we're seeing a documentable rebellion going on against the postwar idea of mere belongingness and sociability. We all agree that Suburbia means America. It's not different, but it's typical. Solve Suburbia's problems and you solve America's problems."...

The fact surrounding all the criticism and self-searching is that most suburbanites are having too good a time to realize that they ought to be unhappy with their condition.

Source: *Time*, June 20, 1960.

5. Dwight D. Eisenhower, Farewell Address, 1961

As President Eisenhower left office in 1961, he reflected on his eight years in the White House and proudly declared America "the strongest, the most influential and most productive nation in the world." Yet, the tone of his Farewell Address as a whole was less triumphant. The Cold War had occupied much of the Eisenhower administration's time and energies. A firm believer in the doctrine of Containment and the "Domino Theory" of geopolitics, whereby the fall of one state to communist influence would lead inevitably to the contamination and fall of its neighbors to the same red creed, Eisenhower had steadily increased the US commitment to halting the spread of communism across the globe by diplomacy and economic power if possible, but by military force if necessary. This was certainly true in Southeast Asia, where he sent economic aid and military "advisors" to help bolster the pro-US regime of Ngo Dinh Diem in South Vietnam against threats from nationalist insurgents supported by the communist regime of Ho Chi Minh in North Vietnam.

Yet if Eisenhower was in many respect a quintessential Cold War Warrior, his Farewell Address expressed grave concerns about the ways in which America might choose to use its military and economic muscle on the global stage. Eisenhower, himself a distinguished soldier who had been the Supreme Commander of the Allied troops in Europe during the final years of World War II, warned his fellow countrymen to beware the enormous and largely unchecked power of the nation's military-industrial complex. In particular, he urged vigilance against the combined efforts of arms manufacturers, the scientific-technological elite, and the military establishment to influence the making of foreign and domestic policy decisions for their own ends.

My fellow Americans:

Three days from now, after a half century of service of our country, I shall lay down the responsibilities of office as, in traditional and solemn ceremony, the authority of the Presidency is vested in my successor.

This evening I come to you with a message of leave-taking and farewell, and to share a few final thoughts with you, my countrymen.

Like every other citizen, I wish the new President, and all who will labor with him, Godspeed. I pray that the coming years will be blessed with peace and prosperity for all.

Our people expect their President and the Congress to find essential agreement on questions of great moment, the wise resolution of which will better shape the future of the nation.

My own relations with Congress, which began on a remote and tenuous basis when, long ago, a member of the Senate appointed me to West Point, have since ranged to the intimate during the war and immediate post-war period, and finally to the mutually interdependent during these past eight years.

In this final relationship, the Congress and the Administration have, on most vital issues, cooperated well, to serve the nation well rather than mere partisanship, and so have assured that the business of the nation should go forward. So my official relationship with Congress ends in a feeling on my part, of gratitude that we have been able to do so much together.

We now stand ten years past the midpoint of a century that has witnessed four major wars among great nations. Three of these involved our own country. Despite these holocausts America is today the strongest, the most influential and most productive nation in the world. Understandably proud of this pre-eminence, we yet realize that America's leadership and prestige depend, not merely upon our unmatched material progress, riches and military strength, but on how we use our power in the interests of world peace and human betterment.

Throughout America's adventure in free government, such basic purposes have been to keep the peace; to foster progress in human achievement, and to enhance liberty, dignity and integrity among peoples and among nations. To strive for less would be unworthy of a free and religious people. Any failure traceable to arrogance or our lack of comprehension or readiness to sacrifice would inflict upon us a grievous hurt, both at home and abroad.

Progress toward these noble goals is persistently threatened by the conflict now engulfing the world. It commands our whole attention, absorbs our very beings. We face a hostile ideology global in scope, atheistic in character, ruthless in purpose, and insidious in method. Unhappily the danger it poses promises to be of indefinite duration. To meet it successfully, there is called for, not so much the emotional and transitory sacrifices of crisis, but rather those which enable us to carry forward steadily, surely, and without complaint the burdens of a prolonged and complex struggle – with liberty the stake. Only thus shall we remain, despite every provocation, on our charted course toward permanent peace and human betterment.

Crises there will continue to be. In meeting them, whether foreign or domestic, great or small, there is a recurring temptation to feel that some spectacular and costly action could become the miraculous solution to all current difficulties. A huge increase in the newer elements of our defenses; development of unrealistic programs to cure every ill in agriculture; a dramatic expansion in basic and applied research – these and many other possibilities, each possibly promising in itself, may be suggested as the only way to the road we wish to travel.

But each proposal must be weighed in light of a broader consideration; the need to maintain balance in and among national programs – balance between the private and the public economy, balance between the cost and hoped for advantages – balance between the clearly necessary and the comfortably desirable; balance between our essential requirements as a nation and the duties imposed by the nation upon the individual; balance between the actions of the moment and the national welfare of the future. Good judgment seeks balance and progress; lack of it eventually finds imbalance and frustration.

The record of many decades stands as proof that our people and their Government have, in the main, understood these truths and have responded to them well in the face of threat and stress. But threats, new in kind or degree, constantly arise. I mention two only.

A vital element in keeping the peace is our military establishment. Our arms must be mighty, ready for instant action, so that no potential aggressor may be tempted to risk his own destruction.

Our military organization today bears little relation to that known by any of my predecessors in peacetime, or indeed by the fighting men of World War II or Korea.

Until the latest of our world conflicts, the United States had no armaments industry. American makers of plowshares could, with time and as required, make swords as well. But now we can no longer risk emergency improvisation of national defense; we have been compelled to create a permanent armaments industry of vast proportions. Added to this, three and a half million men and women are directly engaged in the defense establishment. We annually spend on military security more than the net income of all United States corporations.

This conjunction of an immense military establishment and a large arms industry is new in the American experience. The total influence – economic, political, even spiritual – is felt in every city, every Statehouse, every office of the Federal government. We recognize the imperative need for this development. Yet we must not fail to comprehend its grave implications. Our toil, resources and livelihood are all involved; so is the very structure of our society.

In the councils of government, we must guard against the acquisition of unwarranted influence, whether sought or unsought, by the military-industrial complex. The potential for the disastrous rise of misplaced power exists and will persist.

We must never let the weight of this combination endanger our liberties or democratic processes. We should take nothing for granted. Only an alert and knowledgeable citizenry can compel the proper meshing of the huge industrial and military machinery of defense with our peaceful methods and goals, so that security and liberty may prosper together.

Akin to, and largely responsible for the sweeping changes in our industrial-military posture, has been the technological revolution during recent decades.

In this revolution, research has become central, it also becomes more formalized, complex, and costly. A steadily increasing share is conducted for, by, or at the direction of, the Federal government.

Today, the solitary inventor, tinkering in his shop, has been overshadowed by task forces of scientists in laboratories and testing fields. In the same fashion, the free university, historically the fountainhead of free ideas and scientific discovery, has experienced a revolution in the conduct of research. Partly because of the huge costs involved, a government contract becomes virtually a substitute for intellectual curiosity. For every old blackboard there are now hundreds of new electronic computers.

The prospect of domination of the nation's scholars by Federal employment, project allocations, and the power of money is ever present – and is gravely to be regarded.

Yet, in holding scientific research and discovery in respect, as we should, we must also be alert to the equal and opposite danger that public policy could itself become the captive of a scientific-technological elite.

It is the task of statesmanship to mold, to balance, and to integrate these and other forces, new and old, within the principles of our democratic system – ever aiming toward the supreme goals of our free society.

Another factor in maintaining balance involves the element of time. As we peer into society's future, we – you and I, and our government – must avoid the impulse to live only for today, plundering for, for our own ease and convenience, the precious resources of tomorrow. We cannot mortgage the material assets of our grandchildren without asking the loss also of their political and spiritual heritage. We want democracy to survive for all generations to come, not to become the insolvent phantom of tomorrow.

Down the long lane of the history yet to be written America knows that this world of ours, ever growing smaller, must avoid becoming a community of dreadful fear and hate, and be, instead, a proud confederation of mutual trust and respect.

Such a confederation must be one of equals. The weakest must come to the conference table with the same confidence as do we, protected as we are by our moral, economic, and military strength. That table, though scarred by many past frustrations, cannot be abandoned for the certain agony of the battlefield.

Disarmament, with mutual honor and confidence, is a continuing imperative. Together we must learn how to compose differences, not with arms, but with intellect and decent purpose. Because this need is so sharp and apparent I confess that I lay down my official responsibilities in this field with a definite sense of disappointment. As one who has witnessed the horror and the lingering sadness of war – as one who knows that another war could utterly destroy this civilization which has been so slowly and painfully built over thousands of years – I wish I could say tonight that a lasting peace is in sight.

Happily, I can say that war has been avoided. Steady progress toward our ultimate goal has been made. But, so much remains to be done. As a private citizen, I shall never cease to do what little I can to help the world advance along that road.

So – in this my last good night to you as your President – I thank you for the many opportunities you have given me for public service in war and peace. I trust that in that service you find some things worthy; as for the rest of it, I know you will find ways to improve performance in the future.

You and I – my fellow citizens – need to be strong in our faith that all nations, under God, will reach the goal of peace with justice. May we be ever unswerving in devotion to principle, confident but humble with power, diligent in pursuit of the Nations' great goals.

To all the peoples of the world, I once more give expression to America's prayerful and continuing aspiration:

We pray that peoples of all faiths, all races, all nations, may have their great human needs satisfied; that those now denied opportunity shall come to enjoy it to the full; that all who yearn for freedom may experience its spiritual blessings; that those who have freedom will understand, also, its heavy responsibilities; that all who are insensitive to the needs of others will learn charity; that the scourges of poverty, disease and ignorance will be made to disappear from the earth, and that, in the goodness of time, all peoples will come to live together in a peace guaranteed by the binding force of mutual respect and love.

Source: *Public Papers of the Presidents of the United States: Dwight D. Eisenhower, 1960–61* (Washington, DC: United States Government Printing Office, 1961), pp. 1035–40.

Discussion Questions

1. How do the documents in this chapter challenge or reinforce popular images of the 1950s as an era of social, cultural and political conservatism?
2. From the evidence in these documents what were the main anxieties and problems confronting America at the dawn of the 1960s?
3. Nora Johnson refers to the co-eds she profiles in her article as a "buffer generation." How useful is this concept for thinking about the 1950s more generally?

Chapter 2 The Economy: Abundance, Consumerism, and Poverty

1. Michael Harrington, *The Other America*, 1962

Few books published in America during the early 1960s had more impact than Michael Harrington's The Other America – *a searing indictment of poverty in the United States that ran counter to the era's dominant themes of widespread abundance and perpetual economic growth. As a socialist, Harrington was troubled by the way that American capitalism, for all its success in raising average living standards, actually worked to reproduce inequalities of wealth and opportunity based around differences of race, ethnicity, gender, and class. Writing in the tradition of the best "muckraking" journalism of the Progressive Era and extending more recent critiques of American economic structures, notably John Kenneth Galbraith's* The Affluent Society, *Harrington revealed the plight of some 40 to 50 million impoverished, despondent, and largely neglected Americans. A major best-seller, Harrington's book helped to thrust the issue of poverty into the public consciousness and political arena where presidents John F. Kennedy and Lyndon B. Johnson were among those who fell under its influence. In particular, Johnson's War on Poverty and other aspects of his Great Society programs sought to use federal power to address some of the problems Harrington had identified.*

The poor are increasingly slipping out of the very experience and consciousness of the nation. If the middle class never did like ugliness and poverty, it was at least aware of them. "Across the tracks" was not a very long way to go. There were forays into the slums at Christmas time; there were charitable organizations that brought contact with the poor. Occasionally, almost everyone passed through the Negro ghetto or the blocks of tenements, if only to get downtown to work or to entertainment.

Now the American city has been transformed. The poor still inhabit the miserable housing in the central area, but they are increasingly isolated from contact with, or sight of, anybody else. Middle-class women coming in from Suburbia on a rare trip may catch the merest glimpse of the other America on the way to an evening at the theater, but their children are segregated in suburban schools. The business or professional man may drive along the fringes of slums in a car or bus, but it is not an important experience to him. The failures, the unskilled, the disabled, the aged, and the minorities are right there, across the tracks, where they have always been. But hardly anyone else is.

In short, the very development of the American city has removed poverty from the living, emotional experience of millions upon millions of middle-class Americans. Living out in the suburbs it is easy to assume that ours is, indeed, an affluent society.

This new segregation of poverty is compounded by a well-meaning ignorance. A good many concerned and sympathetic Americans are aware that there is much discussion of urban renewal. Suddenly, driving through the city, they notice that a familiar slum has been torn down and that there are towering, modern buildings where once there had been tenements or hovels. There is a warm feeling of satisfaction, of pride in the way things are working out: the poor, it is obvious, are being taken care of.

The irony in this ... is that the truth is nearly the exact opposite to the impression. The total impact of the various housing programs in postwar America has been to squeeze more and more people into existing slums. More often than not, the modern apartment in a towering building rents at $40 a room or more. For, during the past decade and a half, there has been more subsidization of middle- and upper-income housing than there has been of housing for the poor.

Clothes make the poor invisible too: America has the best-dressed poverty the world has ever known. For a variety of reasons, the benefits of mass production have been spread much more evenly in this area than in many others. It is much easier in the United States to be decently dressed than it is to be decently housed, fed, or doctored. Even people with terribly depressed incomes can look prosperous.

This is an extremely important factor in defining our emotional and existential ignorance of poverty. In Detroit the existence of social classes became much more difficult to discern the day the companies put lockers in the plants. From that moment on, one did not see men in work clothes on the way to the factory, but citizens in slacks and white shirts. This process has been magnified with the poor throughout the country. There are tens of thousands of Americans in the big cities who are wearing shoes, perhaps even a stylishly cut suit or dress, and yet are hungry. It is not a matter of planning, though it almost seems as if the affluent society had given out costumes to the poor so that they would not offend the rest of society with the sight of rags.

Then, many of the poor are the wrong age to be seen. A good number of them (over 8,000,000) are sixty-five years of age or better; an even larger number are under eighteen. The aged members of the other America are often sick, and they cannot move. Another group of them live out their lives in loneliness and frustration: they sit in rented rooms, or else they stay close to a house in a neighborhood that has completely changed from the old days. Indeed, one of the worst aspects of poverty among the aged is that these people are out of sight and out of mind, and alone.

The young are somewhat more visible, yet they too stay close to their neighborhoods. Sometimes they advertise their poverty through a lurid tabloid story about a gang killing. But generally they do not disturb the quiet streets of the middle class.

And finally, the poor are politically invisible. It is one of the cruelest ironies of social life in advanced countries that the dispossessed at the bottom of society are unable to speak for themselves. The people of the other America do not, by far and large, belong to unions, to fraternal organizations, or to political parties. They are without lobbies of their own; they put forward no legislative program. As a group, they are atomized. They have no face; they have no voice....

Out of the thirties came the welfare state. Its creation had been stimulated by mass impoverishment and misery, yet it helped the poor least of all. Laws like unemployment compensation, the Wagner Act, the various farm programs, all these were designed for the middle third in the cities, for the organized workers, and for the upper third in the country, for the big market farmers. If a man works in an extremely low-paying job, he may not even be covered by social security or other welfare programs. If he receives unemployment compensation, the payment is scaled down according to his low earnings.

One of the major laws that was designed to cover everyone, rich and poor, was social security. But even here the other Americans suffered discrimination. Over the years social security payments have not even provided a subsistence level of life. The middle third have been able to supplement the federal pension through private plans negotiated by unions, through joining medical insurance schemes like Blue Cross, and so on. The poor have not been able to do so. They lead a bitter life, and then have to pay for that fact in old age.

Indeed, the paradox that the welfare state benefits those least who need help most is but a single instance of a persistent irony in the other America. Even when the money finally trickles down, even when a school is built in a poor neighborhood, for instance, the poor are still deprived. Their entire environment, their life, their values, do not prepare them to take advantage of the new opportunity. The parents are anxious for the children to go to work; the pupils are pent up, waiting for the moment when their education has complied with the law.

Today's poor, in short, missed the political and social gains of the thirties. They are, as Galbraith rightly points out, the first minority poor in history, the first poor not to be seen, the first poor whom the politicians could leave alone.

The first step toward the new poverty was taken when millions of people proved immune to progress. When that happened, the failure was not individual and personal, but a social product. But once the historic accident takes place, it begins to become a personal fate.

The new poor of the other America saw the rest of society move ahead. They went on living in depressed areas, and often they tended to become depressed human beings. In some of the West Virginia towns, for instance, an entire community will become shabby and defeated. The young and the adventurous go to the city, leaving behind those who cannot move and those who lack the will to do so. The entire area becomes permeated with failure, and that is one more reason the big corporations shy away.

Indeed, one of the most important things about the new poverty is that it cannot be defined in simple, statistical terms. Throughout this book a crucial term is used: aspiration. If a group has internal vitality, a will – if it has aspiration – it may live in dilapidated housing, it may eat an inadequate diet, and it may suffer poverty, but it is not impoverished. So it was in those ethnic slums of the immigrants that played such a dramatic role in the unfolding of the American dream. The people found themselves in slums, but they were not slum dwellers.

But the new poverty is constructed so as to destroy aspiration; it is a system designed to be impervious to hope. The other America does not contain the adventurous seeking a new life and land. It is populated by the failures, by those driven from the land and bewildered by the city, by old people suddenly confronted with the torments of loneliness and poverty, and by minorities facing a wall of prejudice.

In the past, when poverty was general in the unskilled and semi-skilled work force, the poor were all mixed together. The bright and the dull, those who were going to escape into the great society and those who were to stay behind, all of them lived on the same street. When the middle third rose, this community was destroyed. And the entire invisible land of the other Americans became a ghetto, a modern poor farm for the rejects of society and of the economy.

It is a blow to reform and the political hopes of the poor that the middle class no longer understands that poverty exists. But, perhaps more important, the poor are losing their links with the great world. If statistics and sociology can measure a feeling as delicate as loneliness... the other America is becoming increasingly populated by those who do not belong to anybody or anything. They are no longer participants in an ethnic culture from the old country; they are less and less religious; they do not belong to unions or clubs. They are not seen, and because of that they themselves cannot see. Their horizon has become more and more restricted; they see one another, and that means they see little reason to hope. . . .

Finally, one might summarize the newness of contemporary poverty by saying: These are the people who are immune to progress. But then the facts are even more cruel. The other Americans are the victims of the very inventions and machines that have provided a higher living standard for the rest of the society. They are upside-down in the Economy and for them greater productivity often means worse jobs; agricultural advance becomes hunger.

In the optimistic theory, technology is an undisguised blessing. An increase in productivity, the argument goes, generates a higher standard of living for the whole people. And indeed, this has been true for the middle and upper thirds of American society, the people who made such striking gains in the last two decades. It tends to overstate the automatic character of the process, to omit the role of human struggle. . . . Yet it states a certain truth-for those who are lucky enough to participate in it.

But the poor, if they were given to theory, might argue the exact opposite. They might say: Progress is misery.

As the society became more technological, more skilled, those who learn to work the machines, who get the expanding education, move up. Those who miss out at the very start find themselves at a new disadvantage. A generation ago in American life, the majority of the working people did not have high-school educations. But at that time industry was organized on a lower level of skill and competence. And there was sort of continuum in the shop: the youth who left school at sixteen could begin as a laborer, and gradually pick up skill as he went along.

Today the situation is quite different. The good jobs require much more academic preparation, much more skill from the very outset. Those who lack a high-school education tend to be condemned to the underworld – to low-paying service industries, to backward factories, to sweeping and janitorial duties. If the fathers and mothers of the contemporary poor were penalized a generation ago for their lack of schooling, their children will suffer all the more. The very rise in productivity that created more money and better working conditions for the rest of the society can be a menace to the poor....

Poverty in the 1960s is invisible and it is new, and both these factors make it more tenacious. It is more isolated and politically powerless than ever before. It is laced with ironies, not the least of which is that many of the poor view progress upside-down, as a menace and a threat to their lives. And if the nation does not measure up to the challenge of automation, poverty in the 1960s might be on the increase.

Source: Michael Harrington, *The Other America: Poverty in the United States* (New York: Macmillan Publishing Company, 1962), pp. 11–13, 16–21. Reprinted with the permission of Scribner, a Division of Simon & Schuster, Inc. Copyright renewed © 1990 by Stephanie Harrington. All rights reserved.

2. Council of Economic Advisers, *Annual Report*, 1965, 1966

While prosperity was unevenly spread, the strength of the US economy during the 1960s provided a crucial context for many of its most important social, political and cultural developments. This excerpt from the 1965 report of the Council of Economic Advisers – an advisory body set up by Congress after World War II to assist the president in formulating economic policy – captures both a sense of pride in the performance of the economy and an unflinching confidence that growth would continue indefinitely. Interestingly, given the emphasis on free-market principles and the importance of private enterprise, the report is also careful to note the significance of strategic federal interventions to encourage economic growth, with all that seemed to promise in terms of full-employment and greater prosperity throughout the nation.

The Sustained Expansion of 1961–64

As 1965 begins, most Americans are enjoying a degree of prosperity un-matched in their experience, or indeed in the history of their nation. In 1964, some 70 million of them were at work, producing $622 billion worth of goods and services.

The gains of four years of uninterrupted economic expansion had brought fuller pay envelopes, greater sales, larger dividend checks, a higher standard of living, more savings, and a stronger sense of security than ever before. Over that period industrial production grew at an annual rate of 7 percent, and the total output of all goods and services ... increased at an average rate of 5 percent. ... These gains brought jobs to 4 million more persons and raised total consumer income after taxes by 6 percent a year. All this was accomplished with essentially stable prices....

The extent and duration of these gains exceeded the two preceding postwar expansions.... Indeed, in a few months, the duration of this expansion will have surpassed any other on record – except only the prolonged advance before and during World War II.

An overall view of the expansion

This gratifying record reflects the strength and elasticity of the private economy and its favorable response to a series of policy measures deliberately designed to invigorate it. The upturn of 1961 was quick and strong, in part through an early recovery of private demand and in part through forceful policy actions. Prompt steps to boost consumers' purchasing power taken by President Kennedy's administration were later reinforced by increases in Government expenditures necessary to strengthen America's basic defenses and to achieve the precautionary buildup required by the Berlin crisis.

Following the rapid recovery, the outlook appeared favourable in 1962. Many observers, recognizing that there were special explanations for the weakness and brevity of the recovery of 1958–60, expected a return of the vigorous expansionary strength of 1954–57. In fact, conditions had changed. The backlogs of demand for housing, consumer durable goods, and additions to manufacturing plant and equipment, which had existed in 1954–55, were gone. Even after the expansionary fiscal measures of 1961, the federal budget remained more restrictive than it had been in the 1954–57 period. ...

In the course of 1962, the pace of expansion slowed. By mid-1962 it had become apparent that, given the level and structure of federal tax rates, the strength of private demand would be insufficient to carry the economy up to full employment of its resources. Consequently, President Kennedy announced in August that he would propose a major tax bill in 1963, reducing the rates of personal income and corporate profits taxes from levels which had been determined in large part by the need to fight the postwar and Korean [War] inflations. The year 1963 saw prolonged debate over this measure and enactment came only in February 1964. But by mid-1963, increasing confidence that prosperity would be maintained with the aid of the expected tax cut, the continuing support of an expansionary monetary policy, the fuller response of business investment to the 1962 tax measures, and the strong demand for automobiles once again began to accelerate the pace of expansion. Thus, as the Revenue Act of 1964 became effective, the economy was already moving ahead strongly.

The economy in 1964

In its Report a year ago, the Council of Economic Advisers found that "... the outlook this year calls for a significant acceleration in the growth of output. At the midpoint of the forecast range, current dollar GNP for 1964 is estimated to increase 6.5 percent above the level of 1963, and the real GNP about 5 percent ... the more rapid expansion of production in 1964 should lower the unemployment rate. By the end of the year, it is expected to fall to approximately 5 percent." These expectations were realized. Gross National Product (GNP) for the year as a whole exceeded that of 1963 by 6.5 percent and the unemployment rate in December was 5.0 percent.

The optimistic forecast for 1964 depended on the tax cut, and its fulfillment is a measure of the tax cut's accomplishments....

These four years of expansion have demonstrated that the American economy is capable of sustained balanced growth in peacetime. No law of nature compels a free market economy to suffer from recessions or periodic inflations. As the postwar experience of Western Europe and Japan already indicates, future progress need not be interrupted even though its pace may vary from year to year. We need not judge the life expectancy of the current expansion by measuring the time it has already run. The economy is in good health, and its prospects for continued expansion are in no wise dimmed by the fact that the upswing began four years ago rather than one or two years ago. ...

Source: *Annual Report of the Council of Economic Advisers, 1965* (Washington, DC: United States Government Printing Office, 1966), pp. 35–8.

3. Frigidaire, Advertisement for Gemini 19 Refrigerator, 1966

The 1960s was a golden era for the advertising industry. Widespread prosperity, expanding electronic and print media outlets, and a Cold War ideology that made consumerism virtually a patriotic duty, helped to place

Figure 2.1   Frigidaire, Advertisement for Gemini 19 Refrigerator, 1966.

Madison Avenue near the heart of American commerce and lifestyles. No wonder, then, that the advertising industry itself–brash, confident, creative, and lucrative, if also amoral, ruthlessly avaricious, and usually sexist, homophobic, anti-Semitic, and racially blinkered – has become a convenient metaphor for the turbulent cross-currents of the 1960s, as reflected in the critically acclaimed Mad Men *television series launched in 2007.*

The copy and images produced by these [M]Ad Men are a rich source for historians. Although there were relatively few female executives in the industry, clearly women constituted an important market demographic and the manner in which they were courted reveals much about dominant ideas concerning gender, although the messages were often quite mixed. This advertisement for a refrigerator named after NASA's Gemini space program is laden with space-age imagery and technical specifications and seems to speak to a sophisticated, hyper-modern woman. Yet, it still works on the assumption that it is the lot of women to act as custodian of a well-stocked larder that, as the copy repeatedly stresses, is a massive icy monument to middle-class affluence and abundance.

---

4. The Monkees, "Pleasant Valley Sunday," 1967

Originally the brainchild of directors Bob Rafelson and Bert Schneider, the Monkees pop group was created in 1966 to star in a madcap new TV show based loosely on the Beatles' popular movie A Hard Day's Night. *In many ways this artificially manufactured group, formed when Mickey Dolenz, Davy Jones, Mike Nesmith, and Peter Tork responded to a* Daily Variety *advertisement offering "Running parts for 4 insane boys, 17–21," represented the antithesis of the earnest, politicized, and self-consciously artistic folk and rock music that played such an important part in the counterculture of the 1960s. Indeed, while they were never quite the musical novices some believed, session musicians often carried the major burden on the Monkees' early recordings, which included a string of immaculately crafted hit singles such as "Last Train to Clarksville" and "I'm a Believer." "Pleasant Valley Sunday" was composed by veteran songwriters Gerry Goffin and Carole King and became a Number 3 hit single for the Monkees in the summer of 1967. The lyrics, however, represented a significant departure from the love songs that had previously dominated the group's repertoire. With its description of a conformist suburbia, where outward appearance and conspicuous consumption defined status and happiness, the song seemed more in tune with the critiques of traditional American values associated with the New Left and the counterculture. "Pleasant Valley Sunday" heralded the Monkees' growing*

self-consciousness about their own status as a manufactured product – a
perspective that found full, if surreal, expression in a self-mocking feature film
Head and on some of the band's later recordings.

The local rock group down the street
Is trying hard to learn their song
Serenade the weekend squire, who just came out to mow his lawn

Another Pleasant Valley Sunday
Charcoal burning everywhere
Rows of houses that are all the same
And no one seems to care

See Mrs. Gray she's proud today because her roses are in bloom
Mr. Green he's so serene, he's got a TV in every room

Another Pleasant Valley Sunday
Here in status symbol land
Mothers complain about how hard life is
And the kids just don't understand

Creature comfort goals
They only numb my soul and make it hard for me to see
My thoughts all seem to stray, to places far away
I need a change of scenery

Another Pleasant Valley Sunday
Charcoal burning everywhere
Another Pleasant Valley Sunday
Here in status symbol land

Another Pleasant Valley Sunday ...

Source: Written by Gerry Goffin and Carole King © Screen Gems – EMI Music, 1967;
Recorded by The Monkees, June 10–11,1967; Colgems #1007, released on July 10,
1967.

5. *Billboard*, Top Selling Records, 1960–9

*Popular music played a central role in the social and cultural history of the
1960s, but it was also an important factor in the decade's economic history.
Revenue from recordings went up from about $600 million in 1960 to $1.2
billion by 1970. This growth was especially significant among increasingly
affluent young Americans, many of whom used music – whether on record, on
the radio, or at live shows – to express both their attitudinal and economic
independence from an older generation.*

The compilation of data below is drawn from three types of Billboard *record
charts and offers a glimpse into the intersecting social, generational, and
economic forces that lay behind changing musical tastes and patterns of
consumption. It is not a complete picture, of course: record sales and chart
positions alone cannot, for example, do justice to the musical and cultural
importance of Bob Dylan and the folk music revival, nor do they reflect
the exciting experimentations in free jazz that captivated black and white
devotees. Nevertheless, there is much to be learned from these charts. The
existence of a separate "black" Rhythm and Blues (later Soul) chart for much of
this period – as well as the fact that the chart was temporarily abandoned in late
1963, when black and white consumer preferences converged, only to be
resurrected in early 1965 as black tastes diverged again – suggests important
things about the state of race relations and black consciousness during this
period. They also reveal the powerful presence of the black-owned,
Detroit-based Motown label for which artists like Marvin Gaye, Stevie Wonder,
and the Supremes recorded. Until the late 1960s, when rock and pop albums
became more coherent, ambitious, and ultimately popular, the best-selling
albums were often recordings of stage or film musicals, largely consumed by an
adult, rather than a youth, audience. Conversely, although Percy Faith's 1960
movie score hit, "The Theme from a* Summer Place" *was one of the best selling
disks of the entire decade, the singles charts were much more indicative of teen
and youth preferences. Those charts also reflect the enormous commercial
and stylistic impact in the US of the "British Invasion" led by the Beatles and
Rolling Stones.*

Most Popular Top 40 Singles, by Year

1960:   Percy Faith, "The Theme from *A Summer Place*"
1961:   Bobby Lewis, "Tossin' and Turnin'"
1962:   Ray Charles, "I Can't Stop Loving You"
        4 Seasons, "Sherry"
        4 Seasons, "Big Girls Don't Cry"

1963:   Jimmy Gilmer & The Fireballs, "Sugar Shack"
1964:   Beatles, "I Want to Hold Your Hand"
1965:   Rolling Stones, "(I Can't Get No) Satisfaction"
        Beatles, "Yesterday"
1966:   Monkees, "I'm a Believer"
1967:   Lulu, "To Sir With Love"
1968:   Beatles, "Hey Jude"
1969:   5th Dimension, "Aquarius/Let the Sunshine In"
        Zager and Evans, "In the Year 2525"

The criteria for "Most Popular" used here is the number of weeks a recording spent at Number 1 in the Billboard *popular music singles chart. Where more than one song spent the same amount of time at the top of the charts in any given year, all records are included.*

Most Popular Rhythm and Blues Singles, by Year

1960:   Brook Benton and Dinah Washington, "Baby (You've Got What it Takes)"
1961:   Bobby Lewis, "Tossin' and Turnin'"
1962:   Ray Charles, "I Can't Stop Lovin' You"
1963:   Little Stevie Wonder, "Fingertips, Part Two"
1964:   *No separate Rhythm and Blues charts published between November 30, 1963 and January 23, 1965*
1965:   Four Tops, "I Can't Help Myself"
1966:   Temptations, "Ain't too Proud to Beg"
1967:   Aretha Franklin, "Respect"
1968:   Marvin Gaye, "I Heard it Through the Grapevine"
1969:   Marvin Gaye, "Too Busy Thinking about my Baby"

The criteria used here is the number of weeks a recording spent at Number 1 in the Billboard *Rhythm and Blues (or, after August 23, 1969, Soul) singles chart.*

Best Selling Albums, by Year

1960:   *The Sound of Music*, original cast recording
1961:   *Camelot*, original cast recording
1962:   *West Side Story*, soundtrack
1963:   *West Side Story*, soundtrack
1964:   *Hello, Dolly!*, original cast recording
1965:   *Mary Poppins*, soundtrack
1966:   Herb Alpert & The Tijuana Brass, *Whipped Cream & Other Delights*
1967:   Monkees, *More of The Monkees*
1968:   Jimi Hendrix Experience, *Are You Experienced?*
1969:   Iron Butterfly, *In-A-Gadda-Da-Vida*

Sources: Compiled from Joel Whitburn, *Billboard Book of Top 40 Hits, 1955–Present*, 6th rev. edn (New York: Billboard Books, 1996); Joel Whitburn, *Top Rhythm and Blues Records, 1949–1971* (Menomee Falls, WI: Record Research, 1972); and *Billboard*'s annual album sales round-up, 1960–9.

Discussion Questions

1. What were the main criticisms of an apparently booming economy offered, in very different contexts, by Michael Harrington and the Monkees?
2. How does the Report of the Council of Economic Advisers characterize the relationship between the federal government and private enterprise in explaining the widespread economic prosperity of the 1960s?
3. How does the evidence in these documents relating to consumer culture illuminate issues of generation, race, class, and gender in 1960s America?

Chapter 3   The Cold War Context

1. John F. Kennedy, Inaugural Address, 1961

When John F. Kennedy took the oath of office in January 1961, he became the youngest president in American history. He was also the first Catholic to occupy the White House. Such firsts, coupled with his shrewd use of the mass media to project an image of dynamism and innovation for his administration, helped to create a sense of new beginnings and burgeoning possibilities for America at home and abroad. In his Inaugural Address Kennedy boldly asserted the nation's obligation to foster and protect freedom, democracy, and human rights wherever they were challenged, and to use America's economic power and scientific expertise to address issues of poverty around the world. Using rhetoric that betrayed both immediate Cold War anxieties and a commitment to the ideals of the nation's founding fathers, Kennedy called upon Americans to accept the burden of these global responsibilities in terms of a renewal of America's national identity and sense of destiny. The speech's ambition and calls for self-sacrifice in pursuit of worldwide peace, prosperity, and justice was particularly inspirational for a younger generation of Americans. However, Kennedy made virtually no mention of the domestic problems that beset many Americans at this time, notably neglecting to mention the plight of African Americans.

Vice President Johnson, Mr. Speaker, Mr. Chief Justice, President Eisenhower, Vice President Nixon, President Truman, Reverend Clergy, fellow citizens:

We observe today not a victory of party, but a celebration of freedom – symbolizing an end, as well as a beginning – signifying renewal, as well as change. For I have sworn before you and Almighty God the same solemn oath our forebears prescribed nearly a century and three-quarters ago.

The world is very different now. For man holds in his mortal hands the power to abolish all forms of human poverty and all forms of human life. And yet the same revolutionary beliefs for which our forebears fought are still at issue around the globe – the belief that the rights of man come not from the generosity of the state, but from the hand of God.

We dare not forget today that we are the heirs of that first revolution. Let the word go forth from this time and place, to friend and foe alike, that the torch has been passed to a new generation of Americans – born in this century, tempered by war, disciplined by a hard and bitter peace, proud of our ancient heritage, and unwilling to witness or permit the slow undoing of those human rights to which this nation has always been committed, and to which we are committed today at home and around the world.

Let every nation know, whether it wishes us well or ill, that we shall pay any price, bear any burden, meet any hardship, support any friend, oppose any foe, to assure the survival and the success of liberty.

This much we pledge – and more.

To those old allies whose cultural and spiritual origins we share, we pledge the loyalty of faithful friends. United there is little we cannot do in a host of cooperative ventures. Divided there is little we can do – for we dare not meet a powerful challenge at odds and split asunder.

To those new states whom we welcome to the ranks of the free, we pledge our word that one form of colonial control shall not have passed away merely to be replaced by a far more iron tyranny. We shall not always expect to find them supporting our view. But we shall always hope to find them strongly supporting their own freedom – and to remember that, in the past, those who foolishly sought power by riding the back of the tiger ended up inside.

To those people in the huts and villages of half the globe struggling to break the bonds of mass misery, we pledge our best efforts to help them help themselves, for whatever period is required – not because the Communists may be doing it, not because we seek their votes, but because it is right. If a free society cannot help the many who are poor, it cannot save the few who are rich.

To our sister republics south of our border, we offer a special pledge: to convert our good words into good deeds, in a new alliance for progress, to assist free men and free governments in casting off the chains of poverty. But this peaceful revolution of hope cannot become the prey of hostile powers. Let all our neighbors know that we shall join with them to oppose aggression or subversion anywhere in the Americas. And let every other power know that this hemisphere intends to remain the master of its own house.

To that world assembly of sovereign states, the United Nations, our last best hope in an age where the instruments of war have far outpaced the instruments of peace, we renew our pledge of support – to prevent it from becoming merely a forum for invective, to strengthen its shield of the new and the weak, and to enlarge the area in which its writ may run.

Finally, to those nations who would make themselves our adversary, we offer not a pledge but a request: that both sides begin anew the quest for peace, before the dark powers of destruction unleashed by science engulf all humanity in planned or accidental self-destruction.

We dare not tempt them with weakness. For only when our arms are sufficient beyond doubt can we be certain beyond doubt that they will never be employed.

But neither can two great and powerful groups of nations take comfort from our present course – both sides overburdened by the cost of modern weapons, both rightly alarmed by the steady spread of the deadly atom, yet both racing to alter that uncertain balance of terror that stays the hand of mankind's final war.

So let us begin anew – remembering on both sides that civility is not a sign of weakness, and sincerity is always subject to proof. Let us never negotiate out of fear, but let us never fear to negotiate.

Let both sides explore what problems unite us instead of belaboring those problems which divide us.

Let both sides, for the first time, formulate serious and precise proposals for the inspection and control of arms, and bring the absolute power to destroy other nations under the absolute control of all nations.

Let both sides seek to invoke the wonders of science instead of its terrors. Together let us explore the stars, conquer the deserts, eradicate disease, tap the ocean depths, and encourage the arts and commerce.

Let both sides unite to heed, in all corners of the earth, the command of Isaiah – to "undo the heavy burdens, and [to] let the oppressed go free."

And, if a beach-head of cooperation may push back the jungle of suspicion, let both sides join in creating a new endeavor – not a new balance of power, but a new world of law – where the strong are just, and the weak secure, and the peace preserved.

All this will not be finished in the first one hundred days. Nor will it be finished in the first one thousand days; nor in the life of this Administration; nor even perhaps in our lifetime on this planet. But let us begin.

In your hands, my fellow citizens, more than mine, will rest the final success or failure of our course. Since this country was founded, each generation of Americans has been summoned to give testimony to its national loyalty. The graves of young Americans who answered the call to service surround the globe.

Now the trumpet summons us again – not as a call to bear arms, though arms we need – not as a call to battle, though embattled we are – but a call to bear the burden of a long twilight struggle, year in and year out, "rejoicing in hope; patient in tribulation," a struggle against the common enemies of man: tyranny, poverty, disease, and war itself.

Can we forge against these enemies a grand and global alliance, North and South, East and West, that can assure a more fruitful life for all mankind? Will you join in that historic effort?

In the long history of the world, only a few generations have been granted the role of defending freedom in its hour of maximum danger. I do not shrink from this responsibility – I welcome it. I do not believe that any of us would exchange places with any other people or any other generation. The energy, the faith, the devotion which we bring to this endeavor will light our country and all who serve it. And the glow from that fire can truly light the world.

And so, my fellow Americans, ask not what your country can do for you; ask what you can do for your country.

My fellow citizens of the world, ask not what America will do for you, but what together we can do for the freedom of man.

Finally, whether you are citizens of America or citizens of the world, ask of us here the same high standards of strength and sacrifice which we ask of you. With a good conscience our only sure reward, with history the final judge of our deeds, let us go forth to lead the land we love, asking His blessing and His help, but knowing that here on earth God's work must truly be our own.

Source: *Public Papers of the Presidents of the United States: John F. Kennedy, 1961* (Washington, DC: United States Government Printing Office, 1962), pp. 1–3.

2. Robert McNamara, Notes on October 21, 1962, Meeting with the President

On October 14, 1962, a U2 spyplane flying over Cuba took surveillance photographs of construction work on what was quickly identified as a ballistic missile site. Located just 90 miles off the Florida coastline, the site was designed to house short- and intermediate-range Russian-supplied missiles capable of carrying a nuclear payload deep into the heart of the US mainland. The Soviet premier Nikita Khruschev insisted that the missiles were purely defensive in function, designed to protect Fidel Castro's Communist Cuba from invasion by US-sponsored forces, as had been attempted the previous year when the CIA supported a botched invasion by around 1,200 anti-Castro exiles at the Bay of Pigs. President Kennedy and his advisors, however, saw the sites as a clear threat to US security and were determined to have them destroyed. For two weeks, the world watched tremulously as the Cuban Missile Crisis escalated into the most tense episode in the Cold War, with the two major superpowers teetering on the edge of open and potentially apocalyptic conflict.

These "Top Secret" notes, made by Secretary of Defense Robert McNamara after his October 21 meeting with the president and other key advisors, shows the administration groping for an appropriate response to the crisis and reveals a good deal of sentiment for the immediate use of force. Other voices in the administration, notably Attorney General Robert Kennedy, urged restraint and counseled continued diplomatic efforts to defuse the situation.

The day after this meeting, President Kennedy revealed the presence of the missile sites in Cuba to the American public and announced that he was going to establish a naval blockade around Cuba to prevent further Soviet deliveries until the sites were dismantled. Although Kruschev railed against this act of "piracy" and refused to recall a flotilla of ships heading towards Cuba, the move did avoid immediate military engagement and buy time for more negotiations. On October 24, the Russian ships halted and two days later Kruschev agreed to remove the missiles and secure an undertaking from Castro that there would be no offensive weapons on Cuba in the future if the US would pledge not to invade Cuba. Unknown to the US public, another part of the agreement that resolved the crisis also guaranteed that the US would dismantle its own missile sites in Turkey.

---

1. The meeting was held in the Oval Room at the White House and lasted from 11:30 a.m. to approximately 12:30 p.m. In attendance were the Attorney General, General Taylor, General Sweeney and the Secretary of Defense.

2. The Secretary of Defense stated that following the start of an air attack, the initial units of the landing force could invade Cuba within 7 days. The movement of troops in preparation for such an invasion will start at the time of the President's speech. No mobilization of Reserve forces is required for such an invasion until the start of the air strike. General LeMay had stated that the transport aircraft, from Reserve and Guard units,

which would be required for participation in such an invasion can be fully operational within 24 to 48 hours after the call to active duty.

3.   The Secretary of Defense reported that, based on information which became available during the night, it now appears that there is equipment in Cuba for approximately 40 MRBM or IRBM launchers. (Mr. McCone, who joined the group 15 or 20 minutes after the start of the discussion, confirmed this report.) The location of the sites for 36 of these launchers is known. 32 of the 36 known sites appear to have sufficient equipment on them to be included in any air strike directed against Cuba's missile capability.

4.   We believe that 40 launchers would normally be equipped with 80 missiles. John McCone reported yesterday that a Soviet ship believed to be the vessel in which the Soviets have been sending missiles to Cuba has made a sufficient number of trips to that island within recent weeks to offload approximately 48 missiles. Therefore, we assume there are approximately that number on the Island today, although we have only located approximately 30 of these.

5.   General Sweeney outlined the following plan of air attack, the object of which would be the destruction of the known Cuban missile capability.

a.   The 5 surface-to-air missile installations in the vicinity of the known missile sites would each be attacked by approximately 8 aircraft; the 3 MIG airfields defending the missile sites would be covered by 12 U.S. aircraft per field. In total, the defense suppression operations, including the necessary replacement aircraft, would require approximately 100 sorties.

b.   Each of the launchers at the 8 or 9 known sites (a total of approximately 32 to 36 launchers) would be attacked by 6 aircraft. For the purpose, a total of approximately 250 sorties would be flown.

c.   The U.S. aircraft covering the 3 MIG airfields would attack the MIG's if they became airborne. General Sweeney strongly recommended attacks on each of the airfields to destroy the MIG aircraft.

6.   General Sweeney stated that he was certain the air strike would be "successful"; however, even under optimum conditions, it was not likely that all of the known missiles would be destroyed. (As noted in 4 above, the known missiles are probably no more than 60% of the total missiles on the Island.) General Taylor stated, "The best we can offer you is to destroy 90% of the known missiles." General Taylor, General Sweeney and the Secretary of Defense all strongly emphasized that in their opinion the initial air strike

must be followed by strikes on subsequent days and that these in turn would lead inevitably to an invasion.

7. CIA representatives, who joined the discussion at this point, stated that it is probable the missiles which are operational (it is estimated there are now between 8 and 12 operational missiles on the Island) can hold indefinitely a capability for firing with from 2–1/2 to 4 hours' notice. Included in the notice period is a countdown requiring 20 to 40 minutes. In relation to the countdown period, the first wave of our attacking aircraft would give 10 minutes of warning; the second wave, 40 minutes of warning; and the third wave a proportionately greater warning.

8. As noted above, General Sweeney strongly recommended that any air strike include attacks on the MIG aircraft and, in addition, the IL28s. To accomplish the destruction of these aircraft, the total number of sorties of such an air strike should be increased to 500. The President agreed that if an air strike is ordered, it should probably include in its objective the destruction of the MIG aircraft and the IL28s.

9. The President directed that we be prepared to carry out the air strike Monday(1) morning or any time thereafter during the remainder of the week. The President recognized that the Secretary of Defense was opposed to the air strike Monday morning, and that General Sweeney favored it. He asked the Attorney General and Mr. McCone for their opinions:

a. The Attorney General stated he was opposed to such a strike because:
   (1) "It would be a Pearl Harbor type of attack."
   (2) It would lead to unpredictable military responses by the Soviet Union which could be so serious as to lead to general nuclear war.

He stated we should start with the initiation of the blockade and thereafter "play for the breaks."

b. Mr. McCone agreed with the Attorney General, but emphasized he believed we should be prepared for an air strike and thereafter an invasion.

Robert S. McNamara

Source: Washington National Records Center, RG 330, OASD (C) A Files: FRC 71 A 2896, Misc. Papers Regarding Cuba. Top Secret (declassified, September 1985, NLK 78–627).

3. Stanley Kubrick, Terry Southern, and Peter George, *Dr. Strangelove, Or: How I Learned to Stop Worrying and Love the Bomb*, 1964

The terrifying specter of "the Bomb" shaped many aspects of American diplomatic, political, social, economic, and cultural life in the 1960s. Stanley Kubrick's black comedy Dr. Strangelove poked deadly serious fun at the politicians and military leaders who talked about the virtues of making a "first strike" against the Soviet Union, or entertained the possibility of conducting a "contained" nuclear war to halt the spread of communism in South East Asia. The film mocked official government reassurances about the safeguards in place to prevent accidental or premature deployment of America's nuclear option, while also satirizing the concept of Mutually Assured Destruction: MAD rationalized the enormous build up of atomic weaponry on the grounds that increasing the likelihood that any nuclear attack would result in total global annihilation actually reduced the likelihood that either side would risk provoking such a catastrophic conflict. In the movie, Jack D. Ripper, a demented Air Force general, dispatches a bomber wing to launch a preemptive nuclear attack on Russia. In the excerpt below, the US President Merkin Muffley is in the Pentagon War Room being briefed on the situation by the Joint Chiefs of Staff and General Buck Turgidson, a character who – like Jack D. Ripper – was modeled on real-life war-hawk and commander of the Strategic Air Command, General Curtis LeMay.

MUFFLEY: Right. Now, General Turgidson, what's going on here?

TURGIDSON: Mr. President, about thirty-five minutes ago, General Jack Ripper, the commanding General of Burpleson Air Force Base, issued an order to the 34 B-52's of his wing which were airborne at the time as part of a special exercise we were holding called Operation Dropkick. Now, it appears that the order called for the planes to attack their targets inside Russia. The planes are fully armed with nuclear weapons with an average load of 40 megatons each. Now the central display of Russia will indicate the position of the planes. The triangles are their primary targets, the squares are their secondary targets. The aircraft will begin penetrating Russian radar cover within 25 minutes.

MUFFLEY: General Turgidson, I find this very difficult to understand. I was under the impression that I was the only one in authority to order the use of nuclear weapons.

TURGIDSON: That's right sir. You are the only person authorized to do so. And although I hate to judge before all the facts are in, it's beginning to look like General Ripper exceeded his authority.

MUFFLEY: It certainly does. Far beyond the point I would have imagined possible.

TURGIDSON: Well perhaps you're forgetting the provisions of plan R, sir.

MUFFLEY: Plan R?

TURGIDSON: Plan R is an emergency war plan in which a lower echelon commander may order nuclear retaliation after a sneak attack if the normal chain of
command is disrupted. You approved it, sir. You must remember. Surely you must
recall, sir, when Senator Buford made that big hassle about our deterrent lacking
credibility. The idea was for plan R to be a sort of retaliatory safeguard.

MUFFLEY: A safeguard?

TURGIDSON: I admit the human element seems to have failed us here. But the
idea was to discourage the Russkies from any hope that they could knock out
Washington, and yourself, sir, as part of a general sneak attack, and escape
retaliation because of lack of proper command and control.

MUFFLEY: Well I assume then, that the planes will return automatically once they
reach their failsafe points.

TURGIDSON: Well, sir, I'm afraid not. You see the planes were holding at their
failsafe points when the go code was issued. Now, once they fly beyond failsafe
they do not require a second order to proceed. They will fly until they reach
their targets.

MUFFLEY: Then why haven't you radioed the planes countermanding the go code?

TURGIDSON: Well, I'm afraid we're unable to communicate with any of the aircraft.

MUFFLEY: Why?

TURGIDSON: As you may recall, sir, one of the provisions of plan R provides that
once the go code is received the normal SSB radios in the aircraft are switched into
a special coded device, which I believe is designated as CRM114. Now, in order to
prevent the enemy from issuing fake or confusing orders, CRM114 is designed not
to receive at all, unless the message is preceded by the correct three letter code
group prefix.

MUFFLEY: Then do you mean to tell me, General Turgidson, that you will be unable
to recall the aircraft?

TURGIDSON: That's about the size of it. However, we are plowing through every
possible three letter combination of the code. But since there are seventeen
thousand permutations it's going to take us about two and a half days to transmit
them all.

MUFFLEY: How soon did you say the planes would penetrate Russian radar cover?

TURGIDSON: About eighteen minutes from now, sir.

MUFFLEY: Are you in contact with General Ripper?

TURGIDSON: Ah.. No sir, no, General Ripper sealed off the base and cut off all
communications.

MUFFLEY: Where did you get all this information?

TURGIDSON: General Ripper called Strategic Air Command headquarters shortly
after he issued the go code. I have a partial transcript of that conversation if you'd
like me to read it.

MUFFLEY: Read it.

TURGIDSON: The duty officer asked General Ripper to confirm the fact the he had
issued the go code and he said, "Yes gentlemen, they are on their way in and no one

can bring them back. For the sake of our country and our way of life, I suggest you get the rest of SAC in after them, otherwise we will be totally destroyed by red retaliation. My boys will give you the best kind of start, fourteen hundred megatons worth, and you sure as hell won't stop them now. So let's get going. There's no other choice. God willing, we will prevail in peace and freedom from fear and in true health through the purity and essence of our natural fluids. God bless you all." Then he hung up. We're still trying to figure out the meaning of that last phrase, sir.

MUFFLEY: There's nothing to figure out General Turgidson. This man is obviously a psychotic.

TURGIDSON: Well, I'd like to hold off judgment on a thing like that, sir, until all the facts are in.

MUFFLEY: General Turgidson, when you instituted the human reliability tests, you assured me there was no possibility of such a thing ever occurring.

TURGIDSON: Well, I don't think it's quite fair to condemn a whole program because of a single slip up, sir....

TURGIDSON: Mr. President, there are one or two points I'd like to make, if I may.

MUFFLEY: Go ahead, General.

TURGIDSON: One, our hopes for recalling the 843rd bomb wing are quickly being reduced to a very low order of probability. Two, in less than fifteen minutes from now the Russkies will be making radar contact with the planes. Three, when they do, they are going to go absolutely ape, and they're gonna strike back with everything they've got. Four, if prior to this time, we have done nothing further to suppress their retaliatory capabilities, we will suffer virtual annihilation. Now, five, if on the other hand, we were to immediately launch an all out and coordinated attack on all their airfields and missile bases we'd stand a damn good chance of catching 'em with their pants down. Hell, we got a five-to-one missile superiority as it is. We could easily assign three missiles to every target, and still have a very effective reserve force for any other contingency. Now, six, an unofficial study which we undertook of this eventuality, indicated that we would destroy ninety percent of their nuclear capabilities. We would therefore prevail, and suffer only modest and acceptable civilian casualties from their remaining force which would be badly damaged and uncoordinated.

MUFFLEY: General, it is the avowed policy of our country never to strike first with nuclear weapons.

TURGIDSON: Well, Mr. President, I would say that General Ripper has already invalidated that policy.

MUFFLEY: That was not an act of national policy and there are still alternatives left open to us.

TURGIDSON: Mr. President, we are rapidly approaching a moment of truth both for ourselves as human beings and for the life of our nation. Now, the truth is not always a pleasant thing, but it is necessary now make a choice, to choose between two admittedly regrettable, but nevertheless, distinguishable post-war environments: one where you got twenty million people killed, and the other where you got a hundred and fifty million people killed.

MUFFLEY: You're talking about mass murder, General, not war.

TURGIDSON: Mr. President, I'm not saying we wouldn't get our hair mussed. But I do say... no more than ten to twenty million killed, tops. Uh...depending on the breaks.

Source: *Dr. Strangelove, Or: How I Learned to Stop Worrying and Love the Bomb*, movie directed by Stanley Kubrick, Columbia Pictures, 1964. Screenplay by Stanley Kubrick, Terry Southern, and Peter George.

4. Revd. David A. Noebel, *Rhythm, Riots and Revolution*, 1966

During the 1960s, anti-communism shaped many aspects of domestic and cultural life as well as foreign policy. The Revd. David A. Noebel, a close associate of evangelical preacher Billy James Hargis and a minister in Hargis's powerful Tulsa-based Christian Crusade, was convinced that communists and their supporters were using popular music to undermine the religious, moral, and social fabric of the nation by brainwashing America's youth. In a torrent of books, articles, recordings, broadcasts, and in his many sermons and personal appearances, Noebel worked tirelessly to expose the sinister "Red" conspiracy lurking behind youth-oriented music in general and the folk revival and the Beatles in particular. In this excerpt from his 1966 book Rhythms, Riots and Revolution, *Noebel revealed the threat to traditional American values posed by Bob Dylan, offering a distinctly unflattering portrayal of an amoral, communist-influenced Dylan and a lurid, paranoid vision of a massive left-wing conspiracy controlling America's media and popular music industries. Ironically, Noebel, who went on to become founder-president of the arch-conservative Summit Ministries and a collaborator with best-selling Rapture novelist-theologian Tim La Haye, made very shrewd and sophisticated use of the mass media to promote his own uncompromising brand of all-American Christian fundamentalism.*

The crowned prince of rock'n'folk is the extremely popular Bob Dylan. *Newsweek* magazine announced it in very patriotic terminology: "The Patrick Henry of this revolution is twenty-four year old Bob Dylan, a bony prophet-haired poet of protest." Even *Time* magazine admitted, "Folk'n'rock owes its origins to Bob Dylan, 24, folk music's most celebrated contemporary composer." Dylan, a faithful disciple of identified Communist Woody Guthrie, has reached heights never before available to one steeped in the traditions of Communists like Brecht, Lorca, and Yevtushenko. Even Allen Ginsberg, the San Francisco poet who openly advocates promiscuous relations among sexes, says that Dylan is "the most influential poet of his generation." Dylan in turn thinks Ginsberg should have been invited to the Kennedy inauguration instead of Robert Frost.

International Publishers, official Communist publishing firm in the United States, goes into greater historical detail concerning Dylan in its work on Marxist folk music, *Freedom in the Air*. The author, Josh Dunson, is not only an associate editor of the pro-Communist folk journal, *Broadside*, but a recent addition to the *Sing Out!* staff.

According to *Freedom in the Air*, Bob Dylan left the University of Minnesota during his freshman year and bummed around the country. As irony would have it, he was rejected by Folkways Records but accepted by Columbia Records. It seems that, at first, Dylan found himself in the position of having recorded his songs for Columbia and not having them released. However, with time and assistance from extreme leftist John Hammond, Columbia released his topical (pro-Communist) songs in the record album *Freewheelin'* ...

Columbia spent a great deal of money building and advertising the album which included "Blowin' in the Wind," "Hard Rain," "It's All Right" and "Masters of War." In the latter, Dylan expresses bitter hatred toward the generals and war manufacturers who, he says, rule the world and are about to destroy it.... The *Freewheelin'* album made Dylan a national figure and ... International Publishers says of the album *Freewheelin'*, "This record spread more radical ideas to more people in a few short months than all the northern protest meetings and marches since 1960."

But the first and most basic influence on Dylan, according to *Freedom in the Air* "was that of Woody Guthrie." In fact, in *Young Folk Song Book*, Dylan has a "Song to Woody" in which he tells Guthrie about a world that seems sick, tired, torn, and dying although it's hardly been born – no doubt referring to the United States, but assures Guthrie of "a coming new world." One can only surmise whether or not he is referring to William Z. Foster's or Langston Hughes' Soviet America, but then Guthrie would not be interested in any other America. Not only has Guthrie been identified under oath as having been a member of the Communist Party, but Dunson points out that Guthrie wrote a column for the *Daily Worker* entitled, "Woody Sez."

Dylan, as pointed out in our previous chapter on folk music, has been a contributing editor of the pro-Communist *Broadside* journal and a fellow-traveler of the Broadside movement from its inception.... He took part in the great Freedom March on Washington. And even though some maintain Mr. Dylan has lost contact with movements, it should be noted that he "contributes lavishly to SNCC." He also acknowledges that pro-Communist Bertold Brecht is his favorite poet and his attitude toward the United States in contrast to his pro-Russian feelings betrays his conscious motivations....

The International Publishers' book, *Freedom in the Air*, admits that Dylan's best poem is "Hard Rain." Interestingly enough, it also acknowledges that this poem "appears in a poetry anthology edited by a leading American man of letters, Walter Lowenfels." What the book fails to print is the fact that Lowenfels himself has been identified under oath as having been a member of the Communist Party, and that his book *Poets of Today* was published by Communist publishing company, International Publishers. It also failed to point out that *Poets of Today* was highly praised by Gus Hall, leading American Communist Party member, in *Political Affairs*, the recognized theoretical journal of the Communist Party, U.S.A. Dylan's poem is found on page forty-one in the book, and according to copyright acknowledgements, Dylan permitted Lowenfels the usage of his poem. The poem was written at the height of the Cuban missile crisis and was geared to instill fear into the hearts of Americans over the possibility of a nuclear war. Naturally, if we would have backed down, our total capitulation to Communism would have been assured.

For Dylan's usefulness to the Communist Party and his open and defiant attitude toward anti-Communists, the Communist front, Emergency Civil Liberties Committee, presented Dylan with its Tom Paine Award. According to Dunson, Dylan was quite taken aback with ECLC's display of finery, but took the award nevertheless. *The Bob Dylan Story* seeks to soften the blow by pinning the award to that catch-all, "civil rights." Says the Ribakoves, "In December he was given the coveted Tom Paine Award of the Emergency Civil Liberties Committee in recognition of his work for civil rights." However, Mr. and Mrs. Ribakove failed to inform their many readers that the "Emergency Civil Liberties Committee, established in 1951, actually operates as a front for the Communist Party. It has repeatedly assisted, by means of funds and legal aid, Communists involved in Smith Act violations and similar legal proceedings. One of its chief activities has been and still is the dissemination of voluminous Communist propaganda material."

Josh Dunson then seemingly gives away the mystique of Dylan's recent switch from a sloppy, disheveled Castro-looking cultist to the more respectable rock'n'folk composer and singer. Dunson says, "He wants to reach more Americans by using many of the melodic phrases of the Beatles, a popular rock'n'roll group imported from England." He also admits, "In the light of the general level of popular tunes, I think most people would be very pleased if Dylan's latest songs made the hit parade." The trouble is – his songs have not only made the hit parade – but landed right on top! And even now we are informed by Katy Woolston of the *Albuquerque Tribune* that "Hovering on the horizon may be the hairy style of Bob Dylan, folk rock'n'roller from Gallup, classed by music trade journals as the No. 1 influence on teenagers"...

For parents whose daughters believe Dylan to be a fine, uplifting musician, one need only to notice his answer to a question asked recently by a national magazine concerning his kind of girl. Said Dylan, "I want my woman dirty looking as though I'd just found her in some alley. Dirt is very attractive. It triggers the animal emotion. I want dirty long hair hanging all over the place"...

Source: Revd. David A. Noebel, *Rhythm, Riots and Revolution: An Analysis of the Communist Use of Music – The Communist Master Plan* (Tulsa, Oklahoma: Christian Crusade Publications, 1966), pp. 216–23. Reprinted by permission of David A. Noebel.

Discussion Questions

1. How do these documents reflect the influence of "the Bomb" on American foreign policy and domestic culture in the 1960s?
2. John Kennedy's Inaugural Address makes several references to the idea of "freedom" and America's duty to defend it. What do this speech and documents elsewhere in the Reader reveal about how "freedom" was defined in the Cold War context?
3. What were the main substantive and rhetorical features of Revd. Noebel's denunciation of Bob Dylan and what do they reveal about 1960s-style domestic anti-communism?

Chapter 4 The Civil Rights Movement

1. SNCC, Statement of Purpose, 1960

*On February 1, 1960, four black students from North Carolina A&T College
began a sit-in at the Woolworth's lunch counter in downtown Greensboro to
protest the store's refusal to serve African Americans. The Greensboro sit-in
quickly inspired similar demonstrations across the South. In mid-April, around
175 civil rights activists gathered at Shaw University in Raleigh to create a new
organization designed to coordinate the campaign against segregation. Although
students dominated the Shaw meeting and comprised the bulk of the membership
in the newly formed Student Nonviolent Coordinating Committee, SNCC was
also heavily influenced by the veteran civil rights activist Ella Baker, who urged the
students to adopt a "decentralized" and "democratic" structure so as to avoid
over-dependence on a single charismatic leader. The other major influence at Shaw
was the Revd. James Lawson, an experienced exponent of nonviolent direct action
tactics who had pioneered sit-ins in Nashville in the late 1950s. While Baker's
impact was felt in SNCC's emphasis on participatory democracy and grassroots
organizing, SNCC's founding "Statement of Purpose" clearly reflected Lawson's
influence.*

The following Statement of Purpose was adopted in Raleigh, North Carolina, on April 17, 1960, at the first general conference of student movement participants:

We affirm the philosophical or religious ideal of nonviolence as the
foundation of our purpose, the presupposition of our belief, and the manner
of our action.

Nonviolence, as it grows from the Judeo-Christian tradition, seeks a social order of justice permeated by love. Integration of human endeavor represents the crucial first step towards such a society.

Through nonviolence, courage displaces fear. Love transcends hate. Acceptance dissipates prejudice; hope ends despair. Faith reconciles doubt. Peace dominates war. Mutual regards cancel enmity. Justice for all overthrows injustice. The redemptive community supersedes immoral social systems.

By appealing to conscience and standing on the moral nature of human existence, nonviolence nurtures the atmosphere in which reconciliation and justice become actual possibilities.

Source: Marion Barry, 1960, Series I. Chairmen's Files, 1960–9. Subgroup A. Atlanta Office, 1959–72. A-I-1, Student Nonviolent Coordinating Committee Papers, Martin Luther King, Jr. Center for Nonviolent Social Change, Atlanta.

2. Martin Luther King, Jr., "I Have A Dream," 1963

One of the most celebrated orations in American history, Martin Luther King's "I Have a Dream" speech encapsulated the early civil rights movement's efforts to create a land of genuine racial equality and equal opportunity, couching those efforts in terms of America's core values and democratic ideals. King was speaking to a massive interracial crowd and an even larger television audience from the steps of the Lincoln Memorial in Washington DC at the climax of the March on Washington, a nonviolent protest organized by veteran civil rights activist Bayard Rustin and labor leader A. Philip Randolph to draw attention to economic, as well as racial, injustice.

Some critics, notably Malcolm X, who sneered at what he called the "farce on Washington," complained that the original radicalism of the protest had been diluted in order to appease the Kennedy administration, which was supporting the passage of new civil rights legislation in Congress. In fact, amid the visions of racial harmony, King's speech offered a clear warning of growing black impatience with the miserly extent and slovenly pace of meaningful racial change. Presciently King hinted that other, much more radical forces would eclipse the advocates of nonviolent social change if black needs were not quickly addressed.

I am happy to join with you today in what will go down in history as the greatest demonstration for freedom in the history of our nation.

Five score years ago, a great American, in whose symbolic shadow we stand today, signed the Emancipation Proclamation. This momentous decree came as a great beacon light of hope to millions of Negro slaves who had been seared in the flames of withering injustice. It came as a joyous daybreak to end the long night of their captivity.

But one hundred years later, the Negro still is not free. One hundred years later, the life of the Negro is still sadly crippled by the manacles of segregation and the chains of discrimination. One hundred years later, the Negro lives on a lonely island of poverty in the midst of a vast ocean of material prosperity. One hundred years later, the Negro is still languishing in the corners of American society and finds himself an exile in his own land. So we have come here today to dramatize a shameful condition.

In a sense we have come to our nation's capital to cash a check. When the architects of our republic wrote the magnificent words of the Constitution and the Declaration of Independence, they were signing a promissory note to which every American was to fall heir. This note was a promise that all men, yes, black men as well as white men, would be guaranteed the unalienable rights of life, liberty, and the pursuit of happiness.

It is obvious today that America has defaulted on this promissory note insofar as her citizens of color are concerned. Instead of honoring this sacred obligation, America has given the Negro people a bad check, a check which has come back marked "insufficient funds." But we refuse to believe that the bank of justice is bankrupt. We refuse to believe that there are insufficient funds in the great vaults of opportunity of this nation. So we have come to cash this check – a check that will give us upon demand the riches of freedom and the security of justice. We have also come to this hallowed spot to remind America of the fierce urgency of now. This is no time to engage in the luxury of cooling off or to take the tranquilizing drug of gradualism. Now is the time to make real the promises of democracy. Now is the time to rise from the dark and desolate valley of segregation to the sunlit path of racial justice. Now is the time to lift our nation from the quicksands of racial injustice to the solid rock of brotherhood. Now is the time to make justice a reality for all of God's children.

It would be fatal for the nation to overlook the urgency of the moment. This sweltering summer of the Negro's legitimate discontent will not pass until there is an invigorating autumn of freedom and equality. Nineteen sixty-three is not an end, but a beginning. Those who hope that the Negro needed to blow off steam and will now be content will have a rude awakening if the nation returns to business as usual. There will be neither rest nor tranquility in America until the Negro is granted his citizenship rights. The whirlwinds of revolt will continue to shake the foundations of our nation until the bright day of justice emerges.

But there is something that I must say to my people who stand on the warm threshold which leads into the palace of justice. In the process of gaining our rightful place we must not be guilty of wrongful deeds. Let us not seek to satisfy our thirst for freedom by drinking from the cup of bitterness and hatred.

We must forever conduct our struggle on the high plane of dignity and discipline. We must not allow our creative protest to degenerate into physical violence. Again and again we must rise to the majestic heights of meeting physical force with soul force. The marvelous new militancy which has engulfed the Negro community must not lead us to distrust of all white people, for many of our white brothers, as evidenced by their presence here today, have come to realize that their destiny is tied up with our destiny and their freedom is inextricably bound to our freedom. We cannot walk alone.

As we walk, we must make the pledge that we shall march ahead. We cannot turn back. There are those who are asking the devotees of civil rights, "When will you be satisfied?" We can never be satisfied as long as the Negro is the victim of the unspeakable horrors of police brutality. We can never be satisfied, as long as our bodies, heavy with the fatigue of travel, cannot gain lodging in the motels of the highways and the hotels of the cities. We can never be satisfied as long as a Negro in Mississippi cannot vote and a Negro in New York believes he has nothing for which to vote. No, no, we are not satisfied, and we will not be satisfied until justice rolls down like waters and righteousness like a mighty stream.

I am not unmindful that some of you have come here out of great trials and tribulations. Some of you have come fresh from narrow jail cells. Some of you have come from areas where your quest for freedom left you battered by the storms of persecution and staggered by the winds of police brutality. You have been the veterans of creative suffering. Continue to work with the faith that unearned suffering is redemptive.

Go back to Mississippi, go back to Alabama, go back to South Carolina, go back to Georgia, go back to Louisiana, go back to the slums and ghettos of our northern cities, knowing that somehow this situation can and will be changed. Let us not wallow in the valley of despair.

I say to you today, my friends, so even though we face the difficulties of today and tomorrow, I still have a dream. It is a dream deeply rooted in the American dream.

I have a dream that one day this nation will rise up and live out the true meaning of its creed: "We hold these truths to be self-evident: that all men are created equal."

I have a dream that one day on the red hills of Georgia the sons of former slaves and the sons of former slave owners will be able to sit down together at the table of brotherhood.

I have a dream that one day even the state of Mississippi, a state sweltering with the heat of injustice, sweltering with the heat of oppression, will be transformed into an oasis of freedom and justice.

I have a dream that my four little children will one day live in a nation where they will not be judged by the color of their skin but by the content of their character.

I have a dream today.

I have a dream that one day, down in Alabama, with its vicious racists, with its governor having his lips dripping with the words of interposition and nullification; one day right there in Alabama, little black boys and black girls will be able to join hands with little white boys and white girls as sisters and brothers.

I have a dream today.

I have a dream that one day every valley shall be exalted, every hill and mountain shall be made low, the rough places will be made plain, and the crooked places will be made straight, and the glory of the Lord shall be revealed, and all flesh shall see it together.

This is our hope. This is the faith that I go back to the South with. With this faith we will be able to hew out of the mountain of despair a stone of hope. With this faith we will be able to transform the jangling discords of our nation into a beautiful symphony of brotherhood. With this faith we will be able to work together, to pray together, to struggle together, to go to jail together, to stand up for freedom together, knowing that we will be free one day.

This will be the day when all of God's children will be able to sing with a new meaning, "My country, 'tis of thee, sweet land of liberty, of thee I sing. Land where my fathers died, land of the pilgrim's pride, from every mountainside, let freedom ring."

And if America is to be a great nation this must become true. So let freedom ring from the prodigious hilltops of New Hampshire. Let freedom ring from the mighty mountains of New York. Let freedom ring from the heightening Alleghenies of Pennsylvania!

Let freedom ring from the snowcapped Rockies of Colorado!

Let freedom ring from the curvaceous slopes of California!

But not only that; let freedom ring from Stone Mountain of Georgia!

Let freedom ring from Lookout Mountain of Tennessee!

Let freedom ring from every hill and molehill of Mississippi. From every mountainside, let freedom ring.

And when this happens, When we allow freedom to ring, when we let it ring from every village and every hamlet, from every state and every city, we will be able to speed up that day when all of God's children, black men and white men, Jews and Gentiles, Protestants and Catholics, will be able to join hands and sing in the words of the old Negro spiritual, "Free at last! Free at last! Thank God Almighty, we are free at last!"

Source: James M. Washington (ed.), *A Testament of Hope: The Essential Writings and Speeches of Martin Luther King, Jr.* (New York: Harper One, 1990), pp. 217–20. Copyright 1963 Dr. Martin Luther King, Jr.; copyright renewed 1991 Coretta Scott King.

3. Malcolm X, "The Ballot or the Bullet," 1964

During the early 1960s, Malcolm X emerged as one of the most eloquent and influential advocates of Black Nationalism in America. A former petty criminal and drug addict, Malcolm Little embraced the tenets of Elijah Muhammad's Nation of Islam while in jail and, after his release, rose to prominence as a spokesman for Muhammad's organization. Insisting on racial pride and black self-reliance while denouncing America's "white devils" for their many abuses of African Americans, Malcolm brilliantly articulated the simmering anger and frustrations of many African Americans in the urban North. He presented a separatist alternative to the integrationist ethos of the southern struggle and instead of emphasizing nonviolence championed the right of armed self-defense.

By the time he delivered this version of his "The Ballot or the Bullet" speech in Cleveland in April 1964, Malcolm had left Elijah Muhammad's Nation. There were many reasons for the split. Muhammad had clearly become jealous of Malcolm's growing influence and prestige; Malcolm was deeply disillusioned by revelations of Muhammad's philandering and increasingly skeptical about some aspects of the Nation's theology – concerns that would become even greater after Malcolm went on a pilgrimage to Mecca and discovered a much more progressive, racially inclusive form of Islam. Malcolm was also frustrated by Muhammad's reluctance to allow his followers to participate in the kind of political and civil rights activities that were capturing the black imagination in the 1960s. In this election year speech Malcolm critiqued the failure of the US government and the current political system to address African American problems while proposing a move towards Black Nationalism, a credo which he carefully tried to distinguish from simple "anti-white" sentiments. Malcolm attempted to institutionalize his vision in his Organization of African American Unity, but those efforts were cut short when he was assassinated by followers of Elijah Muhammad in February 1965. His ideas, however, would play an important role in the Black Power movement that blossomed in the late 1960s.

The question tonight, as I understand it, is The Negro Revolt, and Where Do We Go From Here? or What Next? In my little humble way of understanding it, it points toward either the ballot or the bullet.

Before we try and explain what is meant by the ballot or the bullet, I would like to clarify something concerning myself. I'm still a Muslim; my religion is still Islam. That's my personal belief. Just as Adam Clayton Powell is a Christian minister who heads the Abyssinian Baptist Church in New York, but at the same time takes part in the political struggles to try and bring about rights to the black people in this country; and Dr. Martin Luther King is a Christian minister down in Atlanta, Georgia, who heads another organization fighting for the civil rights of black people in this country; and Reverend Galamison, I guess you've heard of him, is another Christian minister in New York who has been deeply involved in the school boycotts to eliminate segregated education; well, I myself am a minister, not a Christian minister, but a Muslim minister; and I believe in action on all fronts by whatever means necessary.

Although I'm still a Muslim, I'm not here tonight to discuss my religion. I'm not here to try and change your religion. I'm not here to argue or discuss anything that we differ about, because it's time for us to submerge our differences and realize that it is best for us to first see that we have the same problem, a common problem, a problem that will make you catch hell whether you're a Baptist, or a Methodist, or a Muslim, or a nationalist. Whether you're educated or illiterate, whether you live on the boulevard or in the alley, you're going to catch hell just like I am. We're all in the same boat and we all are going to catch the same hell from the same man. He just happens to be a white man. All of us have suffered here, in this country, political oppression at the hands of the white man, economic exploitation at the hands of the white man, and social degradation at the hands of the white man.

Now in speaking like this, it doesn't mean that we're anti-white, but it does mean we're anti-exploitation, we're anti-degradation, we're anti-oppression. And if the white man doesn't want us to be anti-him, let him stop oppressing and exploiting and degrading us. Whether we are Christians or Muslims or nationalists or agnostics or atheists, we must first learn to forget our differences. If we have differences, let us differ in the closet; when we come out in front, let us not have anything to argue about until we get finished arguing with the man...

1964 threatens to be the most explosive year America has ever witnessed. The most explosive year. Why? It's also a political year. It's the year when all of the white politicians will be back in the so-called Negro community jiving you and me for some votes. The year when all of the white political crooks will be right back in your and my community with their false promises, building up our hopes for a letdown, with their trickery and their treachery, with their false promises which they don't intend to keep. As they nourish these dissatisfactions, it can only lead to one thing, an explosion; and now we have the type of black man on the scene in America today ... who just doesn't intend to turn the other cheek any longer...

I'm not a politician, not even a student of politics; in fact, I'm not a student of much of anything. I'm not a Democrat. I'm not a Republican, and I don't even consider myself an American. If you and I were Americans, there'd be no problem. Those Hunkies that just got off the boat, they're already Americans; Polacks are already Americans; the Italian refugees are already Americans. Everything that came out of Europe, every blue-eyed thing, is already an American. And as long as you and I have been over here, we aren't Americans yet...

No, I'm not an American. I'm one of the 22 million black people who are the victims of Americanism. One of the 22 million black people who are the victims of democracy, nothing but disguised hypocrisy. So, I'm not standing here speaking to you as an American, or a patriot, or a flag-saluter, or a flag-waver – no, not I. I'm speaking as a victim of this American system. And I see America through the eyes of the victim. I don't see any American dream; I see an American nightmare...

These 22 million victims are waking up. Their eyes are coming open. They're beginning to see what they used to only look at. They're becoming politically mature. They are realizing that there are new political trends from coast to coast. As they see these new political trends, it's possible for them to see that every time there's an election the races are so close that they have to have a recount.... When white people are evenly divided, and black people have a bloc of votes of their own, it is left up to them to determine who's going to sit in the White House and who's going to be in the dog house.

It was the black man's vote that put the present administration in Washington, D.C. Your vote, your dumb vote, your ignorant vote, your wasted vote put in an administration in Washington, D.C., that has seen fit to pass every kind of legislation imaginable, saving you until last, then filibustering on top of that....

Four years in office, and just now getting around to some civil-rights legislation. Just now, after everything else is gone, out of the way, they're going to sit down now and play with you all summer long – the same old giant con game that they call filibuster. All those are in cahoots together. Don't you ever think they're not in cahoots together, for the man that is heading the civil-rights filibuster is a man from Georgia named Richard Russell. When Johnson became president, the first man he asked for when he got back to Washington, D.C., was Dicky – that's how tight they are. That's his boy, that's his pal, that's his buddy. But they're playing that old con game. One of them makes believe he's for you, and he's got it fixed where the other one is so tight against you, he never has to keep his promise...,

I say again, I'm not anti-Democrat, I'm not anti-Republican, I'm not anti-anything. I'm just questioning their sincerity, and some of the strategy that they've been using on our people by promising them promises that they don't intend to keep. When you keep the Democrats in power, you're keeping the Dixiecrats in power.... A vote for a Democrat is a vote for a Dixiecrat. That's why, in 1964, it's time now for you and me to become more politically mature and realize what the ballot is for; what we're supposed to get when we cast a ballot; and that if we don't cast a ballot, it's going to end up in a situation where we're going to have to cast a bullet. It's either a ballot or a bullet.

In the North, they do it a different way. They have a system that's known as gerrymandering, whatever that means. It means when Negroes become too heavily concentrated in a certain area, and begin to gain too much political power, the white man comes along and changes the district lines. You may say, Why do you keep saying white man? Because it's the white man who does it. I haven't ever seen any Negro changing any lines. They don't let him get near the line. It's the white man who does this. And usually, it's the white man who grins at you the most, and pats you on the back, and is supposed to be your friend. He may be friendly, but he's not your friend.

So, what I'm trying to impress upon you, in essence, is this: You and I in America are faced not with a segregationist conspiracy, we're faced with a government conspiracy. Everyone who's filibustering is a senator – that's the government. Everyone who's finagling in Washington, D.C., is a congressman – that's the government. You don't have anybody putting blocks in your path but people who are a part of the government. The same government that you go abroad to fight for and die for is the government that is in a conspiracy to deprive you of your voting rights, deprive you of your economic opportunities, deprive you of decent housing, deprive you of decent education. You don't need to go to the employer alone, it is the government itself, the government of America, that is responsible for the oppression and exploitation and degradation of black people in this country. And you should drop it in their lap. This government has failed the Negro. This so-called democracy has failed the Negro. And all these white liberals have definitely failed the Negro....

The political philosophy of black nationalism means that the black man should control the politics and the politicians in his own community; no more. The black man in the black community has to be re-educated into the science of politics so he will know what politics is supposed to bring him in return. Don't be throwing out any ballots. A ballot is like a bullet. You don't throw your ballots until you see a target, and if that target is not within your reach, keep your ballot in your pocket.... Black people are fed up with the dillydallying, pussyfooting, compromising approach that we've been using toward getting our freedom. We want freedom now, but we're not going to get it saying We Shall Overcome. We've got to fight until we overcome.

The economic philosophy of black nationalism is pure and simple. It only means that we should control the economy of our community. Why should white people be running all the stores in our community? Why should white people be running the banks of our community? Why should the economy of our community be in the hands of the white man? Why? If a black man can't move his store into a white community, you tell me why a white man should move his store into a black community. The philosophy of black nationalism involves a re-education program in the black community in regards to economics. Our people have to be made to see that any time you take your dollar out of your community and spend it in a community where you don't live, the community where you live will get poorer and poorer, and the community where you spend your money will get richer and richer....

The social philosophy of black nationalism only means that we have to get together and remove the evils, the vices, alcoholism, drug addiction, and other evils that are destroying the moral fiber of our community. We ourselves have to lift the level of our community, the standard of our community to a higher level, make our own society beautiful so that we will be satisfied in our own social circles and won't be running around here trying to knock our way into a social circle where we're not wanted.

So I say, in spreading a gospel such as black nationalism, it is not designed to make the black man re-evaluate the white man – you know him already – but to make the black man re-evaluate himself. Don't change the white man's mind – you can't change his mind, and that whole thing about appealing to the moral conscience of America – America's conscience is bankrupt. She lost all conscience a long time ago. Uncle Sam has no conscience....

We will work with anybody, anywhere, at any time, who is genuinely interested in tackling the problem head-on, nonviolently as long as the enemy is nonviolent, but violent when the enemy gets violent....

Last but not least, I must say this concerning the great controversy over rifles and shotguns. The only thing that I've ever said is that in areas where the government has proven itself either unwilling or unable to defend the lives and the property of Negroes, it's time for Negroes to defend themselves. Article number two of the constitutional amendments provides you and me the right to own a rifle or a shotgun. It is constitutionally legal to own a shotgun or a rifle. This doesn't mean you're going to get a rifle and form battalions and go out looking for white folks, although you'd be within your rights – I mean, you'd be justified; but that would be illegal and we don't do anything illegal. If the white man doesn't want the black man buying rifles and shotguns, then let the government do its job. . . .

If he's not going to do his job in running the government and providing you and me with the protection that our taxes are supposed to be for, since he spends all those billions for his defense budget, he certainly can't begrudge you and me spending $12 or $15 for a single-shot, or double-action. I hope you understand. Don't go out shooting people, but any time – brothers and sisters, and especially the men in this audience; some of you wearing Congressional Medals of Honor, with shoulders this wide, chests this big, muscles that big – any time you and I sit around and read where they bomb a church and murder in cold blood, not some grownups, but four little girls while they were praying to the same God the white man taught them to pray to, and you and I see the government go down and can't find who did it.

Why, this man – he can find Eichmann hiding down in Argentina somewhere. Let two or three American soldiers, who are minding somebody else's business way over in South Vietnam, get killed, and he'll send battleships, sticking his nose in their business. He wanted to send troops down to Cuba and make them have what he calls free elections – this old cracker who doesn't have free elections in his own country.

No, if you never see me another time in your life, if I die in the morning, I'll die saying one thing: the ballot or the bullet, the ballot or the bullet.

Source: George Breitman (ed.), *Malcolm X Speaks* (New York: Grove Press, Inc., 1965), pp. 23–44. Copyright © 1965, 1989 by Betty Shabazz and Pathfinder Press. Reprinted by permission.

4. Fannie Lou Hamer, Testimony to the Democratic Party National Convention, 1964

A sharecropper scratching a living in Sunflower County, Mississippi,
Mrs. Fannie Lou Hamer was not even aware that voting might be a possibility
for African Americans like herself until she came into contact with SNCC

workers in 1962. Hamer quickly became a charismatic stalwart of voter
registration efforts in Mississippi, where a mixture of white terror and legal
and bureaucratic chicanery meant that less than 2 percent of the adult African
American population was registered to vote in 1960.

In August 1964, after an intense Freedom Summer of voter registration,
Hamer was in the delegation from the bi-racial Mississippi Freedom
Democratic Party (MFDP) that traveled to the Democratic Party's national
convention in Atlantic City, hoping to be seated in place of the regular
exclusively white contingent. Speaking before the Credentials Committee,
which ruled on matters of admission to the Convention, Hamer passionately
indicted Mississippi's racist institutions and recounted her personal
experiences of the discrimination, intimidation, and violence suffered daily by
the state's black inhabitants, particularly those who dared to stand up for their
basic civil and political rights. So damning was her testimony, that President
Johnson interrupted television coverage for a hastily organized press
conference, though many saw Hamer's testimony on later newscasts.

Despite the moral power of its claim to be the only democratically elected
delegation from Mississippi, Johnson's need to maintain the support of
southern whites meant that the MFDP was refused formal recognition at the
Convention and proudly turned down a compromise whereby it would have
received two at-large, non-voting seats. While the MFDP insurgency attracted
widespread sympathy for the plight of Mississippi blacks and increased public
support for black voting rights, many civil rights workers were deeply
disillusioned by what they saw as a betrayal by the Democrats and Lyndon
Johnson in particular. For some, the failure to seat the MFDP at Atlantic City
indicated that mainstream politics remained fundamentally hostile to black
aspirations and revealed serious limitations to the support blacks could expect
from white liberals.

Mr. Chairman, and to the Credentials Committee, my name is Mrs. Fannie
Lou Hamer, and I live at 626 East Lafayette Street, Ruleville, Mississippi,
Sunflower County, the home of Senator James O. Eastland, and Senator
Stennis.

It was the 31st of August in 1962 that eighteen of us traveled twenty-six
miles to the county courthouse in Indianola to try to register to become first-
class citizens. We was met in Indianola by policemen, Highway Patrolmen,
and they only allowed two of us in to take the literacy test at the time. After
we had taken this test and started back to Ruleville, we was held up by the
City Police and the State Highway Patrolmen and carried back to Indianola
where the bus driver was charged that day with driving a bus the wrong color.

After we paid the fine among us, we continued on to Ruleville, and
Reverend Jeff Sunny carried me four miles in the rural area where I had

worked as a timekeeper and sharecropper for eighteen years. I was met there by my children, who told me that the plantation owner was angry because I had gone down to try to register.

After they told me, my husband came, and said the plantation owner was raising Cain because I had tried to register. Before he quit talking the plantation owner came and said, "Fannie Lou, do you know – did Pap tell you what I said?"

And I said, "Yes, sir."

He said, "Well I mean that." He said, "If you don't go down and withdraw your registration, you will have to leave." Said, "Then if you go down and withdraw," said, "you still might have to go because we are not ready for that in Mississippi."

And I addressed him and told him and said, "I didn't try to register for you. I tried to register for myself."

I had to leave that same night.

On the 10th of September 1962, sixteen bullets was fired into the home of Mr. and Mrs. Robert Tucker for me. That same night two girls were shot in Ruleville, Mississippi. Also Mr. Joe McDonald's house was shot in.

And June the 9th, 1963, I had attended a voter registration workshop; was returning back to Mississippi. Ten of us was traveling by the Continental Trailway bus. When we got to Winona, Mississippi, which is Montgomery County, four of the people got off to use the washroom, and two of the people – to use the restaurant – two of the people wanted to use the washroom.

The four people that had gone in to use the restaurant was ordered out. During this time I was on the bus. But when I looked through the window and saw they had rushed out I got off of the bus to see what had happened. And one of the ladies said, "It was a State Highway Patrolman and a Chief of Police ordered us out."

I got back on the bus and one of the persons had used the washroom got back on the bus, too.

As soon as I was seated on the bus, I saw when they began to get the five people in a highway patrolman's car. I stepped off of the bus to see what was happening and somebody screamed from the car that the five workers was in and said, "Get that one there." When I went to get in the car, when the man told me I was under arrest, he kicked me.

I was carried to the county jail and put in the booking room. They left some of the people in the booking room and began to place us in cells. I was placed in a cell with a young woman called Miss Ivesta Simpson. After I was placed in the cell I began to hear sounds of licks and screams, I could hear the sounds of licks and horrible screams. And

I could hear somebody say, "Can you say, 'yes, sir,' nigger? Can you say 'yes, sir'?"

And they would say other horrible names.

She would say, "Yes, I can say 'yes, sir.'"

"So, well, say it."

She said, "I don't know you well enough."

They beat her, I don't know how long. And after a while she began to pray, and asked God to have mercy on those people.

And it wasn't too long before three white men came to my cell. One of these men was a State Highway Patrolman and he asked me where I was from. I told him Ruleville and he said, "We are going to check this."

They left my cell and it wasn't too long before they came back. He said, "You are from Ruleville all right," and he used a curse word. And he said, "We are going to make you wish you was dead."

I was carried out of that cell into another cell where they had two Negro prisoners. The State Highway Patrolmen ordered the first Negro to take the blackjack.

The first Negro prisoner ordered me, by orders from the State Highway Patrolman, for me to lay down on a bunk bed on my face.

I laid on my face and the first Negro began to beat. I was beat by the first Negro until he was exhausted. I was holding my hands behind me at that time on my left side, because I suffered from polio when I was six years old.

After the first Negro had beat until he was exhausted, the State Highway Patrolman ordered the second Negro to take the blackjack.

The second Negro began to beat and I began to work my feet, and the State Highway Patrolman ordered the first Negro who had beat me to sit on my feet – to keep me from working my feet. I began to scream and one white man got up and began to beat me in my head and tell me to hush.

One white man – my dress had worked up high – he walked over and pulled my dress – I pulled my dress down and he pulled my dress back up.

I was in jail when Medgar Evers was murdered.

All of this is on account of we want to register, to become first-class citizens. And if the Freedom Democratic Party is not seated now, I question America. Is this America, the land of the free and the home of the brave, where we have to sleep with our telephones off the hooks because our lives be threatened daily, because we want to live as decent human beings, in America?

Thank you.

Source: "Democratic National Committee-Mississippi Credentials Committee, Atlantic City, NJ, August 22, 1964," Records of the Democratic National Committee, Series II, Box 102, Transcript of Hearing, Lyndon Baines Johnson Presidential Library and Museum, Austin, Texas.

5. Lyndon B. Johnson, "To Fulfill These Rights," 1965

In mid-March 1965, in the wake of the violence perpetrated by Alabama law enforcement officers against nonviolent civil rights marchers demonstrating for the right to vote in Selma, Alabama, President Johnson committed himself to a new law "designed to eliminate illegal barriers to the right to vote." In an electrifying, nationally broadcast message to a joint session of Congress, he insisted that the fate of all Americans and of precious American notions of freedom, justice, and democracy were tightly bound to the success of the civil rights struggle. "Their cause must be our cause too," he explained. "It is not just Negroes, but really it is all of us, who must overcome the crippling legacy of bigotry and injustice," he said, before borrowing a line from the most popular of all the civil rights freedom songs to affirm, "And we shall overcome."

The Voting Rights Bill Johnson sent to Congress was eventually signed into law on August 6, 1965. In the intervening months, Johnson, like many civil rights leaders, began to contemplate the prospects for securing genuine equality for African Americans once the most obvious impediments to black voting had been removed. Overt discrimination in public accommodations, education, and employment had already been outlawed in the Civil Rights Act of 1964. In his Commencement Address at the prestigious historically black Howard University, Johnson made it very clear that after centuries of discrimination and disadvantage the eradication of statutory inequality would be insufficient to secure equality of opportunity, let alone condition, for African Americans. Instead, he emphasized the need to address the particular economic plight of the black community and its attendant social problems – most controversially, the impact of urban poverty and lack of opportunity on the black family – putting this agenda in the context of the kind of federal commitment to the poor and dispossessed in America that characterized his Great Society initiatives.

...Nothing in any country touches us more profoundly, and nothing is more freighted with meaning for our own destiny than the revolution of the Negro American.

In far too many ways American Negroes have been another nation: deprived of freedom, crippled by hatred, the doors of opportunity closed to hope.

In our time change has come to this nation, too. The American Negro, acting with impressive restraint, has peacefully protested and marched, entered the courtrooms and the seats of government, demanding a justice that has long been denied. The voice of the Negro was the call to action. But it is a tribute to America that, once aroused, the courts and the Congress, the President and most of the people, have been the allies of progress.

Legal protection for human rights

Thus we have seen the high court of the country declare that discrimination based on race was repugnant to the Constitution, and therefore void. We have seen in 1957, and 1960, and again in 1964, the first civil rights legislation in this Nation in almost an entire century.

As majority leader of the United States Senate, I helped to guide two of these bills through the Senate. And, as your President, I was proud to sign the third. And now, very soon we will have the fourth – a new law guaranteeing every American the right to vote.

No act of my entire administration will give me greater satisfaction than the day when my signature makes this bill, too, the law of this land.

The voting rights bill will be the latest, and among the most important, in a long series of victories. But this victory – as Winston Churchill said of another triumph for freedom – "is not the end. But it is, perhaps, the end of the beginning."

That beginning is freedom; and the barriers to that freedom are tumbling down. Freedom is the right to share, share fully and equally, in American Society – to vote, to hold a job, to enter a public place, to go to school. It is the right to be treated in every part of our national life as a person equal in dignity and promise to all others.

Freedom is not enough

But freedom is not enough. You do not wipe away the scars of centuries by saying: Now you are free to go where you want, and do as you desire, and choose the leaders you please.

You do not take a person who, for years, has been hobbled by chains and liberate him, bring him up to the starting line of a race and then say, "you are free to compete with all the others," and still justly believe that you have been completely fair.

Thus it is not enough to open the gates of opportunity. All our citizens must have the ability to walk through those gates. This is the next and the more profound stage of the battle for civil rights. We seek not just freedom but opportunity. We seek not just legal equity but human ability, not just equality as a right and a theory but equality as a fact and equality as a result.

For the task to give 20 million Negroes the same chance as every other American to learn and grow, to work and share in society, to develop their abilities – physical, mental and spiritual, and to pursue their individual happiness.

To this end equal opportunity is essential, but not enough, not enough. Men and women of all races are born with the same range of abilities. But ability is not just the product of birth. Ability is stretched or stunted by the family that you live with, and the neighborhood you live in – by the school you go to and the poverty or the richness of your surroundings. It is the product of a hundred unseen forces playing upon the little infant, the child, and finally the man....

Progress for some

This graduating class at Howard University is witness to the indomitable determination of the Negro American to win his way in American life.

The number of Negroes in schools of higher learning has almost doubled in 15 years. The number of nonwhite professional workers has more than doubled in 10 years. The median income of Negro college women tonight exceeds that of white college women. And there are also the enormous accomplishments of distinguished individual Negroes – many of them graduates of this institution, and one of them the first lady ambassador in the history of the United States.

These are proud and impressive achievements. But they tell only the story of a growing middle class minority, steadily narrowing the gap between them and their white counterparts.

A widening gulf

But for the great majority of Negro Americans – the poor, the unemployed, the uprooted, and the dispossessed – there is a much grimmer story. They still, as we meet here tonight, are another nation. Despite the court orders and the laws, despite the legislative victories and the speeches, for them the walls are rising and the gulf is widening.

Here are some of the facts of this American failure.

Thirty-five years ago the rate of unemployment for Negroes and whites was about the same. Tonight the Negro rate is twice as high.

In 1948 the 8 percent unemployment rate for teenage Negro boys was actually less that of whites. By last year that rate had grown to 23 percent, as against 13 percent for whites unemployed.

Between 1949 and 1959, the income of Negro men relative to white men declined in every section of this country. From 1952 to 1963 the median income of Negro families compared to white actually dropped from 57 percent to 53 percent.

In the years 1955 through 1957, 22 percent of experienced Negro workers were out of work at some time during the year. In 1961 through 1963 that proportion had soared to 29 percent.

Since 1947 the number of white families living in poverty has decreased 27 percent while the number of poorer nonwhite families decreased only 3 percent.

The infant mortality of nonwhites in 1940 was 70 percent greater than whites. Twenty-two years later is was 90 percent greater.

Moreover, the isolation of Negro from white communities is increasing, rather than decreasing as Negroes crowd into the central cities and become a city within a city.

Of course Negro Americans as well as white Americans have shared in our rising national abundance. But the harsh fact of the matter is that in the battle for true equality too many – far too many – are losing ground every day.

The causes of inequality

We are not completely sure why this is. We know the causes are complex and subtle. But we do know the two broad basic reasons. And we do know that we have to act.

First, Negroes are trapped – as many whites are trapped – in inherited, gateless poverty. They lack training and skills. They are shut in, in slums, without decent medical care. Private and public poverty combine to cripple their capacities.

We are trying to attack these evils through our poverty program, through our education program, through our medical care and our other health programs, and a dozen more of the Great Society programs that are aimed at the root causes of this poverty.

We will increase, and we will accelerate, and we will broaden this attack in years to come until this most enduring of foes finally yields to our unyielding will.

But there is a second cause – much more difficult to explain, more deeply grounded, more desperate in its force. It is the devastating heritage of long years of slavery; and a century of oppression, hatred, and injustice.

Special nature of Negro poverty

For Negro poverty is not white poverty. Many of its causes and many of its cures are the same. But there are differences – deep, corrosive, obstinate differences – radiating painful roots into the community, and into the family, and the nature of the individual. . . .

The roots of injustice

One of the differences is the increased concentration of Negroes in our cities. More than 73 percent of all Negroes live in urban areas compared with less than 70 percent of the whites. Most of these Negroes live together – a separated people.

Men are shaped by their world. When it is a world of decay, ringed by an invisible wall, when escape is arduous and uncertain, and the saving pressures or a more hopeful society are unknown, it can cripple the youth and it can desolate the man . . . .

Family breakdown

Perhaps most important – its influence radiating to every part of life – is the breakdown of the Negro family structure. For this, most of all, white America must accept responsibility. It flows from centuries of oppression and persecution of the Negro man. It flows from the long years of degradation and discrimination, which have attacked his dignity and assaulted his ability to produce for his family. . . .

Only a minority – less than half – of all Negro children reach the age of 18 having lived all their lives with both of their parents. At this moment, tonight, little less than two-thirds are at home with both of their parents. Probably a majority of all Negro children receive federally-aided public assistance sometime during their childhood.

The family is the cornerstone of our society. More than any other forces it shapes the attitude, the hopes, the ambitions, and the values of the child. And when the family collapses it is the children that are usually damaged. When it happens on a massive scale, the community itself is crippled.

So, unless we work to strengthen the family, to create conditions under which most parents will stay together – all the rest: schools, and playgrounds, and public assistance, and private concern, will never be enough to cut completely the circle of despair and deprivation.

To fulfill these rights

There is no single easy answer to all of these problems.

Jobs are part of the answer. They bring the income which permits a man to provide for his family.

Decent homes in decent surroundings and a chance to learn – an equal chance to learn – are part of the answer.

Welfare and social programs better designed to hold families together are part of the answer.

Care for the sick is part of the answer.

An understanding heart by all Americans is another big part of the answer.

And to all of these fronts – and a dozen more – I will dedicate the expanding efforts of the Johnson administration.

But there are other answers that are still to be found. Nor do we fully understand even all of the problems. Therefore, I want to announce tonight that this fall I intend to call a White House conference of scholars, and experts, and outstanding Negro leaders – men of both races – and officials of Government at every level.

This White House conference's theme and title will be "To Fulfill These Rights."

Its object will be to help the American Negro fulfill the rights which, after the long time of injustice, he is finally about to secure.

To move beyond opportunity to achievement.

To shatter forever not only the barriers of law and public practice, but the walls which bound the condition of many by the color of his skin.

To dissolve, as best we can, the antique enmities of the heart which diminish the holder, divide the great democracy and do wrong – great wrong – to the children of God.

And I pledge you tonight that this will be a chief goal of my administration, and of my program next year, and in the years to come. And I hope, and I pray, and I believe, it will be a part of the program of all America.

Source: *Public Papers of the Presidents of the United States: Lyndon B. Johnson, 1965*, vol. 2 (Washington, DC: United States Government Printing Office, 1966), pp. 635–40.

Discussion Questions

1. What do the documents in this chapter tell us about the significance of both grassroots activism and the federal government in shaping the Freedom Struggle?

2. From reading "I Have a Dream" and "The Ballot or the Bullet," how would you characterize the differences between the approaches of Martin Luther King and Malcolm X to the struggle for African American rights?

3. Collectively, what do these documents reveal about the importance attached by different groups and individuals to voting rights, nonviolence, and the goal of integration?

Chapter 5 The New Left and the Counterculture

1. Students for a Democratic Society, the Port Huron Statement, 1962

In 1960, the radical sociologist C. Wright Mills published an influential essay in the New Left Review *that dismissed as an "unrealistic ... legacy of Victorian Marxism" the traditional left-wing faith that an alienated and dispossessed working class would one day revolt against the brutal exploitation of capitalism and usher in an era of egalitarian socialism. Instead of this romanticization of the working classes, Mills suggested that a vanguard of intellectuals and their students were more likely agents of progressive social change, particularly if they could abandon complacent assumptions about the inevitability of capitalism's demise in favor of more probing analyses of the way that America's intersecting economic, political, social, legal, and military systems actually worked to make the triumph of socialism far from assured.*

The members of the Students for a Democratic Society (SDS) took up Mills's challenge. The Port Huron Statement, largely written by University of Michigan student Tom Hayden, echoed many of Mills's ideas, as well as bearing influences from the civil rights movement, especially from SNCC with its emphasis on participatory democracy and grassroots organizing. SDS became an important national organization, with close ties to the emerging New Left, the antiwar movement and the counterculture – although many SDS stalwarts were frustrated by the failure of some cultural radicals to engage in organized political activities. While riddled with internal tensions, not least around issues of race and gender (SDS was dominated by straight white males, as some of the language of the Statement betrays), SDS offered a sustained critique of American politics, domestic values, and foreign policy until it splintered in the late 1960s.

Introduction: Agenda for a generation

We are people of this generation, bred in at least modest comfort, housed now in universities, looking uncomfortably to the world we inherit.

When we were kids the United States was the wealthiest and strongest country in the world; the only one with the atom bomb, the least scarred by modern war, an initiator of the United Nations that we thought would distribute Western influence throughout the world. Freedom and equality for each individual, government of, by, and for the people – these American values we found good, principles by which we could live as men. Many of us began maturing in complacency.

As we grew, however, our comfort was penetrated by events too troubling to dismiss. First, the permeating and victimizing fact of human degradation, symbolized by the Southern struggle against racial bigotry, compelled most of us from silence to activism. Second, the enclosing fact of the Cold War, symbolized by the presence of the Bomb, brought awareness that we ourselves, and our friends, and millions of abstract "others" we knew more directly because of our common peril, might die at any time. We might deliberately ignore, or avoid, or fail to feel all other human problems, but not these two, for these were too immediate and crushing in their impact, too challenging in the demand that we as individuals take the responsibility for encounter and resolution.

While these and other problems either directly oppressed us or rankled our consciences and became our own subjective concerns, we began to see complicated and disturbing paradoxes in our surrounding America. The declaration "all men are created equal ..." rang hollow before the facts of Negro life in the South and the big cities of the North. The proclaimed peaceful intentions of the United States contradicted its economic and military investments in the Cold War status quo.

We witnessed, and continue to witness, other paradoxes. With nuclear energy whole cities can easily be powered, yet the dominant nation-states seem more likely to unleash destruction greater than that incurred in all wars of human history. Although our own technology is destroying old and creating new forms of social organization, men still tolerate meaningless work and idleness. While two-thirds of mankind suffers undernourishment, our own upper classes revel amidst superfluous abundance. Although world population is expected to double in forty years, the nations still tolerate anarchy as a major principle of international conduct and uncontrolled exploitation governs the sapping of the earth's physical resources. Although mankind desperately needs revolutionary leadership, America rests in national stalemate, its goals ambiguous and tradition-bound instead of informed and clear, its democratic system apathetic and manipulated rather than "of, by, and for the people."

Not only did tarnish appear on our image of American virtue, not only did disillusion occur when the hypocrisy of American ideals was discovered, but we began to sense that what we had originally seen as the American Golden Age was actually the decline of an era. The worldwide outbreak of revolution against colonialism and imperialism, the entrenchment of totalitarian states, the menace of war, overpopulation, international disorder, supertechnology – these trends were testing the tenacity of our own commitment to democracy and freedom and our abilities to visualize their application to a world in upheaval.

Our work is guided by the sense that we may be the last generation in the experiment with living. But we are a minority – the vast majority of our people regard the temporary equilibriums of our society and world as eternally functional parts. In this is perhaps the outstanding paradox; we ourselves are imbued with urgency, yet the message of our society is that there is no viable alternative to the present. Beneath the reassuring tones of the politicians, beneath the common opinion that America will "muddle through," beneath the stagnation of those who have closed their minds to the future, is the pervading feeling that there simply are no alternatives, that our times have witnessed the exhaustion not only of Utopias, but of any new departures as well. Feeling the press of complexity upon the emptiness of life, people are fearful of the thought that at any moment things might be thrust out of control. They fear change itself, since change might smash whatever invisible framework seems to hold back chaos for them now. For most Americans, all crusades are suspect, threatening. The fact that each individual sees apathy in his fellows perpetuates the common reluctance to organize for change. The dominant institutions are complex enough to blunt the minds of their potential critics, and entrenched enough to swiftly dissipate or entirely repel the energies of protest and reform, thus limiting human expectancies. Then, too, we are a materially improved society, and by our own improvements we seem to have weakened the case for further change.

Some would have us believe that Americans feel contentment amidst prosperity–but might it not better be called a glaze above deeply felt anxieties about their role in the new world? And if these anxieties produce a developed indifference to human affairs, do they not as well produce a yearning to believe that there *is* an alternative to the present, that something *can* be done to change circumstances in the school, the workplaces, the bureaucracies, the government? It is to this latter yearning, at once the spark and engine of change, that we direct our present appeal. The search for truly democratic alternatives to the present, and a commitment to social experimentation with them, is a worthy and fulfilling human enterprise, one which moves us and, we hope, others today. On such a basis do we offer this document of our convictions and analysis: as an effort in understanding and changing the conditions of humanity in the late twentieth century, an effort rooted in the ancient, still unfulfilled conception of man attaining determining influence over his circumstances of life.

Values

... A first task of any social movement is to convince people that the search for orienting theories and the creation of human values is complex but worthwhile. We are aware that to avoid platitudes we must analyze the concrete conditions of social order. But to direct such an analysis we must use the guideposts of basic principles. Our own social values involve conceptions of human beings, human relationships, and social systems.

We regard *men* as infinitely precious and possessed of unfulfilled capacities for reason, freedom, and love. In affirming these principles we are aware of countering perhaps the dominant conceptions of man in the twentieth century: that he is a thing to be manipulated, and that he is inherently incapable of directing his own affairs...

Men have unrealized potential for self-cultivation, self-direction, self-understanding, and creativity. It is this potential that we regard as crucial and to which we appeal, not to the human potentiality for violence, unreason, and submission to authority. The goal of man and society should be human independence: a concern not with image of popularity but with finding a meaning in life that is personally authentic; a quality of mind not compulsively driven by a sense of powerlessness, nor one which unthinkingly adopts status values, nor one which represses all threats to its habits, but one which has full, spontaneous access to present and past experiences, one which easily unites the fragmented parts of personal history, one which openly faces problems which are troubling and unresolved; one with an intuitive awareness of possibilities, an active sense of curiosity, an ability and willingness to learn.

This kind of independence does not mean egotistic individualism – the object is not to have one's way so much as it is to have a way that is one's own. Nor do we deify man – we merely have faith in his potential.

Human relationships should involve fraternity and honesty. Human interdependence is contemporary fact; human brotherhood must be willed, however, as a condition of future survival and as the most appropriate form of social relations. Personal links between man and man are needed, especially to go beyond the partial and fragmentary bonds of function that bind men only as worker to worker, employer to employee, teacher to student, American to Russian ....

We would replace power rooted in possession, privilege, or circumstance by power and uniqueness rooted in love, reflectiveness, reason, and creativity. As a social system we seek the establishment of a democracy of individual participation, governed by two central aims: that the individual share in those social decisions determining the quality and direction of his life; that society be organized to encourage independence in men and provide the media for their common participation.

In a participatory democracy, the political life would be based in several root principles:

that decision-making of basic social consequence be carried on by public groupings;

that politics be seen positively, as the art of collectively creating an acceptable pattern of social relations;

that politics has the function of bringing people out of isolation and into community, thus being a necessary, though not sufficient, means of finding meaning in personal life;

that the political order should serve to clarify problems in a way instrumental to their solution; it should provide outlets for the expression of personal grievance and aspiration; opposing views should be organized so as to illuminate choices and facilitate the attainment of goals; channels should be commonly available to relate men to knowledge and to power so that private problems – from bad recreation facilities to personal alienation – are formulated as general issues.

The economic sphere would have as its basis the principles:

that work should involve incentives worthier than money or survival. It should be educative, not stultifying; creative, not mechanical; self-directed, not manipulated, encouraging independence, a respect for others, a sense of dignity, and a willingness to accept social responsibility, since it is this experience that has crucial influence on habits, perceptions and individual ethics;

that the economic experience is so personally decisive that the individual must share in its full determination;

that the economy itself is of such social importance that its major resources and means of production should be open to democratic participation and subject to democratic social regulation.

Like the political and economic ones, major social institutions –
cultural, educational, rehabilitative, and others – should be generally
organized with the well-being and dignity of man as the essential measure
of success.

In social change or interchange, we find violence to be abhorrent because
it requires generally the transformation of the target, be it a human being or
a community of people, into a depersonalized object of hate. It is imperative
that the means of violence be abolished and the institutions – local,
national, international – that encourage non-violence as a condition of
conflict be developed.

These are our central values, in skeletal form. It remains vital to understand their denial or attainment in the context of the modern world.

Source: Alexander Bloom and Wini Breines (eds.), *"Takin' it to the Streets": A
Sixties Reader* (New York: Oxford University Press, 1995; 2nd edn, 2003),
pp. 51–61.

2. Mario Savio, "An End to History," 1964

*While the Port Huron statement suggested that universities could become
important sources for progressive critiques of American society, not all college
administrations were enthusiastic about the spread of youthful dissent on their
campuses. The Berkeley Free Speech Movement (FSM) was formed in the Fall
semester of 1964 to protest efforts by university president Clark Kerr to curb
political speech and other political activities on campus. The simmering
conflict between students and administration had initially boiled over when
the university introduced new regulations to prevent campus organizations
from recruiting volunteers to work on the Mississippi voter registration
project. The administration also disciplined students who continued to use a
stretch of campus called Telegraph Avenue to distribute information about
various causes and organizations, and eventually called the police to arrest a
Congress of Racial Equality activist who, along with representatives of many
other groups, had set up an information booth. A crowd of some 4,000
students surrounded the police and prevented the arrest. FSM was born of this
spontaneous gesture, uniting very disparate campus groups, from SNCC
workers to Young Republicans, who opposed attempts to restrict their right to
air their views. Following many confrontations, including a sit-in involving the
arrest of 770 students, the FSM eventually re-established the students' right to
free speech on campus. In this essay, Mario Savio, a veteran of the Freedom
Summer and one of the most articulate of the FSM leadership, outlines the
major issues at stake for students involved.*

Last summer I went to Mississippi to join the struggle there for civil rights. This fall I am engaged in another phase of the same struggle, this time in Berkeley. The two battlefields may seem quite different to some observers, but this is not the case. The same rights are at stake in both places – the right to participate as citizens in democratic society and the right to due process of law. Further, it is a struggle against the same enemy. In Mississippi an autocratic and powerful minority rules, through organized violence, to suppress the vast, virtually powerless majority. In California, the privileged minority manipulates the university bureaucracy to suppress the students' political expression. That "respectable" bureaucracy masks the financial plutocrats; that impersonal bureaucracy is the efficient enemy in a "Brave New World."

In our free-speech fight at the University of California, we have come up against what may emerge as the greatest problem of our nation – depersonalized, unresponsive bureaucracy. We have encountered the organized status quo in Mississippi, but it is the same in Berkeley. Here we find it impossible usually to meet with anyone but secretaries. Beyond that, we find functionaries who cannot make policy but can only hide behind the rules. We have discovered total lack of response on the part of the policy makers. To grasp a situation which is truly Kafkaesque, it is necessary to understand the bureaucratic mentality. And we have learned quite a bit about it this fall, more outside the classroom than in.

As bureaucrat, an administrator believes that nothing new happens. He occupies an a-historical point of view. In September, to get the attention of this bureaucracy which had issued arbitrary edicts suppressing student political expression and refused to discuss its action, we held a sit-in on the campus. We sat around a police car and kept it immobilized for over thirty-two hours. At last, the administrative bureaucracy agreed to negotiate. But instead, on the following Monday, we discovered that a committee had been appointed, in accordance with usual regulations, to resolve the dispute. Our attempt to convince any of the administrators that an event had occurred, that something new had happened, failed. They saw this simply as something to be handled by normal university procedures.

The same is true of all bureaucracies. They begin as tools, means to certain legitimate goals, and they end up feeding their own existence. The conception that bureaucrats have is that history has in fact come to an end. No events can occur now that the Second World War is over which can change American society substantially. We proceed by standard procedures as we are.

The most crucial problems facing the United States today are the problem of automation and the problem of racial injustice. Most people who will be put out of jobs by machines will not accept an end to events, this historical plateau, as the point beyond which no change occurs.

Negroes will not accept an end to history here. All of us must refuse to accept history's final judgment that in America there is no place in society for people whose skins are dark. On campus students are not about to accept it as fact that the university has ceased evolving and is in its final state of perfection, that students and faculty are respectively raw material and employees, or that the university is to be autocratically run by unresponsive bureaucrats.

Here is the real contradiction: the bureaucrats hold history as ended. As a result significant parts of the population both on campus and off are dispossessed and these dispossessed are not about to accept this a-historical point of view. It is out of this that the conflict has occurred with the university bureaucracy and will continue to occur until that bureaucracy becomes responsive or until it is clear the university cannot function. The things we are asking for in our civil-rights protests have a deceptively quaint ring. We are asking for the due process of law. We are asking for our actions to be judged by committees of our peers. We are asking that regulations ought to be considered as arrived at legitimately only from the consensus of the governed. These phrases are all pretty old, but they are not being taken seriously in America today, nor are they being taken seriously on the Berkeley campus.

I have just come from a meeting with the Dean of Students. She notified us that she was aware of certain violations of university regulations by certain organizations. University friends of Student Non-violent Coordinating Committee, which I represent, was one of these. We tried to draw from her some statement on these great principles, consent of the governed, jury of one's peers, due process. The best she could do was to evade or to present the administration party line. It is very hard to make any contact with the human being who is behind these organizations.

The university is the place where people begin seriously to question the conditions of their existence and raise the issue of whether they can be committed to the society they have been born into. After a long period of apathy during the fifties, students have begun not only to question but, having arrived at answers, to act on those answers. This is part of a growing understanding among many people in America that history has not ended, that a better society is possible, and that it is worth dying for.

This free-speech fight points up a fascinating aspect of contemporary campus life. Students are permitted to talk all they want so long as their speech has no consequences.

One conception of the university, suggested by a classical Christian formulation, is that it be in the world but not of the world. The conception of Clark Kerr by contrast is that the university is part and parcel of this particular stage in the history of American society; it stands to serve the need of American industry; it is a factory that turns out a certain product needed by industry or government. Because speech does often have consequences which might alter this perversion of higher education, the university must put itself in a position of censorship. It can permit two kinds of speech, speech which encourages continuation of the status quo, and speech which advocates changes in it so radical as to be irrelevant in the foreseeable future. Someone may advocate radical change in all aspects of American society, and this I am sure he can do with impunity. But if someone advocates sit-ins to bring about changes in discriminatory hiring practices, this cannot be permitted because it goes against the status quo of which the university is a part. And that is how the fight began here.

The administration of the Berkeley campus has admitted that external, extra-legal groups have pressured the university not to permit students on campus to organize picket lines, not to permit on campus any speech with consequences. And the bureaucracy went along. Speech with consequences, speech in the area of civil rights, speech which some might regard as illegal, must stop.

Many students here at the university, many people in society, are wandering aimlessly about. Strangers in their own lives there is no place for them. They are people who have not learned to compromise, who for example have come to the university to learn to question, to grow, to learn – all the standard things that sound like clichés because no one takes them seriously. And they find at one point or other that for them to become part of society, to become lawyers, ministers, businessmen, people in government, that very often they must compromise those principles which were most dear to them. They must suppress the most creative impulses that they have; this is a prior condition for being part of the system. The university is well structured, well tooled, to turn out people with all the sharp edges worn off, the well-rounded person. The university is well equipped to produce that sort of person, and this means that the best among the people who enter must for four years wander aimlessly much of the time questioning why they are on campus at all, doubting whether there is any point in what they are doing, and looking toward a very bleak existence afterward in a game in which all of the rules have been made up, which one cannot really amend.

It is a bleak scene, but it is all a lot of us have to look forward to. Society provides no challenge. American society in the standard conception it has of itself is simply no longer exciting. The most exciting things going on in America today are movements to change America. America is becoming ever more the utopia of sterilized, automated contentment. The "futures" and "careers" for which American students now prepare are for the most part intellectual and moral wastelands. This chrome-plated consumers' paradise would have us grow up to be well-behaved children. But an important minority of men and women coming to the front today have shown that they will die rather than be standardized, replaceable and irrelevant.

Source: Published originally in *Humanity, an arena of critique and commitment*, No. 2, December 1964. Reprinted with permission of Mario Savio in Alexander Bloom and Wini Breines (eds.), *"Takin' it to the Streets": A Sixties Reader* (New York: Oxford University Press, 1995; 2nd edn, 2003), pp. 89–92.

3. Rick Griffin, *Pow-Wow: A Gathering of the Tribes*, 1967

On January 14, 1967, 20,000 people descended on the Polo Grounds of Golden Gate Park in San Francisco for a "Human Be-In" giving the national news media its first real glimpse of the youthful hippy sub-culture that had been flourishing in the low-rent bohemian district of Haight-Ashbury for several years. According to the florid descriptions of its organizers, the event was dedicated to "a Renaissance of compassion, awareness and love in the Revelation of the unity of all mankind. The Human Be-In is the joyful face-to-face beginning of a new epoch." Within weeks, the hippies of San Francisco and their youthful counterparts throughout the nation were the subject of enormous media attention. Much of that attention focused on the hippies' alternative lifestyles, in particular their long hair, communal living, apparent sexual freedom, and devotions to rock music and consciousness-expanding drugs like LSD.

Underground and alternative newspapers like the San Francisco Oracle *and* Berkeley Barb *played an important part in defining this Bay Area scene, as did the experimental poster designs by artists such as Wes Wilson, Alton Kelley, Victor Moscoso, and Stanley Mouse, many of whom were associated with a loose collective known as the Family Dog. Rick Griffin's poster for the Human Be-In, "A Gathering of the Tribes" as he dubbed it, offered images of Native Americans – a regular symbol of a purer, less avaricious, more communally oriented and environmentally sensitive America for many hippies – and a list of some of the luminaries who appeared at the Polo Grounds, ranging from beat poets Allen Ginsberg and Gary Snyder, to political activists Lenore Kandel and Jerry Rubin, and from key local rock bands like the Grateful Dead and Jefferson Airplane, to the foremost advocate of LSD, former Harvard psychology professor Timothy Leary. Subsequent poster designs, many of them advertising concerts at the Fillmore West or Avalon Ballroom, or for a variety of free festivals, became increasingly colorful and elaborate, reflecting the widespread influence of psychedelic drugs and music. At the same time, the text on these posters become ever-more stylized, often to the point where they were virtually illegible to all except those already in the know.*

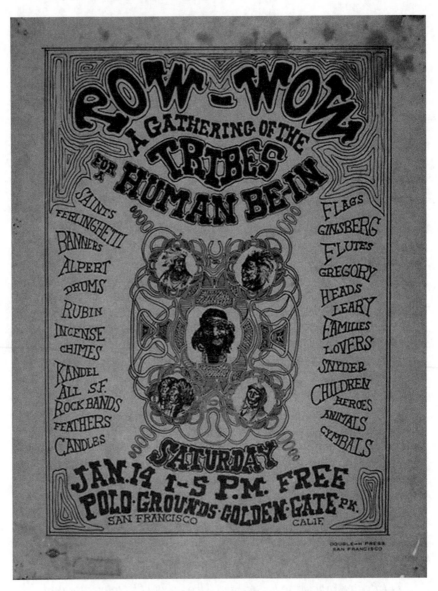

Figure 5.1   Pow-Wow: A Gathering of the Tribes for a Human Be-In, Saturday Jan. 14 1967, Golden Gate Pk. San Francisco. Poster by Rick Griffin.

Source: Special Collections, University of Virginia Library.

4. Warren Hinckle, "A Social History of the Hippies," 1967

This extract from Warren Hinckle's long article on the San Francisco hippie scene for Ramparts *magazine explores the philosophies and practices of the radical communitarian group the Diggers and their most charismatic figure, Emmett Grogan. A loosely organized group of young utopian visionaries, the Diggers rejected consumerism and commercial transactions and strove to establish a "Free City" in Haight-Ashbury where all necessary goods, services, and entertainments would be bartered, exchanged, or given away. Simultaneously highly political, yet avowedly apolitical, and committed both to notions of unfettered individualism – the freedom to do whatever one wanted without censure or official impediment – and to a communalism that required the pursuit of shared, agreed agendas, the Diggers embodied many of the paradoxes that typified the counterculture. Reveling in their outlaw status, the group lived permanently on the edge of the law. Indeed, the Diggers tended to romanticize criminality as a conspicuous rejection of what they considered to be immoral property rights and unsanctioned societal constraints on individual freedom. By the late 1960s, with legal and drug problems rife, the Diggers increasingly looked beyond the city, engaging with the environmental movement and establishing self-sufficient rural communes in northern California.*

Will the Real Frodo Baggins Please Stand Up?

Except for the obvious fact that he wasn't covered with fur, you would have said to yourself that for sure there was old Frodo Baggins, crossing Haight Street. Frodo Baggins is the hero of the English antiquarian J. R. R. Tolkien's classic trilogy, *Lord of the Rings*, absolutely the favorite book of every hippie, about a race of little people called Hobbits who live somewhere in prehistory in a place called Middle Earth. Hobbits are hedonistic, happy little fellows who love beauty and pretty colors. Hobbits have their own scene and resent intrusion, pass the time eating three or four meals a day and smoke burning leaves of herb in pipes of clay. You can see why hippies would like Hobbits.

The hustling, heroic-looking fellow with the mistaken identity was Emmett Grogan, kingpin of The Diggers and the closest thing the hippies in the Haight-Ashbury have to a real live hero. Grogan, twenty-three, with blond, unruly hair, and a fair, freckled Irish face, has the aquiline nose of a leader, but he would prefer to say that he "just presents alternatives." He is in and out of jail seventeen times a week, sometimes busted for smashing a cop in the nose (Grogan has a very intolerant attitude toward policemen), sometimes bailing out a friend, and sometimes, like Monopoly, just visiting. The alternatives he presents are rather disturbing to the hippie bourgeoisie, since he thinks they have no business charging hippies money for their daily needs and should have the decency to give things away free, like The Diggers do, or at least charge the squares and help out the hippies.

Grogan has a very clear view of what freedom means in society ("Why can't I stand on the corner and wait for nobody? Why can't everyone?") and an even clearer view of the social position of the hippie merchants ("They just want to expand their sales, they don't care what happens to people here; they're nothing but goddamn shopkeepers with beards").

Everyone is a little afraid of Grogan in the Haight-Ashbury, including the cops. A one-man crusade for purity of purpose, he is the conscience of the hippie community. He is also a bit of a daredevil and a madman, and could easily pass for McMurphy, the roguish hero in Kesey's novel set in an insane asylum. There is a bit of J. P. Donleavy's *Ginger Man* in him, too . ...

A Psychedelic Grapes of Wrath

Every Bohemian community has its inevitable coterie of visionaries who claim to know what it is all about. But The Diggers are, somehow, different. They are bent on creating a wholly cooperative subculture and, so far, they are not just hallucinating, they are doing it.

Free clothes (used) are there for whomever wants them. Free meals are served every day. Next, Grogan plans to open a smart mod clothing store on Haight Street and give the clothes away free, too (the hippie merchants accused him of "trying to undercut their prices"). He wants to start Digger farms where participants will raise their own produce. He wants to give away free acid, to eliminate junky stuff and end profiteering. He wants cooperative living to forestall inevitable rent exploitation when the Haight-Ashbury becomes chic.

Not since Brook Farm, not since the Catholic Workers, has any group in this dreadfully co-optive, consumer society been so serious about a utopian community.

If Grogan succeeds or fails in the Haight-Ashbury it will not be as important as the fact that he has tried. For he is, at least, providing the real possibility of what he calls, "alternatives" in the down-the-rabbit-hole-culture of the hippies.

Grogan is very hung up on freedom. "Do your thing, what you are, and nothing will ever bother you," he says. His heroes are the Mad Bomber of New York who blissfully blew up all kinds of things around Manhattan over thirty years because he just liked to blow things up, and poet Gary Snyder, whom he considers the "most important person in the Haight-Ashbury" because instead of sitting around sniffing incense and talking about it, he went off to Japan and became a Zen master. "He did it, man."

This is an interesting activist ethic, but it remains doubtful just what the hippies will do. Not that many, certainly, will join Grogan's utopia, because utopias, after all, have a size limit.

The New Left has been flirting with the hippies lately, even to the extent of singing "The [sic] Yellow Submarine" at a Berkeley protest rally, but it looks from here like a largely unrequited love.

The hip merchants will, of course, go on making money. And the youngsters will continue to come to the Haight-Ashbury and do – what?

That was the question put to the hippie leaders at their Summit Meeting. They resolved their goals, but not the means, and the loud noise you heard from outside was probably Emmett Grogan pounding the table with his shoe.

The crisis of the happy hippie ethic is precisely this: it is all right to turn on, but it is not enough to drop out. Grogan sees the issue in the gap "between the radical political philosophy of Jerry Rubin and Mario Savio and psychedelic love philosophy." He, himself, is not interested in the war in Vietnam, but on the other hand he does not want to spend his days like Ferdinand sniffing pretty flowers.

This is why he is so furious at the hip merchants. "They created the myth of this utopia; now they aren't going to do anything about it." Grogan takes the evils of society very personally, and he gets very angry, almost physically sick, when a pregnant fifteen-year-old hippie's baby starves in her stomach, a disaster which is not untypical in the Haight-Ashbury, and which Grogan sees being repeated ten-fold this summer when upwards of two hundred thousand migrant teen-agers and college kids come, as a psychedelic *Grapes of Wrath*, to utopia in search of the heralded turn-on.

The danger in the hippie movement is more than overcrowded streets and possible hunger riots this summer. If more and more youngsters begin to share the hippie political posture of unrelenting quietism, the future of activist, serious politics is bound to be affected. The hippies have shown that it can be pleasant to drop out of the arduous task of attempting to steer a difficult, unrewarding society. But when that is done, you leave the driving to the Hell's Angels.

Source: Originally published in *Ramparts*, vol. 5, no. 9, March 1967, pp. 5–26. Reprinted in Gerald Howard (ed.), *The Sixties* (New York: Washington Square Press, 1982), pp. 207–32.

5. Yippie!, "People, Get Ready," 1968

Yippie!, or the Youth International Party, was formed in December 1967 and offered a chaotic, highly irreverent and stylized blend of protest politics, street theater, absurdist comedy, and countercultural idealism. Spearheaded by Abbie Hoffman, Anita Hoffman, Jerry Rubin, Nancy Kurshan, and Paul Krassner, whose San Francisco-based Realist *newspaper provided an important outlet for Yippie! polemics, the group came to national attention during the bloody events surrounding the August 1968 National Democratic Party Convention in Chicago. By using a network of underground newspapers and distributing thousands of mimeographed fliers, like the one reproduced here, the Yippies encouraged all "rebels, youth spirits, rock minstrels, truth seekers, peacock freaks, poets, barricade jumpers, dances, lovers, [and] artisans," to help stage a "Festival of Life" in Chicago. This was envisaged as a gathering of progressive antiwar forces who would present a positive alternative to what they dubbed the Democrats' "Convention of Death."*

When Chicago's Mayor Daley warned of a hard-line approach to any unruly behavior and unauthorized presence near the Convention, the Yippies responded by threatening to lace the city water supply with LSD and dance naked in the streets. They also offered up their own candidate for president, a pig named Pigasus. Daley was neither amused, nor bluffing. Every night during the Convention, police tear-gassed and clubbed the young people who gathered in nearby Lincoln Park, creating deeply disturbing images that played out on the nation's television screens. Hoffman and Rubin were among the Chicago Eight (later Seven, when Black Panther Bobby Seale was tried separately from the others) arrested for conspiracy to incite a riot. Most Americans had little sympathy for the defendants, whom they saw as radical subversives with no respect for law and order. Others in the New Left and counterculture, however, saw them as outlaw heroes who had taken on the repressive apparatus of the State as represented by the Chicago police. Five of the defendants were convicted on the charge of inciting a riot, though not of conspiracy. That verdict was overturned in 1972 when the trial judge Julius Hoffman – an ultra-conservative jurist who became an arch-villain of the New Left – was reprimanded for his extreme bias in handling the case.

The leaders of the National Democratic Party are planning to meet in Chicago in August; there to enact, for the television audience, all the drama and excitement of an American Political Convention, culminating, it is understood, in the nomination of L. Johnson for President of the United States, and Leader of the Free World.

In the face of this act of sado-masochistic folly the free youth of America will simultaneously hold an enormous International Youth Festival in Chicago; there will be music playing and people swaying, dancing in the streets. Johnson and his delegates, locked in their slaughterhouse conventionhall theatre, will make ugly speeches and play ugly campaign music, while we, the living breathing youth of the world, will make the city a theatre, and every restaurant Alice's. Already, throughout parks and vacant lots in and around Chicago, agents of the Potheads' Benevolent Association have planted hundreds of thousands of pot seeds. The long hot summer of 1968 is expected to produce ideal weather for marijuana growing, and most of the crop should be ready for smoking by the end of August. F r e e people, free pot, free music, free theatre; a whole new culture will manifest itself to the world, rising from the ashes of America. Rock groups will be performing in the parks; newspapers will be printed in the streets; provos and police will play cops and robbers in the department stores; Democrats and dope fiends will chase each other through hotel corridors. Longboats filled with Vikings will land on the shores of Lake Michigan, and discover A m e r i c a ! Chicago will become a river of wild onions!

YOUTH   INTERNATIONAL   PARTY

CHICAGO, AUGUST 25-30, 1968

Yippee!

Figure 5.2 Yippie!, "People, Get Ready," 1968.

Source: The Whole World is Watching, Chicago 1968; members.aol.com/gestalt 768/Chicago1968/overview.htm. Permission by Yippie!

Discussion Questions

1.   Critics have often dismissed the counterculture as narcissistic and escapist, as more interested in style politics than in the substance of serious political engagement. What do the documents in this chapter reveal about the relationship between political and cultural radicalism in the 1960s?
2.   From the documents in this chapter, what were the main elements in New Left and countercultural critiques of American society and values in the 1960s and what alternatives did they propose?
3.   What light do these documents shed on the generational nature of a good deal of social unrest in the 1960s?

Chapter 6   Vietnam

1. Lyndon B. Johnson, Telephone Conversation with Senator Richard Russell, 1964

On becoming president in November 1963, Lyndon Johnson inherited a rapidly deteriorating situation in Southeast Asia and an uncertain American strategy for supporting South Vietnam against internal and external communist threats. In this candid telephone exchange with his old friend and fellow Southern democrat, Senator Richard Russell of Georgia, Johnson admitted that he was extremely gloomy about the prospects for successful American intervention in Vietnam or elsewhere in the region. Yet Johnson was equally unsure of how to disengage the country from its commitment to resist the expansion of communism in Southeast Asia, since to do so could have all manner of political, psychological, and strategic implications for the US and his own career. Russell, with whom Johnson regularly crossed swords concerning the passage of civil rights legislation, sympathized deeply with the president's predicament. The two veteran political fixers agreed that the situation was worsening daily, with few clear-cut policy options that would preserve Johnson's political credibility as a staunch anti-communist, bolster America's international reputation as protector of free nations, while at the same time avoiding a major escalation of the conflict and the need to deploy many more US ground troops.

LBJ: ... What do you think of this Vietnam thing? I'd like to hear you talk a little bit.

RUSSELL: Frankly, Mr. President, if you were to tell me that I was authorized to settle it as I saw fit, I would respectfully decline and not take it.

LBJ: [chuckles]

RUSSELL: It's the damn worst mess I ever saw, and I don't like to brag. I never have been right many times in my life. But I knew that we were going to get into this sort of mess when we went in there. And I don't see how we're ever going to get out of it without fighting a major war with the Chinese and all of them down there in those rice paddies and jungles ... I just don't know what to do.

LBJ: That's the way I've been feeling for six months.

RUSSELL: It appears that our position is deteriorating, And it looks like the more that we try to do for them, the less they're willing to do for themselves. It's just a sad situation. There's no sense of responsibility there on the part of any of their leaders that are bearing it ... It's a hell of a situation. It's a mess. And it's going to get worse. And I don't know what to do. I don't think that the American people are quite ready to send our troops in there to do the fighting. If it came down to an option for us of just sending the Americans in there to do the fighting, which will, of course, eventually lead to a ground war and a conventional war with China, we'd do them a favor every time we killed a coolie, whereas when one of our people got killed, it would be a loss to us. If it got down to ... just pulling out, I'd get out. But then I don't know. There's undoubted some middle ground, some-where. If I was going to get out, I'd get the same crowd that got rid of old Diem to get rid of these people and get some fellow in there that said he wished to hell we *would* get out. That would be a good excuse for getting out...

LBJ: How important is it to us?

RUSSELL: It isn't important a damn bit, with all these new missile systems.

LBJ: Well, I guess it's important to us –

RUSSELL: From a psychological standpoint.

LBJ: I mean, yes, and from the standpoint that we are party to a treaty. And if we don't pay any attention to this treaty, why, I don't guess they think we'll pay attention to any of them.

RUSSELL: Yeah, but we're the only ones paying any attention to it!

LBJ: Yeah, I think that's right....

LBJ: I spend all my days with Rusk and McNamara and Bundy and Harriman and Vance and all those folks that are dealing with it and I would say that it pretty well adds up to them now that, we've got to show some power and some force, that they do not believe – they're kinda like MacArthur in Korea – they don't believe the Chinese Communists will come into this thing. But they don't know and nobody can really be sure. But their feeling is that they won't. And in any event, that we haven't got much choice, that we are treaty-bound, that we are there, that this will be a domino that will kick off a whole list of others, that we've just got to prepare for the worst ... I don't think the people of the country know much about Vietnam and I think they care a hell of a lot less.

RUSSELL: Yeah, I know, but you go to send a whole lot of our boys out there –

LBJ: Yeah, that's right. That's exactly right. That's what I'm talking about. You get a few. We had thirty-five killed – and we got enough hell over thirty-five – this year.

RUSSELL: More than that ... in Atlanta, Georgia, have been killed this year in automobile accidents.

LBJ: That's right, and eighty-three went down in one crash on a 707 in one day, but that doesn't make any difference.... The Republicans are going to make a political issue out of it, every one of them...

RUSSELL: It's a tragic situation. It's just one of those places where you can't win. Anything you do is wrong.... I have thought about it. I have worried about it. I have prayed about it.

LBJ: I don't believe we can do anything –

RUSSELL: It frightens me 'cause it's my country involved over there and if we get into there on any considerable scale, there's no doubt in my mind but that the Chinese will be in there and we'd be fighting a danged conventional war against our secondary potential threat and it'd be a Korea on a much bigger scale and a worse scale.... If you go from Laos and Cambodia and Vietnam and bring North Vietnam into it, too, it's the damndest mess on earth. The French report that they lost 250,000 men and spent a couple of billion of their money and two billion of ours down there and just got the hell whipped out of them....

LBJ: You don't have any doubt but what if we go in there and get 'em up against the wall, the Chinese Communists are gonna come in?

RUSSELL: No sir, no doubt about it.

LBJ: That's my judgment, and our people don't think so.... The whole question, as I see it is, is it more dangerous for us to let things go as they're going now, deteriorating every day –

RUSSELL: I don't think we can let it go, Mr. President, indefinitely.

LBJ: Than it would be for us to move in.

RUSSELL: We got to either move in or move out.

LBJ: That's about what it is.

RUSSELL: You can make a tremendous case for moving out, not as good a one for moving in, but–.... It would be more consistent with the attitude of the American people and their general reactions to go in, because they could understand that better. But getting out, even after we go in and get bogged down in there in a war with China, it's going to be a hell of a mess. It would be worse than where we are now, to some extent, and that's what makes it so difficult.... I don't know how much Russia – they want to cause us all the trouble they can – is there any truth in their theory that they are really at odds with China?

LBJ: They are, but they'd go with them as soon as the fight started. They wouldn't forsake that Communist philosophy...

RUSSELL: Hell, there ain't any way you can move into the North. You know as well as I do that we've tried that from the infiltration, guerilla war standpoint with disastrous results.

LBJ: Lodge, Nixon, Rockefeller, Goldwater all say move. Eisenhower –

RUSSELL: Bomb the North and kill old men, women, and children?

LBJ: They say pick out an oil plant or pick out a refinery or something like that. Take out selected targets. Watch this trail they're coming down. Try to bomb them out of them, when they're coming in.

RUSSELL: Oh, hell! That ain't worth a hoot. That's just impossible.

LBJ: McNamara said yesterday that in Korea that LeMay and all of 'em were going to stop all of those tanks. There's ninety came through. They turned all the Air Force loose on them. They got one. Eighty-nine come on through....

RUSSELL: If we had a man running the government over there that told us to get out, we could sure get out.

LBJ: That's right, but you can't do that.... Wouldn't that pretty well fix us in the eyes of the world though and make it look mighty bad?

RUSSELL: I don't know [chuckles]. We don't look too good right now. You'd look pretty good, I guess, going in there with all the troops and sending them all in there, but I'll tell you it'll be the most expensive venture this country ever went into.

LBJ: I've got a little old sergeant that works for me over at my house and he's got six children and I just put him up as the United States Army, Air Force, and Navy every time I think about making this decision and think about sending that father of those six kids in there. And what the hell are we going to get out of doing it? It just makes the chills run up my back.

RUSSELL: It does me. I just can't see it.

LBJ: I just haven't got the nerve to do it, and I don't see any other way out of it.

Source: Michael R. Beschloss (ed.), *Taking Charge: The Johnson White House Tapes, 1963–1964* (New York: Simon & Schuster, 1997), pp. 363–70. Reprinted with the permission of Simon & Schuster, Inc. Copyright © 1997 by Michael R. Beschloss.

2. US Congress, Tonkin Gulf Resolution, 1964

On August 4, 1964, President Lyndon Johnson informed the American public that US navy ships had come under unprovoked attack from North Vietnamese gunboats while cruising in the Gulf of Tonkin. In fact, the circumstances surrounding this attack were far from clear. The US destroyer Maddox *had indeed come under torpedo fire a few days earlier. But that incident had occurred when the* Maddox *was secretly assisting South Vietnamese commando raids on the North Vietnamese coast and the US vessel had apparently fired the first shots, hitting a North Vietnamese gunboat, before fleeing unscathed. Far from backing off from this high-risk covert policy of support for South Vietnamese military operations, Johnson sent a second destroyer into the Gulf and, on the night of August 4, the* Turner Joy *opened fire, allegedly responding to another North Vietnamese attack, although even Johnson was skeptical about whether any such provocation had occurred. Fearful lest his hawkish Republican opponent in the forthcoming presidential election, Barry Goldwater, might exploit his lack of success, or any perceived lack of resolve, in fighting the communist takeover of Vietnam, and advised by Secretary of State Dean Rusk and Defense Secretary Robert McNamara that these skirmishes represented a golden opportunity to increase public and congressional support for what they believed would be a decisive military push in the region, Johnson used the occasion to call for virtually unlimited powers to stop aggression in Vietnam. With the American public and Capitol Hill deliberately misled about the extent to which American forces were already engaged in the conflict in Vietnam and the circumstances of the recent incidents, the Tonkin Gulf Resolutions – which had actually been drafted several months earlier – passed unanimously in the House and by a vote of 88–2 in the Senate. In the absence of any formal Congressional declaration of war, Presidents Johnson and Nixon both used the Resolutions as authority to wage war in Vietnam.*

Joint Resolution

To promote the maintenance of international peace and security in southeast Asia.

Whereas naval units of the Communist regime in Vietnam, in violation of the principles of the Charter of the United Nations and of international law, have deliberately and repeatedly attacked United States naval vessels lawfully present in international waters, and have thereby created a serious threat to international peace; and

Whereas these attackers are part of a deliberate and systematic campaign of aggression that the Communist regime in North Vietnam has been waging against its neighbors and the nations joined with them in the collective defense of their freedom; and

Whereas the United States is assisting the peoples of southeast Asia to protect their freedom and has no territorial, military or political ambitions in that area, but desires only that these people should be left in peace to work out their destinies in their own way: Now, therefore be it

Resolved by the Senate and House of Representatives of the United States of America in Congress assembled, That the Congress approves and supports the determination of the President, as Commander in Chief, to take all necessary measures to repel any armed attack against the forces of the United States and to prevent further aggression.

Section 2. The United States regards as vital to its national interest and to world peace the maintenance of international peace and security in southeast Asia. Consonant with the Constitution of the United States and the Charter of the United Nations and in accordance with its obligations under the Southeast Asia Collective Defense Treaty, the United States is, therefore, prepared, as the President determines, to take all necessary steps, including the use of armed force, to assist any member or protocol state of the Southeast Asia Collective Defense Treaty requesting assistance in defense of its freedom.

Section 3. This resolution shall expire when the President shall determine that the peace and security of the area is reasonably assured by international conditions created by action of the United Nations or otherwise, except that it may be terminated earlier by concurrent resolution of the Congress.

Source: *Congressional Record* (Washington, DC: US Government Printing Office, 1964), Proceedings and Debates of the 88th Congress, Second Session, volume 110, part 14, p. 18132.

3. US State Department, *Aggression from the North*, 1965

This report was written in February 1965, just six months after the Gulf of Tonkin incident and on the eve of a major escalation of the country's military involvement in Vietnam. Operation Rolling Thunder, the large-scale bombing of North Vietnamese military targets, began on March 2, and on March 8 the first US combat troops arrived. By the end of the year, troop strength had reached 184,300, compared with 23,310 in 1964. In what would become a familiar mantra, the State Department defended the presence of US forces in Vietnam by explaining that they were there to defend the freedom of South Vietnam, and by extension democracy around the world, against communist aggression. Following the defeat of US-supported French colonial forces by Viet Minh nationalists led by Ho Chi Minh, Indochina had been partitioned at the 17th parallel as part of the Geneva Accords of July 1954. This was supposed to be a temporary measure designed to separate the warring nationalist and pro-French forces until a permanent settlement could be negotiated. The State Department, however, operated as if the division was permanent and generally ignored the possibility of any real sympathy in South Vietnam for the prospect of reunification with the North, preferring to see any such moves as driven wholly by communist ambition. Thus, the US insisted that it was not interfering in a civil war, but defending a sovereign democratic nation from communist attack.

Not everyone was convinced by this rationale. As early as February 2, 1965, the Daily Cal had reported "Get the troops out of Vietnam" slogans appearing on campus walls at Berkeley, where shortly afterwards former Free Speech Movement activists organized about 100 students in one of the nation's first antiwar demonstrations. By mid-April 1965, SDS was able to attract between 15,000 and 30,000 protesters to an antiwar rally in Washington, DC. The battle lines for one of the most divisive issues of the 1960s, the legitimacy of the American presence in Vietnam, were already being drawn.

South Vietnam is fighting for its life against a brutal campaign of terror and armed attack inspired, directed, supplied, and controlled by the Communist regime in Hanoi. This flagrant aggression has been going on for years, but recently the pace has quickened and the threat has now become acute.

The war in Vietnam is a new kind of war, a fact as yet poorly understood in most parts of the world. Much of the confusion that prevails in the thinking of many people, and even governments, stems from this basic misunderstanding. For in Vietnam a totally new brand of aggression has been loosed against an independent people who want to make their way in peace and freedom.

Vietnam is not another Greece, where indigenous guerrilla forces used friendly neighboring territory as a sanctuary.

Vietnam is not another Malaya, where Communist guerrillas were, for the most part, physically distinguishable from the peaceful majority they sought to control.

Vietnam is not another Philippines, where Communist guerrillas were physically separated from the source of their moral and physical support.

Above all, the war in Vietnam is not a spontaneous and local rebellion against the established government.

There are elements in the Communist program of conquest directed against South Vietnam common to each of the previous areas of aggression and subversion. But there is one fundamental difference. In Vietnam a Communist government has set out deliberately to conquer a sovereign people in a neighboring state. And to achieve its end, it has used every resource of its own government to carry out its carefully planned program of concealed aggression. North Vietnam's commitment to seize control of the South is no less total than was the commitment of the regime in North Korea in 1950. But knowing the consequences of the latter's undisguised attack, the planners in Hanoi have tried desperately to conceal their hand. They have failed and their aggression is as real as that of an invading army.

This report is a summary of the massive evidence of North Vietnamese aggression obtained by the Government of South Vietnam. This evidence has been jointly analyzed by South Vietnamese and American experts.

The evidence shows that the hard core of the Communist forces attacking South Vietnam were trained in the North and ordered into the South by Hanoi. It shows that the key leadership of the Vietcong (VC), the officers and much of the cadre, many of the technicians, political organizers, and propagandists have come from the North and operate under Hanoi's direction. It shows that the training of essential military personnel and their infiltration into the South is directed by the Military High Command in Hanoi. In recent months new types of weapons have been introduced in the VC army, for which all ammunition must come from outside sources. Communist China and other Communist states have been the prime suppliers of these weapons and ammunition, and they have been channeled primarily through North Vietnam.

The directing force behind the effort to conquer South Vietnam is the Communist Party in the North, the Lao Dong (Workers) Party. As in every Communist state, the party is an integral part of the regime itself. North Vietnamese officials have expressed their firm determination to absorb South Vietnam into the Communist world.

Through its Central Committee, which controls the Government of the North, the Lao Dong Party directs the total political and military effort of the Vietcong. The Military High Command in the North trains the military men and sends them into South Vietnam. The Central Research Agency, North Vietnam's central intelligence organization, directs the elaborate espionage and subversion effort....

Under Hanoi's overall direction the Communists have established an extensive machine for carrying on the war within South Vietnam. The focal point is the Central Office for South Vietnam with its political and military subsections and other specialized agencies. A subordinate part of this Central Office is the liberation Front for South Vietnam. The front was formed at Hanoi's order in 1960. Its principle function is to influence opinion abroad and to create the false impression that the aggression in South Vietnam is an indigenous rebellion against the established Government.

For more than 10 years the people and the Government of South Vietnam, exercising the inherent right of self-defense, have fought back against these efforts to extend Communist power south across the 17th parallel. The United States has responded to the appeals of the Government of the Republic of Vietnam for help in this defense of the freedom and independence of its land and its people.

In 1961 the Department of State issued a report called "A Threat to the Peace." It described North Vietnam's program to seize South Vietnam. The evidence in that report had been presented by the Government of the Republic of Vietnam to the International Control Commission (ICC).

A special report by the ICC in June 1962 upheld the validity of that evidence. The Commission held that there was "sufficient evidence to show beyond reasonable doubt" that North Vietnam had sent arms and men into South Vietnam to carry out subversion with the aim of overthrowing the legal Government there. The ICC found the authorities in Hanoi in specific violation of four provisions of the Geneva Accords of 1954.

Since then, new and even more impressive evidence of Hanoi's aggression has accumulated. The Government of the United States believes that evidence should be presented to its own citizens and to the world. It is important for free men to know what has been happening in Vietnam, and how, and why. That is the purpose of this report...

The record is conclusive. It establishes beyond question that North Vietnam is carrying out a carefully conceived plan of aggression against the South. It shows that North Vietnam has intensified its efforts in the years since it was condemned by the International Control Commission. It proves that Hanoi continues to press its systematic program of armed aggression into South Vietnam. This aggression violates the United Nations Charter. It is directly contrary to the Geneva Accords of 1954 and of 1962 to which North Vietnam is a party. It is a fundamental threat to the freedom and security of South Vietnam.

The people of South Vietnam have chosen to resist this threat. At their request, the United States has taken its place beside them in their defensive struggle.

The United States seeks no territory, no military bases, no favored position. But we have learned the meaning of aggression elsewhere in the postwar world, and we have met it.

If peace can be restored in South Vietnam, the United States will be ready at once to reduce its military involvement. But it will not abandon friends who want to remain free. It will do what must be done to help them. The choice now between peace and continued and increasingly destructive conflict is one for the authorities in Hanoi to make.

Source: *US Department of State Bulletin*, March 22, 1965.

4. Country Joe and the Fish, "I Feel Like I'm Fixin'-To-Die Rag," 1965/1967

Although the most famous public rendition of Country Joe McDonald's classic antiwar song came at the Woodstock Festival in August 1969, the first version of the song was actually written in the summer of 1965 and appeared on an EP (extended play) record given out free with an underground San Francisco newspaper called Rag Baby. *McDonald, raised in a politically radical family, had served for a while in the US Navy before becoming a conspicuous part of the Bay Area's vibrant arts and folk music scene as a writer and musician.*

In 1967, "I Feel Like I'm Fixin'-To-Die Rag" was re-recorded as the title track of the second album released by Country Joe and the Fish. It soon became a popular anthem of the burgeoning antiwar movement: a rollicking, irreverent folk-rock version of the kind of hostile critique of the deceitfulness and hubris of American foreign policy that Senator J. William Fulbright of Arkansas had unleashed in his 1966 book, The Arrogance of Power. *In a countercultural echo of Eisenshower's Farewell Address, McDonald laid the blame for the deepening Vietnam crisis firmly at the door of the government, the military establishment, and the arms industry.*

Now come on all of you big strong men,
Uncle Sam needs your help again.
He's got himself in a terrible jam
Way down yonder in Vietnam
So put down your books and pick up a gun,
We're gonna have a whole lotta fun.

Chorus:
And it's one, two, three,
What are we fighting for?
Don't ask me, I don't give a damn,
Next stop is Vietnam;
And it's five, six, seven,
Open up the pearly gates,
Well there ain't no time to wonder why,
Whoopee! We're all gonna die.

Well, come on generals, let's move fast;
Your big chance has come at last.
Gotta go out and get those reds –
The only good commie is the one who's dead
And you know that peace can only be won
When we've blown 'em all to Kingdom Come.

Chorus:
Well, come on Wall Street, don't move slow,
Why man, this is War-a-go-go.
There's plenty good money to be made
By supplying the Army with the tools of the trade,
Just hope and pray that if they drop the bomb,
They drop it on the Viet Cong.

Chorus:
Well, come on mothers throughout the land,
Pack your boys off to Vietnam.
Come on fathers, don't hesitate,
Send 'em off before it's too late.
Be the first one on your block
To have your boy come home in a box.

Source: "I Feel Like I'm Fixin'-To-Die Rag," Original release on *Rag Baby*, Talking Issue, EP, 1965. © 1965 – renewed 1993 Alkatraz Corner Music BMI. Words and Music by Joe McDonald.

5. Corporal Jon Johnson, Letter to Mom & Dad & Peggy, 1966

Between the summer of 1965 and the spring of 1967, US troop levels in Vietnam increased dramatically to around 400,000. The intensity of the fighting also increased on all fronts. Since the Vietcong refused to be drawn into pitched battles with US troops, American ground forces resorted to "search-and-destroy" campaigns to flush out and eliminate the Vietcong and their sympathizers from the villages and countryside of South Vietnam. On such missions, the body count – the number of dead Vietnamese – was the primary index of "success" for the Pentagon, even though US troops struggled to differentiate between hostile, sympathetic, and neutral Vietnamese. Whole villages were sometimes destroyed in a largely futile effort to root out communist sympathizers. At the same time, massive aerial bombing raids continued, alongside the widespread use of poisonous defoliants like Agent Orange and napalm – liquid fire bombs that incinerated everything in their path – that were designed to deprive the Vietcong of their jungle refuge. Search-and-destroy tactics, bombing, and the new technologies of war combined to devastate the environment and killed many non-combatants as well as enemy forces. Not only was the escalation of the US war effort largely ineffectual in military terms, in that it failed to crush the Vietcong, but it also helped to alienate many ordinary South Vietnamese citizens, who suffering from the increasingly desperate and indiscriminate use of lethal force by American forces, began to loathe the US presence in their country.

Meanwhile, as US casualty rates increased with no end to the conflict in sight, rumblings of discontent about both the official rationale for US involvement in Vietnam and the manner in which the war was being prosecuted became louder. Around 1,400 American soldiers died in 1965, another 5,000 during 1966. Behind such crude statistics were the stories of the individuals who fought, often with great courage, in an alien, inhospitable place that was unrelenting in its physical and psychological demands, for a cause that seemed increasingly elusive. One of those soldiers was Marine Corps Corporal Jon Johnson, who was deployed to serve in the notoriously hostile Mekong Delta as part of Delta Company, 1st Battalion, 5th Marine Regiment, 1st Marine Division. In Spring 1966, he wrote to his wife and parents back in Sidney, Ohio, describing the horrors of combat.

---

8 April 1966

Dear Mom & Dad & Peggy,

Operation Jackstay is over. I guess now I'm a veteran. Nothing they could have done would have prepared us for this. We now know the training in Hawaii and the Philippines was a piece of cake. God doesn't know about the Mekong Delta, He didn't create that hellhole. I think when He rested, the devil slipped one in on him. They told us before we went in that we were the first American unit to operate that far south in the war. I think everyone else had more brains. Maybe when I'm out of the Marines I'll be proud of this, I'm just too tired to feel anything.

We lost some good guys. How do you explain this in a letter? One minute they were there, then dead. I have no idea why I'm still here. Our third night into the operation we set up on the high ground, what there was of it, and all of a sudden I heard a shell coming in. It was the most horrifying sound I could imagine. I was in position with another guy, George from Boston, and it was as dark as it could be. I can't describe that sound. It would be close if I said it sounded like a freight train coming out of the sky. No warning, just that sound. My instincts told me that it was up and to my left. Just as I looked that way it hit about 100 feet from me. The flash of light and explosion was tremendous. It knocked me stupid. Next thing I knew I was laying on my back wondering why the voices were so far away, and my head felt like there was a basketball inside trying to get out. For some reason George kept asking me if I was dead, and I thought why the hell didn't he shut up. Finally things started coming back into focus and I heard the screams. I told George to get ready because I thought there was going to be an attack soon. Then I noticed I was on his right. I was on his left before the shell hit. Sgt. Joyce comes running by and asked for help with the wounded. All we could do was crawl around in the darkness feeling for bodies. I found the foot of someone and told him. He had a red lens flashlight and turned it on. It was Sgt. Herrera, dead. I went back to my position, and the corpsman was working on George. He had been hit in the leg with shrapnel but would remain with us. The shell killed two and wounded nine. That was it, just one shell. But my God what a price.

We're on our way back to Subic Bay now to pick up replacements and take on supplies. The whole atmosphere has changed. No more chicken shit stuff. After Subic we're going on another operation. They say this one is near the DMZ. It has to be better than the Mekong Delta.

Sorry to be so down in the dumps. I'm just tired, very tired. Don't expect many letters because we have no idea when we will return to Vietnam. I don't take writing gear with me on an operation. Wouldn't have time to write anyway.

I'm supposed to feel something for those we lost. Wish to God I knew what.

Love You Mom–Love You Dad.

I love you Peggy.

Your son & husband,

Jon

Source: Bill Adler (ed.), *Letters from Vietnam* (New York: Ballantine Books/Presidio Press, 2004).

6. CBS News, "Saigon Under Fire," 1968

On January 30, 1968, Vietcong forces supplemented by regular North Vietnamese troops launched a series of surprise attacks throughout South Vietnam to coincide with Tet, the Vietnamese New Year holiday. Just weeks after General William C. Westmoreland, commander of the US forces in Vietnam, had assured the American public that the enemy was on the brink of defeat, it had managed to mount a simultaneous assault on 36 provincial capitals, 64 district capitals, and 5 of the 6 largest cities in the South, including the capital Saigon where a small group of fighters even breached the US Embassy compound.

In purely military terms, the Tet Offensive was a limited success: the Vietcong were unable to hold onto any of their gains and lost thousands of troops. Yet in propaganda terms it was a major victory. The shock of the attacks severely dented the confidence of the American people in both the wisdom of US policy in Southeast Asia and the truthfulness of their government in explaining the progress of the war. In this extract from a January 31 CBS-TV newscast, reporter Mike Wallace describes the attack on the Embassy, fellow newsman Robert Schakne interviews a dissembling General Westmoreland, who tries to spin the day's events as a US victory, while White House correspondent Dan Rather reports on the inadequacy of Pentagon and government plans to deal with the renewed Vietcong threat.

Within a month of Tet, even the dean of American news broadcasting Walter Cronkite had joined those who felt that the war was unwinnable and that the US's only option was to pursue a negotiated peace. When Cronkite, the most respected, popular, and trustworthy journalist in the nation, told viewers that "to say that we are mired in stalemate seems the only realistic, yet unsatisfactory conclusion," Lyndon Johnson realised that the credibility of his administration's Vietnam policy had been fatally damaged. In April 1968, Lyndon Johnson announced that he would not seek another term as president and North Vietnam agreed to preliminary pace talks with the US in Paris. The war, however, would drag on for another 6 years, spilling over into adjacent countries and costing thousands more lives.

WALLACE: Good evening. I'm Mike Wallace.

With a bold series of raids during the last three days, the enemy in Vietnam has demolished the myth that Allied military strength controls that country. The Communists hit the very heart of Saigon, the capital of South Vietnam, and at least ten cities which correspond to state capitals here in the United States. And then, as if to demonstrate that no place in that war-torn nation is secure, they struck at least nine American military strongholds and unnumbered field positions. Tonight the magnitude of those raids became apparent in the U.S. Command's report on casualties. The Communists paid a heavy toll for their strikes, almost 5,000 dead, including 660 in Saigon alone, and almost 2,000 captured. But Allied casualties also are high: 232 Americans killed, 929 wounded; 300 South Vietnamese killed, 747 wounded, and that toll is expected to climb.

The enemy's well-coordinated attacks occurred throughout South Vietnam, but the most dramatic demonstration of his boldness and capability came at the very symbol of America's presence in Vietnam, the brand new U.S. Embassy building there. CBS News Correspondent Robert Schakne reports.

SCHAKNE: The American Embassy is under siege; only the besiegers are Americans. Inside, in part of the building, are the Vietcong terror squads that charged in during the night. Military Police got back into the compound of the $2.5 million Embassy complex at dawn. Before that a platoon of Vietcong were in control. The Communist raiders never got into the main chancery building; a handful of Marines had it blocked and kept them out. But the raiders were everywhere else. By daylight (voice drowned out by gunfire). No one, unless identified, was allowed in the street. An Australian Military Policeman was standing guard, firing warning shots to keep the street clear.

Outside the building knots of Military Policemen held positions. There were bursts of wild shooting in the streets, perhaps snipers in other buildings and there had been casualties. The bodies of two Military Policemen who died as they tried to assault the compound lay near their jeep across the boulevard. But even after the Military Police fought their way back inside, there was more fighting to do. The raiders were still about the compound. They may have been a suicide cadre. In the end none of them were to surrender.

This is where the Vietcong raiders broke in. They sneaked up and blasted a hold in the reinforced concrete fence surrounding the compound. They were inside before anyone knew it. They had the big Embassy wall to protect them. But none of the raiders lived to tell of their exploit. By eight o'clock, five hours after they first broke in, almost all of them were dead. Nineteen bodies were counted. All in civilian clothes, they had been armed with American M-16 rifles and also rocket-launchers and rockets. They had explosives, their purpose apparently to destroy the Embassy. In that purpose they did not succeed.

The fighting went on for a total of six hours before the last known Vietcong raider was killed. They were rooted out of bushes, from outlying buildings, and then the last one, the nineteenth, from the small residence of the Embassy's Mission Coordinator, George Jacobson, who had been hiding out all alone, all morning. ...

Saigon had been on the alert for Vietcong terror attacks during the night, but for some reason the Embassy guard was not increased. Just two Military Policemen at one gate, a handful of Marines inside. There wasn't anyone to stop the Vietcong when they came. General William Westmoreland came by soon after. His version was that all this represented a Vietcong defeat.

WESTMORELAND: In some way the enemy's well-laid plans went afoul. Some superficial damage was done to the building. All of the enemy that entered the compound as far as I can determine were killed. Nineteen bodies have been found on the premises – enemy bodies. Nineteen enemy bodies have been found on the premises.

SCHAKNE: General, how would you assess yesterday's activities and today's? What is the enemy doing? Are these major attacks?

(Sound of explosions)

WESTMORELAND: That's POD setting off a couple of M-79 duds, I believe.

SCHAKNE: General, how would you assess the enemy's purposes yesterday and today?

WESTMORELAND: The enemy very deceitfully has taken advantage of the Tet truce in order to create maximum consternation within South Vietnam, particularly in the populated areas. In my opinion this is diversionary to his main effort, which he had planned to take place in Quang Tri Province, from Laos, toward Khesanh and across the Demilitarized Zone. This attack has not yet materialized; his schedule has probably been thrown off balance because of our very effective air strikes.

Now yesterday the enemy exposed himself by virtue of this strategy, and he suffered great casualties. When I left my office late yesterday, approximately eight o'clock, we – we had accounted for almost 700 enemy killed in action. Now we had suffered some casualties ourselves, but they were small by comparison. My guess is, based on my conversations with my field commanders, that there were probably – there were probably far more than 700 that were killed. Now by virtue of this audacious action by the enemy, he has exposed himself, he has become more vulnerable. As soon as President Thieu, with our agreement, called off the truce, U.S. and American [AVRN?] troops went on the offensive and pursued the enemy aggressively.

SCHAKNE: When they built this Embassy, it was first to be a secure building. This Embassy was designed as a bomb-proof, attack-proof building, but it turned out, when the VC hit us, it wasn't attack-proof enough. Robert Schakne, CBS News, Saigon.

WALLACE: Washington regards the enemy raids as the first step in a strategy aimed at strengthening their hand for any peace talks which may develop, and captured Communist documents lend weight to the theory.

CBS News White House Correspondent Dan Rather reports.

RATHER: We knew this was coming – a well-coordinated series of enemy raids against South Vietnamese cities. Our intelligence even pinpointed the exact day it would happen. What we did not know was where. This is the official story, as given out by White House news secretary George Christian, who went on to say there was no way to completely insulate yourself against this kind of thing if the enemy is willing to sacrifice large numbers of men.

But if we knew it was coming, even to the exact day, Christian was asked, why wasn't extra protection placed around such an obvious place as the Saigon Embassy? The White House spokesman paused, then said, "I just don't know." At the Pentagon a high-ranking source said, "There simply were more of them and they were better than we expected."

Washington is startled but not panicked by the latest series of events. President Johnson privately is warning Congressmen that intelligence reports indicate the whole month of February will be rough in Southeast Asia. Mr. Johnson is emphasizing that the enemy's winter offensive is only beginning. Dan Rather, CBS News, Washington.

WALLACE: The drama of the battle for Saigon captured most attention, but the South Vietnamese capital was only one of the Communist targets. In a moment we'll return with battle film from another city.

(Announcement)

WALLACE: The U.S. Command's battle communiqué indicates that the Allies repulsed most of the enemy's attacks, but this success was not universal. In an assault today the Communists captured half of the Central Highlands city of Kontum and the Vietcong flag flies in the center of the northern city of Hue. The enemy claims also to control Quang Tri City, also in I Corps in the north, a claim as yet unconfirmed by the Allies.

But one place where American and South Vietnamese troops turned back the enemy was at Nhatrang, a coastal city about 190 miles northeast of Saigon. In peacetime a pleasant resort city, now Nhatrang is the headquarters for the Fifth Special Forces, the Green Berets; and the Green Berets were in the thick of the fighting. The Communist attack there had begun around midnight, and it developed into a street fight which, as you see here, carried over into the daylight hours. The enemy's apparent goal in this fight, down the street, was a provincial prison where many important Vietcong were held. During this battle many innocent civilians, friendly to the Allies, were trapped in their homes between the lines of fire between VC and the Green Berets. It was only after twelve hours of battle that the area was secure enough to call those civilians out to safety.

The Communist raids had a stunning impact, all of them, around the world, and the question is, what is it that the enemy is after in these attacks. Certainly he does not believe that these suicide assaults by terrorists squads are going to radically change the course of the war in Vietnam; but there can be no doubt that these attacks are calculated to impress indelibly on public opinion in North and South Vietnam and in the United States the resourcefulness and the determination of the Vietcong and his ability to strike almost at will any place in South Vietnam if he is willing to pay the price.

The story of the past three days, with heavy emphasis, of course, on American and South Vietnamese casualties will be trumpeted throughout Vietnam and around the world by Hanoi. Whether all of this is a prelude to an expression that Hanoi is willing now to go to the negotiation table remains to be seen, but there is little doubt that there will be more such stories from Khesanh and elsewhere in South Vietnam in the bitter month of February that lies ahead.

Mike Wallace, CBS News, New York.

ANNOUNCER: This has been a CBS News Special Report: "Saigon Under Fire."

Source: Irwin Unger and Debi Unger (eds.), *The Times Were a Changin': The Sixties Reader* (New York: Three Rivers Press, 1998), pp. 266–70.

Discussion Questions

1. What do the documents in this chapter suggest were the main reasons for US involvement in Vietnam?
2. What special insights into the Vietnam war and the antiwar movement are provided by first-hand testimony and artistic creations such as Cpl. Jon Johnson's letter home and Country Joe McDonald's song?
3. How much do these documents suggest that the US government was ultimately to blame for the defeat in Vietnam?

Chapter 7   Gender and Sexuality

1. Betty Friedan, *The Feminine Mystique*, 1963

The Feminine Mystique *was a seminal text in the development of the women's liberation movement with its careful delineation of what Betty Friedan called the "problem that has no name": the pervasive cult of domesticity which restricted many American women to a life defined largely by their function as homemakers, mothers, and wives. Despite widespread material abundance and outward appearances of comfort and satisfaction, Friedan found deep wells of frustration and anxiety among American women, snared by the social and cultural power of a male-defined, media-reinforced "feminine mystique" that confined them to a very narrow range of acceptable lifestyle choices and left their other capacities, aspirations, and needs unrecognized. Friedan's own career, which combined journalism and motherhood, offered a reminder that some women did manage to escape, if only partially, the shackles of the cult of domesticity. Moreover, as a heterosexual middle-class white professional and a graduate of the prestigious Smith College, her insights often had more resonance for educated women of her own class, race, and sexual orientation than they did for poor, black, Hispanic women or lesbians. Nevertheless,* The Feminine Mystique *endures as a sharp analysis of the position of many women in America in the early 1960s, simultaneously identifying and helping to usher in the modern feminist movement.*

The problem lay buried, unspoken, for many years in the minds of American women. It was a strange stirring, a sense of dissatisfaction, a yearning that women suffered in the middle of the twentieth century in the United States. Each suburban wife struggled with it alone. As she made the beds, shopped for groceries, matched slipcover material, ate peanut butter sandwiches with her children, chauffeured Cub Scouts and Brownies, lay beside her husband at night – she was afraid to ask even of herself the silent question – "Is this all?"

For over fifteen years there was no word of this yearning in the millions of words written about women, for women, in all the columns, books and articles by experts telling women their role was to seek fulfillment as wives and mothers. Over and over women heard in voices of tradition and of Freudian sophistication that they could desire no greater destiny than to glory in their own femininity. Experts told them how to catch a man and keep him, how to breastfeed children and handle their toilet training, how to cope with sibling rivalry and adolescent rebellion; how to buy a dishwasher, bake bread, cook gourmet snails, and build a swimming pool with their own hands; how to dress, look, and act more feminine and make marriage more exciting; how to keep their husbands from dying young and their sons from growing into delinquents. They were taught to pity the neurotic, unfeminine, unhappy women who wanted to be poets or physicists or presidents. They learned that truly feminine women do not want careers, higher education, political rights – the independence and the opportunities that the old-fashioned feminists fought for. Some women, in their forties and fifties, still remembered painfully giving up those dreams, but more of the younger women no longer thought about them. A thousand expert voices applauded their femininity, their adjustment, their new maturity. All they had to do was devote their lives from earliest girlhood to finding a husband and bearing children....

In a New York hospital, a woman had a nervous breakdown when she found she could not breastfeed her baby. In other hospitals, women dying of cancer refused a drug which research had proved might save their lives: its side effects were said to be unfeminine. "If I have only one life, let me live it as a blonde," a larger-than-life-sized picture of a pretty, vacuous woman proclaimed from newspaper, magazine, and drugstore ads. And across America, three out of every ten women dyed their hair blonde. They ate a chalk called Metrecal, instead of food, to shrink to the size of the thin young models. Department-store buyers reported that American women, since 1939, had become three and four sizes smaller. "Women are out to fit the clothes, instead of vice-versa," one buyer said.

Interior decorators were designing kitchens with mosaic murals and original paintings, for kitchens were once again the center of women's lives. Home sewing became a million-dollar industry. Many women no longer left their homes, except to shop, chauffeur their children, or attend a social engagement with their husbands. Girls were growing up in America without ever having jobs outside the home. In the late fifties, a sociological phenomenon was suddenly remarked: a third of American women now worked, but most were no longer young and very few were pursuing careers. They were married women who held part-time jobs, selling or secretarial, to put their husbands through school, their sons through college, or to help pay the mortgage. Or they were widows supporting families. Fewer and fewer women were entering professional work. The shortages in the nursing, social work, and teaching professions caused crises in almost every American city. Concerned over the Soviet Union's lead in the space race, scientists noted that America's greatest source of unused brain-power was women. But girls would not study physics: it was "unfeminine." A girl refused a science fellowship at Johns Hopkins to take a job in a real-estate office. All she wanted, she said, was what every other American girl wanted – to get married, have four children and live in a nice house in a nice suburb.

The suburban housewife – she was the dream image of the young American women and the envy, it was said, of women all over the world. The American housewife – freed by science and labor-saving appliances from the drudgery, the dangers of childbirth and the illnesses of her grandmother. She was healthy, beautiful, educated, concerned only about her husband, her children, her home. She had found true feminine fulfillment. As a housewife and mother, she was respected as a full and equal partner to man in his world. She was free to choose automobiles, clothes, appliances, supermarkets; she had everything that women ever dreamed of.

In the fifteen years after World War II, this mystique of feminine fulfillment became the cherished and self-perpetuating core of contemporary American culture. Millions of women lived their lives in the image of those pretty pictures of the American suburban housewife, kissing their husbands goodbye in front of the picture window, depositing their station-wagonsful of children at school, and smiling as they ran the new electric waxer over the spotless kitchen floor. They baked their own bread, sewed their own and their children's clothes, kept their new washing machines and dryers running all day. They changed the sheets on the beds twice a week instead of once, took the rug-hooking class in adult education, and pitied their poor frustrated mothers, who had dreamed of having a career. Their only dream was to be perfect wives and mothers; their highest ambition to have five children and a beautiful house, their only fight to get and keep their husbands. They had no thought for the unfeminine problems of the world outside the home; they wanted the men to make the major decisions. They gloried in their role as women, and wrote proudly on the census blank: "Occupation: housewife" ....

If the woman had a problem in the 1940's and 1950's, she knew that something must be wrong with her marriage, or with herself. Other women were satisfied with their lives, she thought. What kind of a woman was she if she did not feel this mysterious fulfillment waxing the kitchen floor? She was so ashamed to admit her dissatisfaction that she never knew how many other women shared it ....

In 1960, the problem that has no name burst like a boil through the image of the happy American housewife. In the television commercials the pretty housewives still beamed over their foaming dishpans and *Time*'s cover story on "The Suburban Wife, and American Phenomenon," protested: "Having too good a time ... to believe that they should be unhappy." But the actual unhappiness of the American housewife was suddenly being reported – from the *New York Times* and *Newsweek* to *Good Housekeeping* and C.B.S. Television ....

It is no longer possible to ignore that voice, to dismiss the desperation of so many American women. This is not what being a woman means, no matter what the experts say. For human suffering there is a reason; perhaps the reason has not been found because the right questions have not been asked, or pressed far enough. I do not accept the answer that there is no problem because American women have luxuries that women in other times and lands never dreamed of; part of the strange newness of the problem is that it cannot be understood in terms of the age-old material problems of man: poverty, sickness, hunger, cold. The women who suffer this problem have a hunger that food cannot fill. It persists in women whose husbands are struggling interns and law clerks, or prosperous doctors and lawyers; in wives of workers and executives who make $5,000 a year or $50,000. It is not caused by lack of material advantages; it may not even be felt by women preoccupied with desperate problems of hunger, poverty or illness. And women who think it will be solved by more money, a bigger house, a second car, moving to a better suburb, often discover it gets worse.

It is no longer possible today to blame the problem on loss of femininity: to say that education and independence and equality with men have made American women unfeminine. I have heard so many women try to deny this dissatisfied voice within themselves because it does not fit the pretty picture of femininity the experts have given them. I think, in fact, that this is the first clue to the mystery: the problem cannot be understood in the generally accepted terms by which scientists have studied women, doctors have treated them, counselors have advised them, and writers have written about them. Women who suffer this problem, in whom this voice is stirring, have lived their whole lives in the pursuit of feminine fulfillment. They are not career women (although career women may have other problems); they are women whose greatest ambition has been marriage and children. For the oldest of these women, these daughters of the American middle class, no other dream was possible. The ones in their forties and fifties who once had other dreams gave them up and threw themselves joyously into life as housewives. For the youngest, the new wives and mothers, this was the only dream. They are the ones who quit high school and college to marry, or marked time in some job in which they had no real interest until they married. These women are very "feminine" in the usual sense, and yet they still suffer the problem....

If I am right, the problem that has no name stirring in the minds of so many American women today is not a matter of loss of femininity or too much education, or the demands of domesticity. It is far more important than anyone recognizes. It is the key to these other new and old problems which have been torturing women and their husbands and children, and puzzling their doctors and educators for years. It may well be the key to our future as a nation and a culture. We can no longer ignore that voice within women that says: "I want something more than my husband and my children and my home."

Source: Betty Friedan, *The Feminine Mystique* (New York: W. W. Norton, 1963), pp. 13–29. Copyright © 1983, 1974, 1973, 1963 by Betty Friedan. Used by permission of W. W. Norton & Company, Inc.

2. *US News & World Report*, "The Pill," 1966

Few scientific or commercial innovations have had as much impact on American society as the Pill. In 1960 the tablets became widely available, offering a highly effective way to prevent unwanted pregnancy without interfering in any way with the mechanics of sexual intercourse. Although birth control remained illegal in parts of the country until the Supreme Court's 1965 Griswold v. Connecticut ruling – and contraception could still be denied to unmarried women until the Court ruled against such discrimination in 1972 – by the end of the 1960s, some 8.5 million American women were using this form of birth control. This new reproductive technology and the changing attitudes toward human sexuality that had been increasingly evident since World War II combined to cement in place the notion of a sexual revolution. Some were thrilled by these developments; others were appalled.

In the summer of 1966, the conservative newsmagazine US News & World Report *carried an extensive report on the social and cultural effects of the Pill*

and concluded that it was having a generally damaging effect on the moral
health of the nation, particularly at a time when other traditional instruments of
sexual restraint, such as schools, the church, and the family, were losing their
influence on young people. The report neatly summarized many of the anxieties
about the new permissiveness of the 1960s that would fuel the social
conservatism of the next half century.

An era of vast change in sexual morality now is developing in America.

Fear is being expressed that the nation may be heading into a time of "sexual anarchy."

Just six years ago the birth-control pill came onto the market. Today –

- College girls everywhere are talking about the pill, and many are using it. The pill is turning up in high schools, too.
- City after city is pushing distribution of the pill to welfare recipients, including unmarried women.
- Tens of thousands of Roman Catholic couples are turning to the pill as a means of practicing birth control.

These and other trends are expected to accelerate in times just ahead as laboratories perfect the long term "contraceptive shot" and the retroactive pill which wards off pregnancy even if taken after sexual intercourse.

Result: Widespread concern is developing about the impact of the pill on morality.

Being asked are these questions: With birth control so easy and effective, is the last vestige of sexual restraint to go out the window? Will mating become casual and random – as among the animals? Recently, John Alexander, general director of the Inter-Varsity Christian Fellowship, which has its head-quarters in Chicago, said: "I think it is certain that the pill will tear down the barriers for more than a few young people hitherto restrained by fear of pregnancy – and this will be even more true when the 'retroactive pill' comes on the market. I am very much afraid that sexual anarchy could develop."

The nation's Presbyterian leaders, at their 178th General Assembly, warned recently of increasing "confusion about the meaning of sex," which they ascribed, in large part, to new methods of birth control such as the pill.

Disquiet is voiced even by an official of Planned Parenthood-World Population, which actively promotes birth control. Dr. Donald B. Strauss said: "The two great supports of sexual morality in the past – fear of disease and fear of pregnancy – have now, happily, been largely removed. ... This, I submit, leaves our generation of parents with a problem that largely remains unsolved."

Early promiscuity

The dimensions of that problem are being outlined daily by signs of growing sexual promiscuity among America's young.

The Connecticut State Department of health recently estimated that one 13-year-old girl in every six in the State will become pregnant out of wedlock, before she is 20.

Almost countless incidents have been reported, across the U.S., of teenage girls in high school carrying birth control pills.

In some cases, these have been supplied by their parents.

"Sex clubs" at high schools are reported from time to time.

On the East Coast, high school girls of the middle and upper income classes join a steady traffic reported among college girls who fly to Puerto Rico for legalized abortions.

Recently a freshman at one of the East's most exclusive girls' colleges told her parents that, when a group in her class visited an Ivy League university as a weekend guests, her classmates stayed the night at motels with boys – some whom they had never seen before and might never see again.

Such occurrences, she said, were commonplace and there were eight or nine pregnancies in her class during the past academic year. Girls declining to engage in sex relations were regarded as "squares," she said.

A different outlook

Seen as playing an important role in the form of "sexual anarchy" among youngsters is a new attitude towards morality. An official at Mills College in Oakland, CA, reported that "there is less talk than there used to be about right or wrong – the question today is more, 'Is the individual making a wise decision for her future?'"

It is not just the young people who are causing worries about the nation's sexual morality. Marital infidelity is becoming accepted by many Americans as being of little importance. A "wife swapping" scandal made headlines in California, while Long Island's suburbs were rocked by police accounts of housewives earning money as prostitutes – some with the knowledge and consent of their husbands.

"A whole new world"

As many clergymen and educators see it, the pill is becoming a major element in the crumbling of past standards of sexual morality – especially among the young. A woman teacher at a small college in upstate New York said: "When you talk to the girls today, you're talking in a whole new world. They know how to get the pill. They think a girl is a fool not to use it if – and it's a big 'if' – she is seriously in love. Promiscuity is still frowned upon, but it's not equated with morals. It's a matter of personal pride." . . .

Changing attitudes

Until recently, church pressure was a curb on private, as well as public, clinics for birth control among the poor.

Today, however, welfare administrators everywhere are turning to the pill as a means of keeping women from producing large broods, many illegitimate, to be supported by the public treasury.

New York, Chicago and Washington D.C., at first limited birth-control services among the poor to married women. Now unmarried women, too, are getting the pill in those cities.

A number of officials and clergymen are voicing concern over this trend. Unchecked, they say, it could lead to official endorsement of the idea that sexual promiscuity is acceptable as long as pregnancy does not result. The Rev. Dexter L. Hanley, S.J., of Georgetown University's law school, told a Senate subcommittee on May 10: "There are those who sincerely feel that the distribution of information and supplies to the unmarried will encourage promiscuity and a breakdown of public morality. . . . If contraceptive advice is to be distributed to the unmarried, two things will be necessary . . . [firstly] adequate counseling and increased attention to family values . . . secondly, doctors and counselors will have to be able to exercise discretion."

Still another moral dilemma is arising from use of the pill – this one involving Roman Catholic married couples. Recently a Government-financed study showed that 21 percent of Catholic wives under the age of 45 have used, or are using, birth control pills despite the Church's ban on all unapproved means of family planning. The comparable figure for Protestant wives was 29 percent. . . .

What sociologists think

Sociologists point out that the pill, itself, is only one element in the danger of moral anarchy. Dr. Mary S. Calderone, executive director of Sex Information and Education Council of the U.S., said: "Society provides young people with far too many examples of sex irresponsibly used. High-school kids see sex used as a commercial come on, as an end in itself, presented to them. If the pill hadn't come along, we would be excited about whatever methods were being used."

Even so, the pill is becoming a major factor in the problem. Six million American women are using it. This sudden and overwhelming popularity has caused a few physicians to caution that physical effects over the long run are not thoroughly known. But neither these reservations nor the moral issues are dimming enthusiasm felt by many Americans. One social worker said: "The pill is so clean and simple, and sure, that everybody who hears about it wants it. And I tell everybody about it."

Crisis ahead?

Less enthusiastic are many Americans who feel that the pill is making moral choices much more difficult for a lot of people, and could precipitate a crisis in sexual morality.

Recently the Right Rev. Richard S. Emrich, Episcopal Bishop of Michigan, said: "the existence of the pill opens up dangerous possibilities.... It provides an invitation to premarital sex. There must be limitations and restrictions on the use of sex if we are to remain a civilized people."

Source: *US News & World Report*, "The Pill: How it is Affecting U.S. Morals, Family Life," July 11, 1966. Copyright U.S. News & World Report, L.P. Reprinted with permission.

3. National Organization for Women, Bill of Rights, 1967

The National Organization for Women (NOW) was formed in 1966, largely by middle-class heterosexual white women who were disappointed by, among other examples of sexism in American society, the federal government's failure to enforce the provisions of Title VII of the 1964 Civil Rights Act that forbade discrimination in employment on the basis of sex. At the local level, NOW was more often to be found working with union organizers to pursue better employment opportunities, conditions, and remuneration for a wide range of American women. Moreover, even at the national level, NOW radicalized and diversified somewhat during the later 1960s in response to the emergence of much more militant and multicultural feminist voices and a new emphasis on the politics of sexuality. Nonetheless, NOW remained essentially liberal and reformist rather than revolutionary in its goals, as outlined in its initial

Statement of Purpose, drafted by Betty Friedan and adopted at the group's organizing conference in October 29, 1966, and in the Bill of Rights adopted at NOW's first national meeting in November 1967.

I.   Equal Rights Constitutional Amendment
II.   Enforce Law Banning Sex Discrimination in Employment
III.   Maternity Leave Rights in Employment and in Social Security Benefits
IV.   Tax Deduction for Home and Child Care Expenses for Working Parents
V.   Child Day Care Centers
VI.   Equal and Unsegregated Education
VII.   Equal Job Training Opportunities and Allowances for Women in Poverty
VIII. The Right of Women to Control Their Reproductive Lives

WE DEMAND:

I.   That the U.S. Congress immediately pass the Equal Rights Amendment to the Constitution to provide that "Equality of rights under the law shall not be denied or abridged by the United States or by any State on account of sex," and that such then be immediately ratified by the several States.

II.   That equal employment opportunity be guaranteed to all women, as well as men, by insisting that the Equal Employment Opportunity Commission enforces the prohibitions against racial discrimination.

III.   That women be protected by law to ensure their rights to return to their jobs within a reasonable time after childbirth without loss of seniority or other accrued benefits, and be paid maternity leave as a form of social security and/or employee benefit.

IV.   Immediate revision of tax laws to permit the deduction of home and child-care expenses for working parents.

V.   That child-care facilities be established by law on the same basis as parks, libraries, and public schools, adequate to the needs of children from the pre-school years through adolescence, as a community resource to be used by all citizens from all income levels.

VI.   That the right of women to be educated to their full potential equally with men be secured by Federal and State legislation, eliminating all discrimination and segregation by sex, written and unwritten, at all levels of education, including colleges, graduate and professional schools, loans and fellowships, and Federal and State training programs such as the Job Corps.

VII. The right of women in poverty to secure job training, housing, and family allowances on equal terms with men, but without prejudice to a parent's right to remain at home to care for his or her children; revision of welfare legislation and poverty programs which deny women dignity, privacy, and self-respect.

VIII. The right of women to control their own reproductive lives by removing from the penal code laws limiting access to contraceptive information and devices, and by repealing penal laws governing abortion.

Source: Reprinted with permission of the National Organization for Women. This is a historical document and may not reflect the current language or priorities of the organization.

4. Redstockings Manifesto, 1969

Founded by Shulamith Firestone and Ellen Willis in 1969, the Redstockings were a radical feminist group who combined direct-action protests with "consciousness-raising" efforts designed to forge a united female front to combat the intersecting evils of patriarchy and free-market capitalism. Far more militant than NOW, the Redstockings emphasized how all women needed to be brought to recognition of their shared status as an oppressed class. They also rejected the emphasis by other groups on securing full and equal access to the social, economic, and political opportunities of American life as it was then configured, believing that to pursue such goals was to be complicit in perpetuating male domination and multiple forms of economic, social, political, sexual, and psychological oppression on grounds of sex and sexual orientation. Inspired by the consciousness-raising work of Kathie Sarachild, who had changed her given name from Amatniek to honor her maternal ancestry, the Redstockings encouraged women to question the male-defined "natural order of things" in their private lives and in the broader workings of US society and culture.

I. After centuries of individual and preliminary political struggle, women are uniting to achieve their final liberation from male supremacy. Redstockings is dedicated to building this unity and winning our freedom.

II. Women are an oppressed class. Our oppression is total, affecting every facet of our lives. We are exploited as sex objects, breeders, domestic servants, and cheap labor. We are considered inferior beings, whose only purpose is to enhance men's lives. Our humanity is denied. Our prescribed behavior is enforced by the threat of physical violence.

Because we have lived so intimately with our oppressors, in isolation from each other, we have been kept from seeing our personal suffering as a political condition. This creates the illusion that a woman's relationship with her man is a matter of interplay between two unique personalities, and can be worked out individually. In reality, every such relationship is a *class* relationship, and the conflicts between individual men and women are *political* conflicts that can only be solved collectively.

III.   We identify the agents of our oppression as men. Male supremacy is the oldest, most basic form of domination. All other forms of exploitation and oppression (racism, capitalism, imperialism, etc.) are extensions of male supremacy: men dominate women, a few men dominate the rest. All power structures throughout history have been male-dominated and male-oriented. Men have controlled all political, economic and cultural institutions and backed up this control with physical force. They have used their power to keep women in an inferior position. *All men* receive economic, sexual, and psychological benefits from male supremacy. *All men* have oppressed women.

IV.   Attempts have been made to shift the burden of responsibility from men to institutions or to women themselves. We condemn these arguments as evasions. Institutions alone do not oppress; they are merely tools of the oppressor. To blame institutions implies that men and women are equally victimized, obscures the fact that men benefit from the subordination of women, and gives men the excuse that they are forced to be oppressors. On the contrary, any man is free to renounce his superior position provided that he is willing to be treated like a woman by other men.

We also reject the idea that women consent to or are to blame for their own oppression. Women's submission is not the result of brainwashing, stupidity, or mental illness but of continual, daily pressure from men. We do not need to change ourselves, but to change men.

The most slanderous evasion of all is that women can oppress men. The basis for this illusion is the isolation of individual relationships from their political context and the tendency of men to see any legitimate challenge to their privileges as persecution.

V.   We regard our personal experience, and our feelings about that experience, as the basis for an analysis of our common situation. We cannot rely on existing ideologies as they are all products of male supremacist culture. We question every generalization and accept none that are not confirmed by our experience.

Our chief task at present is to develop female class consciousness through sharing experience and publicly exposing the sexist foundation of all our institutions. Consciousness-raising is not "therapy," which implies the existence of individual solutions and falsely assumes that the male-female relationship is purely personal, but the only method by which we can ensure that our program for liberation is based on the concrete realities of our lives.

The first requirement for raising class consciousness is honesty, in private and in public, with ourselves and other women.

VI.   We identify with all women. We define our best interest as that of the poorest, most brutally exploited woman.

We repudiate all economic, racial, educational or status privileges that divide us from other women. We are determined to recognize and eliminate any prejudices we may hold against other women.

We are committed to achieving internal democracy. We will do whatever is necessary to ensure that every woman in our movement has an equal chance to participate, assume responsibility, and develop her political potential.

VII.   We call on all our sisters to unite with us in struggle.

We call on all men to give up their male privileges and support women's liberation in the interest of our humanity and their own.

In fighting for our liberation we will always take the side of women against their oppressors. We will not ask what is "revolutionary" or "reformist," only what is good for women.

The time for individual skirmishes has passed. This time we are going all the way.

July 7, 1969, New York City

Source: The Redstockings Manifesto was issued in New York City on July 7, 1969. It first appeared as a mimeographed flyer, designed for distribution at women's liberation events. Further information about the Manifesto and other materials from the 1960s rebirth years of feminism is available from the Redstockings Women's Liberation Archives for Action at www.redstockings.org.

5. Lucian Truscott IV, "Gay Power Comes to Sheridan Square," 1969

On June 27, 1969, police raided the Stonewall Inn, a well known gay bar in New York's Greenwich Village, intending to enforce an obscure New York State liquor authority ruling that no drinking establishment could admit more than three homosexual customers at the same time. Weary of this kind of discrimination and harassment, the gay patrons at the Stonewall resisted arrest, injuring several policemen in the process. For several successive days, gay men and women and their supporters swarmed the streets of Greenwich Village, chanting "Gay Power" in a spontaneous uprising that was actually decades in the making. For many the Stonewall Riots marked the beginning of a new phase in the struggle for recognition of gay rights, stimulating greater acceptance of a variety of sexual orientations and encouraging the public expression of gay pride. For others, Stonewall represented yet another example of lawlessness and the demise of traditional moral and family values.

Lucian Truscott's eyewitness account of the symbolic birth of the gay liberation movement appeared in the Village Voice *newspaper – itself an important vehicle for the counterculture and New Left. Fully immersed in the events he was witnessing, Truscott's article is a classic example of what was known in the late 1960s and early 1970s as the New Journalism, whereby writers like Tom Wolfe, Norman Mailer and Hunter Thompson gave dramatic, participant-observer accounts of important social, cultural and political phenomena.*

Sheridan Square this weekend looked like something from a William Burroughs novel as the sudden specter of "gay power" erected its brazen head and spat out a *fairy* tale the likes of which the area has never seen.

The forces of faggotry, spurred by a Friday night raid on one of the city's largest, most popular and longest lived gay bars, the Stonewall Inn, rallied Saturday night in an unprecedented protest against the raid and continued Sunday night to assert presence, possibility, and pride until the early hours of Monday morning. "I'm a faggot, and I'm proud of it!" "Gay Power!" "I like boys!" – these and many other slogans were heard all three nights as the show of force by the city's finery met the force of the city's finest. The result was a kind of liberation, as the gay brigade emerged from the bars, back rooms, and bedrooms of the village and became street people.

Cops entered the Stonewall for the second time in a week just before midnight on Friday. It began as a small raid – only two patrolmen, two detectives, and two policewomen were involved. But as the patrons trapped inside were released one by one, a crowd started to gather on the street. It was initially a festive gathering, composed mostly of Stonewall boys who were waiting around for friends still inside or to see what was going to happen. Cheers would go up as favorites would emerge from the door, strike a pose, and swish by the detective with a "Hello there, fella." The stars were in their element. Wrists were limp, hair was primped, and reactions to the applause were classic. "I gave them the gay power bit, and they loved it, girls." "Have you seen Maxine? Where *is* my wife – I told her not to go far."

Suddenly the paddywagon arrived and the mood of the crowd changed. Three of the more blatant queens – in full drag – were loaded inside, along with the bartender and doorman, to a chorus of catcalls and boos from the crowd. A cry went up to push the paddywagon over, but it drove away before anything could happen. With its exit, the action waned momentarily. The next person to come out was a dyke, and she put up a struggle – from car to door to car again. It was at that moment that the scene became explosive. Limp wrists were forgotten. Beer cans and bottles were heaved at the windows, and a rain of coins descended on the cops. At the height of the action, a bearded figure was plucked from the crowd and dragged inside. It was Dave Van Ronk, who had come from the Lion's Head to see what was going on. He was later charged with having thrown an object at the police.

Three cops were necessary to get Van Ronk away from the crowd and into the Stonewall. The exit left no cops on the street, and almost by signal the crowd erupted into cobblestone and bottle heaving. The reaction was solid, they were "pissed." The trashcan I was standing on was nearly yanked out from under me as a kid tried to grab it for use in the windowsmashing melee. From nowhere came an uprooted parking meter – used as a battering ram on the Stonewall door. I heard several cries of "Let's get some gas," but the blaze of flame which soon appeared in the window of the Stonewall was still a shock. As the wood barrier behind the glass was beaten open, the cops inside turned a firehose on the crowd. Several kids took the opportunity to cavort in the spray, and their momentary glee served to stave off what was rapidly becoming a full-scale attack. By the time the fags were able to regroup forces and come up with another assault, several carloads of police reinforcements had arrived, and in minutes the streets were clear.

A visit to the Sixth Precinct revealed the fact that 13 persons had been arrested on charges which ranged from Van Ronk's felonious assault of a police officer to the owners' illegal sale and storage of alcoholic beverages without a license. Two police officers had been injured in the battle with the crowd. By the time the last cop was off the street Saturday morning, a sign was going up announcing that the Stonewall would reopen that night. It did.

Protest set the tone for "gay power" activities on Saturday. The afternoon was spent boarding up the windows of the Stonewall and chalking them with signs of the new revolution. "We are Open," "There is all college boys and girls in here," "Support Gay Power – C'mon in, girls," "Insp. Smyth looted our: money, jukebox, cigarette mach, telephones, safe, cash register, and the boys tips." Among the slogans were two carefully clipped and bordered copies of the Daily News story about the previous night's events, which was anything but kind to the gay cause.

The real action Saturday was that night in the street. Friday night's crowd had returned and was being led in "gay power" cheers by a group of gay cheerleaders. "We are the Stonewall girls/ We wear our hair in curls/ We have no underwear/ We show our pubic hairs!" The crowd was gathered across the street from the Stonewall and was growing with the additions of onlookers, Eastsiders, and rough street people who saw a chance for a little action. Though dress had changed from Friday night's gayery to Saturday night street clothes, the scene was a command performance for queens. If Friday night had been pick-up night, Saturday was date night! Hand-holding, kissing, and posing accented each of the cheers with homosexual liberation that had appeared only fleetingly on the street before. One-liners were as practiced as if they had been used for years. "I just want you all to know," quipped a platinum blond with obvious glee, "that sometimes being homosexual is a big pain in the ass." Another allowed as how he had become a "left-deviationist." And on and on.

The quasi-political tone of the street scene was looked upon with disdain by some, for radio news announcements about the previous night's "gay power" chaos had brought half of Fire Island's Cherry Grove running back to home base to see what they had left behind. The generation gap existed even here. Older boys had strained looks on their faces and talked in concerned whispers as they watched the up-and-coming generation take being gay and flaunt it before the masses.

As the "gay power" chants on the street rose in frequency and volume, the crowd grew restless. The front of the Stonewall was losing its attraction, despite efforts by the owners to talk the crowd back into the club. "C'mon in and see what da pigs done to us," they growled. "We're honest business-men here. We're American-born boys. We run a legitimate joint here. There ain't nuttin bein' done wrong in dis place. Everybody come and see."

The people on the street were not to be coerced. "Let's go down the street and see what's happening girls," someone yelled.

And down the street went the crowd, smack into the Tactical Patrol Force, who had been called earlier to disperse the crowd and were walking west on Christopher from Sixth Avenue. Formed in a line, the TPF swept the crowd back to the corner of Waverly Place, where they stopped. A stagnant situation there brought on some gay tomfoolery in the form of a chorus line facing the line of helmeted and club-carrying cops. Just as the line got into a full kick routine, the TPF advanced again and cleared the crowd of screaming gay powerites down Christopher to Seventh Avenue. The street and park were then held from both ends, and no one was allowed to enter – naturally causing a fall-off in normal Saturday night business, even at the straight Lion's Head and 55. The TPF positions in and around the square were held with only minor incident – one busted head and a number of scattered arrests – while the cops amused themselves by arbitrarily breaking up small groups of people up and down the avenue. The crowd finally dispersed around 3:30 a.m. The TPF had come and they had conquered, but Sunday was already there, and it was to be another story.

Sunday night was a time for watching and rapping. Gone were the "gay power" chants of Saturday, but not the new and open brand of exhibitionism. Steps, curbs, and the park provided props for what amounted to the Sunday fag follies as returning stars from the previous night's performances stopped by to close the show for the weekend.

It was slow going. Around 1 a.m. a non-helmeted version of the TPF arrived and made a controlled and very cool sweep of the area, getting everyone moving and out of the park. That put a damper on posing and primping, and as the last buses were leaving Jerseyward, the crowd grew thin. Allen Ginsberg and Taylor Mead walked by to see what was happening and were filled in on the previous evenings' activities by some of the gay activists. "Gay power! Isn't that great!" Allen said. "We're one of the largest minorities in the country – 10 percent, you know. It's about time we did something to assert ourselves."

Ginsberg expressed a desire to visit the Stonewall – "You know, I've never been in there" – and ambled on down the street, flashing peace signs and helloing the TPF. It was a relief and a kind of joy to see him on the street. He lent an extra umbrella of serenity to the scene with his laughter and quiet commentary on consciousness, "gay power" as a new movement, and the various implications of what had happened. I followed him into the Stonewall, where rock music blared from speakers all around a room that might have come right from a Hollywood set of a gay bar. He was immediately bouncing and dancing wherever he moved.

He left, and I walked east with him. Along the way he described how things used to be. "You know, the guys there were so beautiful – they've lost that wounded look that fags all had 10 years ago." It was the first time I had heard that crowd described as beautiful.

We reached Cooper Square, and as Ginsberg turned to head toward home, he waved and yelled, "Defend the fairies!" and bounced on across the square. He enjoyed the prospect of "gay power" and is probably working on a manifesto for the movement right now. Watch out. The liberation is under way.

Source: Lucian Truscott IV, "Gay Pride Comes to Sheridan Square," *Village Voice*, July 3, 1969, pp. 1, 18.

6. Ruth Miller, Testimony to Senate Hearing on an Equal Rights Amendment, 1970

While issues of sexual freedom and psychological empowerment animated many of those at the forefront of the feminist movement of the 1960s, traditional concerns for expanded employment opportunities and more equitable treatment in the workplace continued to prompt a great deal of activity. The Equal Pay Act of 1963 and Title VII of the Civil Rights Act of 1964, along with the creation of the Office of Equal Employment Opportunity, helped improve matters for many women, although benefits were not equally distributed across all races and classes. Some women, particularly those associated with NOW and other organizations with a heavy concentration of business and professional women, believed their ambitions could only truly be met through the passage of an Equal Rights Amendment (ERA).

The value of an ERA had been the subject of intense debate among women's groups since the 1920s: supporters argued that outlawing any laws or practices that discriminated on the grounds of gender would produce a much-sought-after "level playing field" for women; opponents feared that it would bring to an end recognition of the distinct contribution and unique needs of women in American society, along with legislation specifically crafted to protect their rights. In the mid-to-late 1960s, opposition to the prospect of an ERA stimulated strong grassroots opposition from conservatives associated with Phyllis Schafly, who contended that such an amendment would undermine "proper" family structure, diminish women's special status as mothers and homemakers, make women eligible for the military draft, and even legitimize homosexuality. As the testimony of Ruth Miller (a California official of the Amalgamated Clothing Union of America) to a Senate Sub-Committee investigating the case for an ERA revealed, many female labor activists were similarly hostile, although their objections tended to focus more on the practical implications for working women of losing protective legislation based on gender differences. In spring 1972, Congress passed the ERA, but the proposed amendment expired in 1982, having failed by three states to secure the 38 votes necessary for ratification.

It is interesting to note that in most of the present political activity concerning women, and particularly by those who support this amendment, the "forgotten majority" are the workingwomen, these millions of women employed in the factories, fields, and service industries of the Nation. And this is where the effect of passage of this amendment would be most sorely felt.

It is quite apparent that the leadership in support of the amendment is composed mainly of middle-class professional and semiprofessional women, an infinitesmal percentage of the more than 30 million in the work force. Most of this huge work force is unskilled and semi-skilled work.

Since the turn of the century, a 70-year period, most States, including my own State of California, have enacted statutes designed to benefit working people. In essence, these laws and regulations were based on humane considerations. The primary concern was protection of health, safety, and general welfare of the people affected. Thus, we have had limitations on hours of work, minimum pay, restrictions on weightlifting, plus provisions for good lighting, seating, ventilation, rest periods and the like. The thrust has always been an attempt to remove extremes of possible exploitation in the areas of low wages, long hours, and other substandard working conditions.

These State regulations largely apply to women.

Justification for passage of these laws for one sex was found in the amply demonstrated fact that women lent themselves more readily to the extremes of exploitation.

The proponents of the equal rights amendment claim these labor standards have outlived their usefulness, and the effect of the removal of protective labor standards would virtually be nil.

I would like to examine those assertions in the light of California law and on the advice of attorneys that the passage of the proposed amendment would, in one fell swoop, nullify those standards.

California regulations with regard to the employment of women flow from two sources: the State labor code and the 14 wage orders issued by the Industrial Welfare Commission of the Industrial Relations Department. Each of the 14 wage and working conditions orders provides, among other standards, for a $1.65 minimum wage per hour. This, of course, means every woman whether employed in interstate or intrastate commerce is protected by this minimum, close to 2 million people. Should the equal rights amendment prevail and nullify the orders, women employed in interstate commerce in low-paying jobs, could immediately suffer the threat of a 5-cent-per-hour reduction in earnings. This particularly poignant figure at that wage level and the danger is compounded by the added problem of a 6.2 percent unemployment rate in the State today. But worse than that is the plight of the girl employed in intrastate industry who would be completely at the mercy of her employer in the absence of the orders.

Even more dramatic would be the plight of farmworkers – and California has a tremendous agricultural industry. Farmworker women, too, after much struggle, won the $1.65 minimum wage. The Federal minimum under the 1966 amendments to the Fair Labor Standards Act brought farmworkers to the level of $1.30 per hour beginning February 1, 1969. There are well over 100,000 women farmworkers in California. They earn close to the minimum wage; only a very small percentage are in interstate commerce and few are covered by the benefits of collective bargaining agreements.

Those who would so cavalierly cast out these protections should give pause when they think of the workingwoman, who earns a mere $1.65 per hour, faced with a possible reduction of 35 cents per hour if she is one of the lucky few in interstate commerce. If not she would have no minimum wage protection at all.

California is one of seven States which presently have minima for women only. Before taking the responsibility for seeing women workers – and they represent better than one-third of the total work force – deprived of this significant protection, the proponents of the amendment you are considering would be well advised to seek their remedy in the extension of minimum wage protections to the entire work force in each of these States.

The same reasoning can be applied to such provisions in California orders as rest periods, good ventilation, lighting, meal periods, reporting pay, et cetera, which should, in my view, be applied to the entire work force.

The two most difficult areas in terms of the present discussion are weight lifting regulations and limitations on hours of work. Proponents of the proposed amendment say these regulations lead to discriminatory practices against women, bar them from promotions and prevent them from enjoying the benefits of overtime work.

Let me hasten to say that many States, my own included, explicitly exempt women in the professions and certain creative activities from the provisions of the law. Unfortunately, these proponents place the blame for discriminatory practices against women, including lack of promotions, in the wrong place. There is no question in my mind that women are discriminated against at the hiring in level on wages and job responsibilities and promotional opportunities. They are continuously confined to accepted women's work and at women's wages. But the fault is in the social and cultural attitudes of the Nation, not in protective laws. And the remedy must relate to its source and not an extraneous area. The removal of protective labor standards will not and the passage of the equal rights amendment cannot eliminate overt and subtle cultural practices....

It was an examination of the question of weight lifting which led my union by convention action in May of 1970 to conclude:

Regulations on weight lifting should be revised in accordance with standards set by competent authorities on the basis of physical characteristics, without regard to sex.

The major assault on state protective legislation has, however, been on the proponents of repeal of this limitation that it is discriminatory against the female worker vis-à-vis the male employee; that inability to work overtime not only denies extra income but promotional opportunity. They seek redress in repeal of these limitations at the State level or through passage of equal rights amendments....

No evaluation of the merits of keeping hours limitations can be valid without giving thought to the duality of the role of women in the work force. Almost three out of five women workers are married and living with their husbands. Two out of five are mothers, and 11 million have children under 18 years of age. Consider that a women who works 8 hours a day at the job is away from home between 9 and 10 hours each day depending on transportation problems. In most cases, she does the marketing, food preparation, cleaning, laundry. She is the one who mainly cares for children, home, husband. Extension of the workday for her not only makes her availability uncertain but serves as an open sesame into making her labor endless hours during the day and night. She has little time for anything but tasks.

In 1967, a serious and partially successful attempt was made to extend the hours of work for women in California. No issue in my memory has so incensed the members of my union more than the possibility of being required to work more than 8 hours per day. I am pleased to report we retained the 8-hour standard. It is important to note, too, that California law always permitted a sixth day of work at time and one-half. The same is true of our union contracts. I have repeatedly been told by our women members that when Saturday work is required it causes excessive hardship for them in terms of their home responsibilities. And these are women who work because they must and, at best, have moderate incomes.

It cannot be denied that in some few cases women who cannot work overtime in the light of state hours limitations suffer discrimination. But this must be weighted against the welfare and responsibilities of the vast majority who should not carry the burden for a few....

Source: United States Congress, Senate Committee on the Judiciary, *Equal Rights 1970: Hearings before the Committee on the Judiciary*, 91st Cong., 2nd sess., September 9, 10, 11, and 15, 1970 (Washington, DC: United States Government Printing Office, 1970).

Discussion Questions

1. How do the diverse sources in this chapter help us to understand the causes, character and consequences of the "sexual revolution" of the 1960s?
2. What do the statements from NOW, the Redstockings, and Ruth Miller reveal about key differences within the "women's liberation movement" of the 1960s?
3. Why is personal testimony, whether in Betty Friedan's account of the "Feminine Mystique" or the New Journalism of Lucian Truscott, such a valuable source for understanding changing attitudes to gender and sexuality in the 1960s?

Chapter 8   Conservatism and the New Right

1. Billy Graham, "The National Purpose," 1960

By 1960 Billy Graham was already one of America's most prominent evangelists. Ordained in the Southern Baptist Convention in 1939, the North Carolina native harnessed the potential of the mass media to his indefatigable sense of divine calling to launch a series of phenomenally successful crusades across America and around the globe. Literally millions of people saw, heard, or read Graham's message, prompting many to declare themselves "born-again" as they accepted Christ as their personal savior.

Given his enormous prestige and popularity, Graham's views on many aspects of American life were keenly sought. In June 1960, Wisconsin Democratic Senator William Proxmire requested that one of the preacher's magazine columns should be included in the Congressional Record, *since he felt it offered important insights into the state of US morals, morale and purposefulness at the start of the new decade. Graham's analysis was firmly rooted in the kinds of traditional, faith-based values which provided the bedrock of a resurgent political and social conservatism in the 1960s.*

Mr. PROXMIRE: Mr. President, a recent substantial contribution to a great debate over our national purpose currently being conducted in the columns of *Life* magazine and the *New York Times* has been written by the Reverend Billy Graham.

This man, who has been unsurpassed in recent years in the capacity to instill spiritual inspiration in vast numbers of people throughout the world, surprised me by his prescription for a revised national purpose....

Mr. President, I ask unanimous consent that this article be printed in the RECORD as follows: NATIONAL PURPOSE: GRAHAM DIAGNOSIS – MORAL AND SPIRITUAL CANCER FOUND IN STRESS ON PERSONAL COMFORT.

A few months ago I played golf with a man who looked and acted as though he enjoyed perfect health. Today he is dead. In spite of outward appearance he had a virulent form of cancer which within a short time took his life.

I am convinced that regardless of the outward appearance of prosperity within the corporate life of America today there is present a form of moral and spiritual cancer which can ultimately lead to our destruction unless the disease is treated and the trend reversed.

Many thoughtful Americans are disturbed because as a nation we seem bereft of a sense of purpose. We have the mood and stance of a people who have arrived and have nowhere else to go.

Some of our most outstanding citizens are warning us with statements that are reminiscent of the flaming prophets of old who prophesied the doom of nations that refused to change their moral course.

Distorted values

George F. Kennan, the historian and former American Ambassador to the Soviet Union, recently said: "If you ask me whether a country – with no highly developed sense of national purpose, with the overwhelming accent of life on personal comfort, with a dearth of public services and a surfeit of privately sold gadgetry, with insufficient social discipline even to keep its major industries running without grievous interruption – if you ask me whether such a country has over the long run good chances of competing with a purposeful, serious and disciplined society such as that of the Soviet Union, I must say that the answer is 'No.'" ...

Moral lift needed

America is in desperate need of a moral and spiritual transfusion that will cause her to recapture the strength of individualism. Mass-produced machinery has given rise to the mass-produced man. We are inclined to think like the Joneses, dress like the Joneses, build houses like the Joneses. We have become status conscious and have built for ourselves sets of status symbols....

Spirit is lacking

Second, we need to recapture the Spirit of '76. While we encourage nationalism for ambitious smaller nations abroad, we discourage it at home.

Patriotism in America seems to be "old hat." If a man gets out and waves
the American flag, he is now suspect or called a reactionary.

We applaud the nationalistic demonstrations in other countries. Perhaps
we need a few demonstrations for America . . . .

Comdr. Vincent J. Lonergan, a Roman Catholic chaplain, warned participants at the White House on Children and Youth recently that "far too
many of (our youth) have been led to believe that patriotism is a phony
virtue, that military service is an intolerable burden to be avoided as a
plague; of if imposed upon them, to be carried out grudgingly, without
pride, without honor. It is extremely important that we imbue them with
the spirit of intelligent sacrifice that is our heritage as Americans."

What a heartening thing it would be to see the people of America making
the Spirit of '76 the spirit of 1960.

Too much leisure

Third we need to recapture hardness and discipline in our national life. Our
excessive allotment of leisure in an affluent society is making dullards out
of us. Thousands of our young men are not even able to pass the Army
physical examination. We play too much and work too little. We overspeak,
overdrink, oversex, and overplay, but few of us are overexercised.

We have become surfeited in this land of plenty. Our sedentary way of
life has brought an alarming rash of coronaries and related illnesses.
We may be the richest people in the world, but we are far from being the
sturdiest.

The Bible warns: "Woe to them that are at ease in Zion." We need to
recapture the love and dedication of hard work.

Fourth, we must recapture the courage of our fathers. The chairman of
the history department of one of our great universities recently confided in
me, "We have become a nation of cowards."

I challenged him on this statement, but his arguments were convincing.
The great courage that once was so characteristic of America and
Americans seems to be going. Many of our military leaders are deeply
concerned about the disappearance of the will to fight for what we believe.
We seem to be content to sit within the security of our homes and watch the

brave western heroes on television doing the things that inwardly we wish we had the courage to do....

Odds too easy

Fifth, we must recapture the American challenge.... The rise of the beat-niks is at least partially a pitiful attempt to find a challenge. Dr. Robert Lindner, the late Baltimore psychoanalyst, wrote the book, *Rebel Without a Cause.*

Dr. Lindner found that American youth feel they are so surrounded by conformity that they rebel for the sake of rebelling. This is the psychological basis of much of our teenage delinquency.

We need a challenge such as our forefathers had when they transformed this wilderness into a civilized nation. While the challenge of the present hour may take different forms, I believe it is even greater than what the early Americans faced. What is the American challenge? What is our reason for existence? There are a thousand challenges that should stir our emotions and demand the dedication of every fiber of our being. Some of them may be:

The challenge to be on the side of the little people of the world, the hungry, the homeless, the friendless, the oppressed, the discriminated against, the captives and those who live in countries where there is no freedom.

The challenge to throw political expediency to the wind if necessary and do what we know is morally right because it is right.

The challenge of sharing our immense wealth with others.

The challenge of electing men with moral courage to high office who will be ruthless with the gangsters that operate on such a wide scale throughout the Nation.

The challenge of selling the American ideal and dreams to the world.

The challenge of humility to admit our failures, to repent of our sins, and to unashamedly serve God.

The challenge of solving the worldwide problems of ignorance, disease, and poverty.

The challenge of finding the individual peace and joy that is so lacking in the good life in modern America.

The challenge of contentment with what we have, remembering the words of the Apostle Paul, "I have learned that in whatsoever state I find myself therewith to be content."

American still has a glorious future if we rise to the challenges, opportunities, and responsibilities of the hour. If we fail, may God help us.

Sixth, we must recapture our moral strength and out faith in God.

Some surveys of American life have been alarming and discouraging. We now know that cheating is accepted practice in our society. Morals have become irrelevant or relative – no longer are there moral absolutes. Success at any price is our maxim. We excuse our immorality by saying, "Everybody is doing it."

Many of our modern educators have decreed that we are what we are because of external pressures and that each of us is a victim of environment or inherent tendencies and that we cannot help what we are.

This is totally contrary to the teachings of Holy Scripture. The Bible teaches us that we are responsible for our moral choices.

We cannot possibly exist if we reject the time-honoured moral absolutes of the Ten Commandments and the Sermon on the Mount. The Scripture says:

"Righteousness exalteth a nation, but sin is a reproach to any people." ...

Maudlin sentiments ...

It is absolutely impossible to change society and reverse the moral trend unless we ourselves are changed from the inside out. Many needs transformation or conversion. Unless we Americans are willing to humbly accept the diagnosis of the "Book" upon which our culture was largely founded – and to accept its remedy – we are going to continue along the road to disaster and ruin.

The Scriptures warn: "To whom much is given, much is required." Because our privileges have been greater, our responsibilities are greater, thus, a Holy God requires more of the American people than of any nation in the history or the world with the possible exception of Israel. Out only way to moral reform is through repentance of our sins and a return to God ...

Source: *Congressional Record*, Proceedings and Debates of the 86th Congress, second session, 106, part 9 (June 6, 1960), pp. 11859–60.

2. Young Americans for Freedom, Sharon Statement, 1960

Young Americans for Freedom (YAF) was formed during a conference held at the family estate of conservative ideologue William F. Buckley, in Sharon, Connecticut, in September 1960. The Sharon Statement emerged from this gathering, offering an important blueprint for modern American conservatism. Anxious about the extent of federal intervention in the lives of individuals, in the internal affairs of the several states, and in the operation of the economy, the

Statement affirmed what YAF held to be the quintessential American values of individual freedom and commitment to a free market economy. Equally alarmed by the ever-present threat that communism presented to the American way of life, YAF also called for an uncompromising foreign policy dedicated to the single-minded protection of American interests around the globe. As chapters were formed on campuses across the nation, YAF provided energetic support for Barry Goldwater's ill-fated 1964 presidential bid and offered an important conservative counterpoint to the radical and liberal politics conventionally associated with the youth of the 1960s. Perhaps even more importantly, YAF offered an early, college-based example of the kind of innovative grassroots organizing which would eventually lead to the triumph of the New Right and the eclipse of the economic and social liberalism initially associated with the New Deal and latterly with the Great Society programs of Lyndon Johnson.

In this time of moral and political crises, it is the responsibility of the youth of America to affirm certain eternal truths.

WE, as young conservatives, believe:

THAT foremost among the transcendent values is the individual's use of his God-given free will, whence derives his right to be free from the restrictions of arbitrary force;

THAT liberty is indivisible, and that political freedom cannot long exist without economic freedom;

THAT the purpose of government is to protect those freedoms through the preservation of internal order, the provision of national defense, and the administration of justice;

THAT when government ventures beyond these rightful functions, it accumulates power, which tends to diminish order and liberty;

THAT the Constitution of the United States is the best arrangement yet devised for empowering government to fulfill its proper role, while restraining it from the concentration and abuse of power;

THAT the genius of the Constitution- the division of powers- is summed up in the clause that reserves primacy to the several states, or to the people, in those spheres not specifically delegated to the Federal government;

THAT the market economy, allocating resources by the free play of supply and demand, is the single economic system compatible with the requirements of personal freedom and constitutional government, and that it is at the same time the most productive supplier of human needs;

THAT when government interferes with the work of the market economy, it tends to reduce the moral and physical strength of the nation; that when it takes from one man to bestow on another, it diminishes the incentive of the first, the integrity of the second, and the moral autonomy of both;

THAT we will be free only so long as the national sovereignty of the United States is secure; that history shows periods of freedom are rare, and can exist only when free citizens concertedly defend their rights against all enemies;

THAT the forces of international Communism are, at present, the greatest single threat to these liberties;

THAT the United States should stress victory over, rather than coexistance with, this menace; and

THAT American foreign policy must be judged by this criterion: does it serve the just interests of the United States?

Source: Alexander Bloom and Wini Breines (eds.), *Takin' it to the Streets: A Sixties Reader* (New York and Oxford: Oxford University Press, 1995; 2nd edn, 2003), pp. 290–1.

3. US Supreme Court, *Abington v. Schempp*, 1963

In 1962 the Supreme Court ruled by a 7–1 majority in the case of Engel v. Vitale *that compulsory morning prayers in a New York school violated the Establishment Clause of the First Amendment to the Constitution, which expressly forbids any effort to establish or promote an official state religion. A year later in the case of* Abington v. Schempp *the Court reaffirmed its basic position, with Justice Potter Stewart again the only dissenting opinion. Both of these decisions provoked outrage and dismay from churchgoing Americans and from various conservative groups already alarmed by what they saw as a troublesome decline in America's religious and moral values. In the midst of the civil rights revolution in the South, Alabama Representative George Andrews had responded to* Engel *by complaining, "They put the Negroes in the schools, and now they've driven God out," while Senator Harry Byrd of Virginia openly hoped that the majority of schools would ignore the Supreme Court decisions. This is pretty much what happened as conservatives, particularly those based in the South, made the fight for school prayer a cornerstone of their quest to save America from the twin evils of liberalism and atheism. At the time of the Supreme Court rulings, only 12 states legally required Bible readings in their schools; 6 of those 12 were located in the South, while another two southern states, Mississippi and Texas, had laws that specifically permitted the practice. By 1966, in flagrant defiance of the Supreme Court's rulings, nearly 50 percent of all Southern school districts still*

*required compulsory Bible reading and/or school prayer, whereas
other regions of the country reported equivalent levels of only
2–5 percent.*

Mr. Justice Clark delivered the opinion of the Court.

Once again we are called upon to consider the scope of the provision of
the First Amendment to the United States Constitution which declares that
"Congress shall make no law respecting an establishment of religion, or
prohibiting the free exercise thereof...." These companion cases present
the issues in the context of state action requiring that schools begin each day
with readings from the Bible.... In light of the history of the First Amendment and of our cases interpreting and applying its requirements, we hold
that the practices at issue and the laws requiring them are unconstitutional
under the Establishment Clause, as applied to the States through the Fourteenth Amendment....

It is true that religion has been closely identified with our history and
government. As we said in Engel v. Vitale, *370 U.S. 421*, 434 (1962), "The
history of man is inseparable from the history of religion. And ... since the
beginning of that history many people have devoutly believed that 'More things
are wrought by prayer than this world dreams of.'" In Zorach v. Clauson, *343
U.S. 306*, 313 (1952), we gave specific recognition to the proposition that "[w]e
are a religious people whose institutions presuppose a Supreme Being." The fact
that the Founding Fathers believed devotedly that there was a God and that the
unalienable rights of man were rooted in Him is clearly evidenced in their
writings, from the Mayflower Compact to the Constitution itself. This background is evidenced today in our public life through the continuance in our
oaths of office from the Presidency to the Alderman of the final supplication,
"So help me God." Likewise each House of the Congress provides through its
Chaplain an opening prayer, and the sessions of this Court are declared open by
the crier in a short ceremony, the final phrase of which invokes the grace of
God.... Indeed, only last year an official survey of the country indicated that
64% of our people have church membership, Bureau of the Census, U.S.
Department of Commerce, *Statistical Abstract of the United States* (83d ed.
1962), 48, while less than 3% profess no religion whatever. Id., at p. 46. It can
be truly said, therefore, that today, as in the beginning, our national life reflects
a religious people who, in the words of Madison, are "earnestly praying, as ...
in duty bound, that the Supreme Lawgiver of the Universe ... guide them into
every measure which may be worthy of his [blessing....]," Memorial and
Remonstrance Against Religious Assessments, quoted in Everson v. Board of
Education, *330 U.S. 1*, 71–72 (1947)...

This is not to say, however, that religion has been so identified with our history and government that religious freedom is not likewise as strongly imbedded in our public and private life. Nothing but the most telling of personal experiences in religious persecution suffered by our forebears, see Everson v. Board of Education, supra, at 8–11, could have planted our belief in liberty of religious opinion any more deeply in our heritage .... This freedom to worship was indispensable in a country whose people came from the four quarters of the earth and brought with them a diversity of religious opinion. Today authorities list 83 separate religious bodies, each with membership exceeding 50,000, existing among our people, as well as innumerable smaller groups. Bureau of the Census. Op. cit., supra, at 46–47.

The wholesome "neutrality" of which this Court's cases speak thus stems from a recognition of the teachings of history that powerful sects or groups might bring about a fusion of governmental and religious functions or a concert or dependency of one upon the other to the end that official support of the State or Federal Government would be placed behind the tenets of one or of all orthodoxies. This the Establishment Clause prohibits. And a further reason for neutrality is found in the Free Exercise Clause, which recognizes the value of religious training, teaching and observance and, more particularly, the right of every person to freely choose his own course with reference thereto, free of any compulsion from the state ....

Applying the Establishment Clause principles to the cases at bar we find that the States are requiring the selection and reading at the opening of the school day of verses from the Holy Bible and the recitation of the Lord's Prayer by the students in unison. These exercises are prescribed as part of the curricular activities of students who are required by law to attend school. They are held in the school buildings under the supervision and with the participation of teachers employed in those schools. None of these factors, other than compulsory school attendance, was present in the program upheld in Zorach v. Clauson. The trial court in No. 142 has found that such an opening exercise is a religious ceremony and was intended by the State to be so. We agree with the trial court's finding as to the religious character of the exercises. Given that finding, the exercises and the law requiring them are in violation of the Establishment Clause.

... The State contends ... that the program is an effort to extend its benefits to all public school children without regard to their religious belief. Included within its secular purposes, it says, are the promotion of moral values, the contradiction to the materialistic trends of our times, the perpetuation of our institutions and the teaching of literature. The case came up on demurrer, of course, to a petition which alleged that the uniform practice under the rule had been to read from the King James version of the Bible and that the exercise was sectarian. The short answer, therefore, is that the religious character of the exercise was admitted by the State. But even if its purpose is not strictly religious, it is sought to be accomplished through readings, without comment, from the Bible. Surely the place of the Bible as an instrument of religion cannot be gainsaid, and the State's recognition of the pervading religious character of the ceremony is evident from the rule's specific permission of the alternative use of the Catholic Douay version as well as the recent amendment permitting non-attendance at the exercises. None of these factors is consistent with the contention that the Bible is here used either as an instrument for nonreligious moral inspiration or as a reference for the teaching of secular subjects.

The conclusion follows that ... the laws require religious exercises and such exercises are being conducted in direct violation of the rights of the appellees and petitioners. Nor are these required exercises mitigated by the fact that individual students may absent themselves upon parental request, for that fact furnishes no defense to a claim of unconstitutionality under the Establishment Clause. See Engel v. Vitale, supra, at 430. Further, it is no defense to urge that the religious practices here may be relatively minor encroachments on the First Amendment. The breach of neutrality that is today a trickling stream may all too soon become a raging torrent and, in the words of Madison, "it is proper to take alarm at the first experiment on our liberties." Memorial and Remonstrance Against Religious Assessments, quoted in Everson, supra, at 65.

It is insisted that unless these religious exercises are permitted a "religion of secularism" is established in the schools. We agree of course that the State may not establish a "religion of secularism" in the sense of affirmatively opposing or showing hostility to religion, thus "preferring those who believe in no religion over those who do believe." Zorach v. Clauson, supra, at 314. We do not agree, however, that this decision in any sense has that effect. In addition, it might well be said that one's education is not complete without a study of comparative religion or the history of religion and its relationship to the advancement of civilization. It certainly may be said that the Bible is worthy of study for its literary and historic qualities. Nothing we have said here indicates that such study of the Bible or of religion, when presented objectively as part of a secular program of education, may not be effected consistently with the First Amendment. But the exercises here do not fall into those categories. They are religious exercises, required by the States in violation of the command of the First Amendment that the Government maintain strict neutrality, neither aiding nor opposing religion.

Finally, we cannot accept that the concept of neutrality, which does not permit a State to require a religious exercise even with the consent of the majority of those affected, collides with the majority's right to free exercise of religion. While the Free Exercise Clause clearly prohibits the use of state action to deny the rights of free exercise to anyone, it has never meant that a majority could use the machinery of the State to practice its beliefs....

The place of religion in our society is an exalted one, achieved through a long tradition of reliance on the home, the church and the inviolable citadel of the individual heart and mind. We have come to recognize through bitter experience that it is not within the power of government to invade that citadel, whether its purpose or effect be to aid or oppose, to advance or retard....

Source: US Supreme Court, *Abington School Dist. V. Schempp*, 374 US 203 (1963). Appeal from the United States District Court for the Eastern District of Pennsylvania, No. 142. Argued February 27–28, 1963. Decided June 17, 1963.

4. Ronald Reagan, "A Time For Choosing," 1964

This impassioned but folksy national television address on behalf of Republican presidential candidate Barry Goldwater marked the emergence of former actor Ronald Reagan as a major new voice in American politics. Although Goldwater was unsuccessful in his bid for the White House, Reagan's address, sometimes referred to reverentially as "The Speech," articulated many of the concerns that would inspire the rise of the New Right over the next few years. Reagan condemned the excesses and costs of "big government," denounced the liberal social and economic reforms of the Great Society and War on Poverty as stepping stones towards socialism, and criticized a "soft" appeasing foreign policy towards the Soviet Union that he felt was weakening the nation's security and threatening freedom around the world. These messages struck a resonant chord with much of middle America. Two years later Reagan inflicted a heavy defeat on liberal incumbent Edmund "Pat" Brown to become Governor of California, a post to which he was re-elected in 1970. Having lost the Republican Party presidential nomination in 1976 he won it and the presidency in 1980, confirming the conservative ascendancy in modern American politics.

I have spent most of my life as a Democrat. I recently have seen fit to follow another course. I believe that the issues confronting us cross party lines. Now, one side in this campaign has been telling us that the issues of this election are the maintenance of peace and prosperity. The line has been used "We've never had it so good."

But I have an uncomfortable feeling that this prosperity isn't something on which we can base our hopes for the future. No nation in history has ever survived a tax burden that reached a third of its national income. Today, 37 cents of every dollar earned in this country is the tax collector's share, and yet our government continues to spend $17 million a day more than the government takes in. We haven't balanced our budget 28 out of the last 34 years. We have raised our debt limit three times in the last twelve months, and now our national debt is one and a half times bigger than all the combined debts of all the nations in the world. We have $15 billion in gold in our treasury – we don't own an ounce. Foreign dollar claims are $27.3 billion, and we have just had announced that the dollar of 1939 will now purchase 45 cents in its total value.

As for the peace that we would preserve, I wonder who among us would like to approach the wife or mother whose husband or son has died in South Vietnam and ask them if they think this is a peace that should be maintained indefinitely. Do they mean peace, or do they mean we just want to be left in peace? There can be no real peace while one American is dying some place in the world for the rest of us. We are at war with the most dangerous enemy that has ever faced mankind in his long climb from the swamp to the stars, and it has been said if we lose that war, and in doing so lose this way of freedom of ours, history will record with the greatest astonishment that those who had the most to lose did the least to prevent its happening. Well, I think it's time we ask ourselves if we still know the freedoms that were intended for us by the Founding Fathers.

Not too long ago two friends of mine were talking to a Cuban refugee, a businessman who had escaped from Castro, and in the midst of his story one of my friends turned to the other and said, "We don't know how lucky we are." And the Cuban stopped and said, "How lucky you are! I had some-place to escape to." In that sentence he told us the entire story. If we lose freedom here, there is no place to escape to. This is the last stand on Earth. And this idea that government is beholden to the people, that it has no other source of power except to sovereign people, is still the newest and most unique idea in all the long history of man's relation to man. This is the issue of this election. Whether we believe in our capacity for self-government or whether we abandon the American Revolution and confess that a little intellectual elite in a far-distant capital can plan our lives for us better than we can plan them ourselves....

In this vote-harvesting time, they use terms like the "Great Society," or as we were told a few days ago by the President, we must accept a "greater government activity in the affairs of the people." But they have been a little more explicit in the past and among themselves – and all of the things that

I now will quote have appeared in print. These are not Republican accusations. For example, they have voices that say "the cold war will end through acceptance of a not undemocratic socialism." Another voice says that the profit motive has become outmoded, it must be replaced by the incentives of the welfare state; or our traditional system of individual freedom is incapable of solving the complex problems of the 20th century. Senator Fulbright has said at Stanford University that the Constitution is outmoded. He referred to the president as our moral teacher and our leader, and he said he is hobbled in his task by the restrictions in power imposed on him by this antiquated document. He must be freed so that he can do for us what he knows is best. And Senator Clark of Pennsylvania, another articulate spokesman, defines liberalism as "meeting the material needs of the masses through the full power of centralized government." Well, I for one resent it when a representative of the people refers to you and me – the free man and woman of this country – as "the masses." This is a term we haven't applied to ourselves in America. But beyond that, "the full power of centralized government" – this was the very thing the Founding Fathers sought to minimize. They knew that governments don't control things. A government can't control the economy without controlling people. And they know when a government sets out to do that, it must use force and coercion to achieve its purpose. They also knew, those Founding Fathers, that outside of its legitimate functions, government does nothing as well or as economically as the private sector of the economy....

We were told four years ago that 17 million people went to bed hungry each night. Well, that was probably true. They were all on a diet. But now we are told that 9.3 million families in this country are poverty-stricken on the basis of earning less than $3,000 a year. Welfare spending is 10 times greater than in the dark depths of the Depression. We are spending $45 billion on welfare. Now do a little arithmetic, and you will find that if we divided the $45 billion up equally among those 9 million poor families, we would be able to give each family $4,600 a year, and this added to their present income should eliminate poverty! Direct aid to the poor, however, is running only about $600 per family. It would seem that someplace there must be some overhead.

So now we declare "war on poverty".... Now, do they honestly expect us to believe that if we add $1 billion to the $45 million we are spending, one more program to the 30-odd we have – and remember, this new program doesn't replace any, it just duplicates existing programs – do they believe that poverty is suddenly going to disappear by magic?....

I think we are for an international organization, where the nations of the world can seek peace. But I think we are against subordinating American interests to an organization that has become so structurally unsound that today you can muster a two-thirds vote on the floor of the General Assembly among the nations that represent less than 10 percent of the world's population. I think we are against the hypocrisy of assailing our allies because here and there they cling to a colony, while we engage in a conspiracy of silence and never open our mouths about the millions of people enslaved in Soviet colonies in the satellite nations.

I think we are for aiding our allies by sharing of our material blessings with those nations which share in our fundamental beliefs, but we are against doling out money government to government, creating bureaucracy, if not socialism, all over the world....

No government ever voluntarily reduces itself in size. Government programs, once launched, never disappear. Actually, a government bureau is the nearest thing to eternal life we'll ever see on this Earth. Federal employees number 2.5 million, and federal, state, and local, one out of six of the nation's work force is employed by the government. These proliferating bureaus with their thousands of regulations have cost us many of our constitutional safeguards. How many of us realize that today federal agents can invade a man's property without a warrant? They can impose a fine without a formal hearing, let alone a trial by jury, and they can seize and sell his property in auction to enforce the payment of that fine. In Chico County, Arkansas, James Wier overplanted his rice allotment. The government obtained a $17,000 judgment, and a U.S. marshal sold his 950-acre farm at auction. The government said it was necessary as a warning to others to make the system work. Last February 19 at the University of Minnesota, Norman Thomas, six-time candidate for President on the Socialist Party ticket, said, "If Barry Goldwater became President, he would stop the advance of socialism in the United States." I think that's exactly what he will do....

If you and I have the courage to tell our elected officials that we want our national policy based upon what we know in our hearts is morally right. We cannot buy our security, our freedom from the threat of the bomb by committing an immorality so great as saying to a billion now in slavery behind the Iron Curtain, "Give up your dreams of freedom because to save our own skin, we are willing to make a deal with your slave masters."...

Admittedly there is a risk in any course we follow other than this, but every lesson in history tells us that the greater risk lies in appeasement, and this is the specter our well-meaning liberal friends refuse to face – that their policy of accommodation is appeasement, and it gives no choice between peace and war, only between fight and surrender. If we continue to accommodate, continue to back and retreat, eventually we have to face the final demand – the ultimatum. And what then? When Nikita Khrushchev has told his people he knows what our answer will be? He has told them that we are retreating under the pressure of the Cold War, and someday when the time comes to deliver the ultimatum, our surrender will be voluntary because by that time we will have weakened from within spiritually, morally, and economically. He believes this because from our side he has heard voices pleading for "peace at any price" or "better Red than dead," or as one commentator put it, he would rather "live on his knees than die on his feet." And therein lies the road to war, because those voices don't speak for the rest of us.

You and I know and do not believe that life is so dear and peace so sweet as to be purchased at the price of chains and slavery. If nothing in life is worth dying for, when did this begin – just in the face of this enemy? Or should Moses have told the children of Israel to live in slavery under the pharaohs? Should Christ have refused the cross? Should the patriots at Concord Bridge have thrown down their guns and refused to fire the shot heard 'round the world? The martyrs of history were not fools, and our honored dead who gave their lives to stop the advance of the Nazis didn't die in vain. Where, then, is the road to peace? . . . .

You and I have the courage to say to our enemies, "There is a price we will not pay." There is a point beyond which they must not advance. This is the meaning in the phrase of Barry Goldwater's "peace through strength" . . . .

You and I have a rendezvous with destiny. We will preserve for our children this, the last best hope of man on Earth, or we will sentence them to take the last step into a thousand years of darkness . . . .

Source: An extract from the speech "A Time for Choosing" from *Speaking My Mind: Selected Speeches* by Ronald Reagan, published by Hutchinson. Reprinted by permission of The Random House Group Ltd. Reprinted by permission of Simon & Schuster. Reprinted by permission of the Ronald Reagan Presidential Foundation. Copyright © 1989 by Ronald W. Reagan.

5. Herblock, "Wallace For President," 1968

The 1968 presidential election season was characterized by deepening anxieties about Vietnam, the perceived decline in traditional social and moral values, and the apparent escalation of violence and lawlessness in America. That violence, as evidenced by the increasingly militant rhetoric of Black Power leaders like Stokely Carmichael and H. Rap Brown, the murders of Martin Luther King, Jr. in April and Robert F. Kennedy in June, a new round of urban "race" riots following King's assassination, and major disturbances between police and student antiwar demonstrators at the Democratic Party's national convention in Chicago, encouraged eventual winner Republican

Richard Nixon and independent candidate George Wallace to stress law and order issues in their campaign rhetoric. Both candidates also decried what they saw as the excessive meddling of the federal government in the social and economic lives of the American people under Lyndon Johnson's "Great Society" programs. However, as this editorial cartoon by Herblock (Herbert Block) suggests, some felt that Wallace's emphasis on law and order and states rights concealed a more fundamental racial appeal to white voters. Simultaneously expressing, exploiting, and intensifying what became known as the "white backlash" to further federal efforts to improve opportunities for African Americans and other minority groups – not to mention women – the segregationist icon and former Alabama governor won the support of nearly ten million voters across the nation. The cartoon appeared in the Washington Post *where Herblock consistently produced some of the most trenchant political and social commentary of the era.*

Figure 8.1   "We'll let the Overcoat out all the way, and the robe will hardly show at all." – A 1968 Herblock Cartoon.

Source: *Washington Post,* February 11, 1968, p. C6. Copyright by The Herb Block Foundation. Courtesy of the Library of Congress.

6. Richard M. Nixon, Presidential Nomination Acceptance Speech, 1968

In accepting the Republican Party's nomination for the presidency, Richard Nixon reached out to the "silent majority" of Americans for whom the major social, cultural, and political developments of the 1960s were a nightmare. As the Vietnam War raged with no end in sight, Nixon used the occasion to skewer the Johnson administration's inability to secure victory, despite overwhelming military and economic advantages. Pledging himself to achieving an "honorable end" to the conflict, Nixon rolled his critique of the war effort into a sweeping attack on successive Democratic administrations, which he chastised for failing to maintain both American prestige abroad and fidelity to traditional American values at home. Describing a nation ailing from rampant crime, urban riots, racial conflict, flag-burning antiwar protestors, drug use, sexual permissiveness, spendthrift government, and a pervasive lack of respect for authority, Nixon invoked many of the sources of discontent for middle America in an age of great social ferment. He assured voters that he would address these problems and restore America's sense of pride and purposefulness through honest government and a commitment, not to the kinds of massive governmental social and economic spending programs that had characterized Johnson's Great Society, but to the kind of private enterprise which had made America the richest nation in history and which, he argued, was still the best way to guarantee all Americans a shot at the American Dream. In the November election, Nixon won a narrow victory over Democratic Party nominee Hubert Humphrey.

Mr. Chairman, delegates to this convention, my fellow Americans.

The choice we make in 1968 will determine not only the future of America but the future of peace and freedom in the world for the last third of the Twentieth Century.

And the question that we answer tonight: can America meet this great challenge?

For a few moments, let us look at America, let us listen to America to find the answer to that question.

As we look at America, we see cities enveloped in smoke and flame.

We hear sirens in the night.

We see Americans dying on distant battlefields abroad.

We see Americans hating each other; fighting each other; killing each other at home.

And as we see and hear these things, millions of Americans cry out in anguish.

Did we come all this way for this?

Did American boys die in Normandy, and Korea, and in Valley Forge for this?

Listen to the answer to those questions.

It is another voice. It is the quiet voice in the tumult and the shouting.

It is the voice of the great majority of Americans, the forgotten Americans – the non-shouters; the non-demonstrators.

They are not racists or sick; they are not guilty of the crime that plagues the land.

They are black and they are white – they're native born and foreign born – they're young and they're old.

They work in America's factories.

They run America's businesses.

They serve in government.

They provide most of the soldiers who died to keep us free.

They give drive to the spirit of America.

They give lift to the American Dream.

They give steel to the backbone of America. They are good people, they are decent people; they work, and they save, and they pay their taxes, and they care.

Like Theodore Roosevelt, they know that this country will not be a good place for any of us to live in unless it is a good place for all of us to live in.

This I say to you tonight is the real voice of America. In this year 1968, this is the message it will broadcast to America and to the world.

Let's never forget that despite her faults, America is a great nation.

And America is great because her people are great....

America is in trouble today not because her people have failed but because her leaders have failed. And what America needs are leaders to match the greatness of her people....

When the strongest nation in the world can be tied down for four years in a war in Vietnam with no end in sight; when the richest nation in the world can't manage its own economy; when the nation with the greatest tradition of the rule of law is plagued by unprecedented lawlessness; when a nation that has been known for a century for equality of opportunity is torn by unprecedented racial violence; and when the President of the United States cannot travel abroad or to any major city at home without fear of a hostile demonstration – then it's time for new leadership for the United States of America.

My fellow Americans, tonight I accept the challenge and the commitment to provide that new leadership for America. And I ask you to accept it with me....

The time has come for honest government in the United States of America.

And so tonight I do not promise the millennium in the morning.

I don't promise that we can eradicate poverty, and end discrimination, eliminate all danger of war in the space of four, or even eight years. But, I do promise action – a new policy for peace abroad; a new policy for peace and progress and justice at home.

Look at our problems abroad. Do you realize that we face the stark truth that we are worse off in every area of the world tonight than we were when President Eisenhower left office eight years ago. That's the record. And there is only one answer to such a record of failure and that is a complete housecleaning of those responsible for the failures of that record. The answer is a complete re-appraisal of America's policies in every section of the world.

We shall begin with Vietnam.

We all hope in this room that there is a chance that current negotiations may bring an honorable end to that war. And we will say nothing during this campaign that might destroy that chance.

But if the war is not ended when the people choose in November, the choice will be clear. Here it is.

For four years this Administration has had at its disposal the greatest military and economic advantage that one nation has ever had over another in any war in history.

For four years, America's fighting men have set a record for courage and sacrifice unsurpassed in our history.

For four years, this Administration has had the support of the Loyal Opposition for the objective of seeking an honorable end to the struggle.

Never has so much military and economic and diplomatic power been used so ineffectively.

And if after all of this time and all of this sacrifice and all of this support there is still no end in sight, then I say the time has come for the American people to turn to new leadership – not tied to the mistakes and the policies of the past. That is what we offer to America.

And I pledge to you tonight that the first priority foreign policy objective of our next Administration will be to bring an honorable end to the war in Vietnam...

And as we commit to new policies for America tonight, let us make one further pledge:

For five years hardly a day has gone by when we haven't read or heard a report of the American flag being spit on; an embassy being stoned; a library being burned; or an ambassador being insulted some place in the world.

And each incident reduced respect for the United States until the ultimate insult inevitably occurred....

My friends, we live in an age of revolution in America and in the world. And to find the answers to our problems, let us turn to a revolution, a revolution that will never grow old. The world's greatest continuing revolution, the American Revolution.

The American Revolution was and is dedicated to progress, but our founders recognized that the first requisite of progress is order.

Now, there is no quarrel between progress and order – because neither can exist without the other.

So let us have order in America – not the order that suppresses dissent and discourages change but the order which guarantees the right to dissent and provides the basis for peaceful change.

And tonight, it is time for some honest talk about the problem of order in the United States.

Let us always respect, as I do, our courts and those who serve on them. But let us also recognize that some of our courts in their decisions have gone too far in weakening the peace forces as against the criminal forces in this country and we must act to restore that balance....

And to those who say that law and order is the code word for racism, there and here is a reply:

Our goal is justice for every American. If we are to have respect for law in America, we must have laws that deserve respect....

For the past five years we have been deluged by government programs for the unemployed; programs for the cities; programs for the poor. And we have reaped from these programs an ugly harvest of frustration, violence and failure across the land.

And now our opponents will be offering more of the same – more billions for government jobs, government housing, government welfare.

I say it is time to quit pouring billions of dollars into programs that have failed in the United States of America....

We are a great nation. And we must never forget how we became great.

America is a great nation today not because of what government did for people – but because of what people did for themselves over a hundred-ninety years in this country.

So it is time to apply the lessons of the American Revolution to our present problem.

Let us increase the wealth of America so that we can provide more generously for the aged; and for the needy; and for all those who cannot help themselves.

But for those who are able to help themselves – what we need are not more millions on welfare rolls – but more millions on payrolls in the United States of America.

Instead of government jobs, and government housing, and government welfare, let government use its tax and credit policies to enlist in this battle the greatest engine of progress ever developed in the history of man – American private enterprise....

And let us build bridges, my friends, build bridges to human dignity across that gulf that separates black America from white America.

Black Americans, no more than white Americans, they do not want more government programs which perpetuate dependency.

They don't want to be a colony in a nation.

They want the pride, and the self-respect, and the dignity that can only come if they have an equal chance to own their own homes, to own their own businesses, to be managers and executives as well as workers, to have a piece of the action in the exciting ventures of private enterprise.

I pledge to you tonight that we shall have new programs which will provide that equal chance....

I see a day when Americans are once again proud of their flag. When once again at home and abroad, it is honored as the world's greatest symbol of liberty and justice.

I see a day when the President of the United States is respected and his office is honored because it is worthy of respect and worthy of honor.

I see a day when every child in this land, regardless of his background, has a chance for the best education our wisdom and schools can provide, and an equal chance to go just as high as his talents will take him.

I see a day when life in rural America attracts people to the country, rather than driving them away.

I see a day when we can look back on massive breakthroughs in solving the problems of slums and pollution and traffic which are choking our cities to death.

I see a day when our senior citizens and millions of others can plan for the future with the assurance that their government is not going to rob them of their savings by destroying the value of their dollars.

I see a day when we will again have freedom from fear in America and freedom from fear in the world.

I see a day when our nation is at peace and the world is at peace and everyone on earth – those who hope, those who aspire, those who crave liberty – will look to America as the shining example of hopes realized and dreams achieved....

My fellow Americans, the long dark night for America is about to end.

The time has come for us to leave the valley of despair and climb the mountain so that we may see the glory of the dawn – a new day for America, and a new dawn for peace and freedom in the world.

Source: *Congressional Record*, 90th Congress, Second Session, 114, part 20 (September 16, 1968), pp. 26881–3.

7. Spiro Agnew, Television News Coverage, 1969

In the late 1960s, Richard Nixon's vice-president Spiro Theodore Agnew earned a reputation as one of the most outspoken conservative critics of what he saw as the disastrous liberal tendencies evident in many areas of American life and culture. On November 13, 1969 he delivered a speech prepared by administration aide Pat Buchanan and delivered in the wake of a televised address by Nixon explaining why the US should retain its commitment to an increasingly unpopular war in Vietnam. In it, Agnew railed against a conspiracy by hostile elements in the national news media to destroy the administration's credibility. He also criticized the powerful and unaccountable liberal cabal he believed controlled the three television news networks for helping to undermine America's self-confidence, respect for law, and deference to authority with a constant stream of sensational and negative images. Ironically, all three networks, ABC, CBS and NBC, broadcast Agnew's speech live.

Tonight I want to discuss the importance of the television news medium to the American people. No nation depends more on the intelligent judgment of its citizens. No medium has a more profound influence over public opinion. Nowhere in our system are there fewer checks on vast power. So, nowhere should there be more conscientious responsibility exercised than by the news media. The question is, "Are we demanding enough of our television news presentations?" "And are the men of this medium demanding enough of themselves?"

Monday night a week ago, President Nixon delivered the most important address of his Administration, one of the most important of our decade. His subject was Vietnam. My hope, as his at that time, was to rally the American people to see the conflict through to a lasting and just peace in the Pacific. For 32 minutes, he reasoned with a nation that has suffered almost a third of a million casualties in the longest war in its history.

When the President completed his address – an address, incidentally, that he spent weeks in the preparation of – his words and policies were subjected to instant analysis and querulous criticism. The audience of 70 million Americans gathered to hear the President of the United States was inherited by a small band of network commentators and self-appointed analysts, the majority of whom expressed in one way or another their hostility to what he had to say....

One commentator twice contradicted the President's statement about the exchange of correspondence with Ho Chi Minh. Another challenged the President's abilities as a politician. A third asserted that the President was following a Pentagon line. Others, by the expressions on their faces, the tone of their questions, and the sarcasm of their responses, made clear their sharp disapproval....

Now every American has a right to disagree with the President of the United States and to express publicly that disagreement. But the President of the United States has a right to communicate directly with the people who elected him, and the people of this country have the right to make up their own minds and form their own opinions about a Presidential address without having a President's words and thoughts characterized through the prejudices of hostile critics before they can even be digested....

The purpose of my remarks tonight is to focus your attention on this little group of men who not only enjoy a right of instant rebuttal to every Presidential address, but, more importantly, wield a free hand in selecting, presenting, and interpreting the great issues in our nation. First, let's define that power.

At least 40 million Americans every night, it's estimated, watch the network news. Seven million of them view A.B.C., the remainder being divided between N.B.C. and C.B.S. According to Harris polls and other studies, for millions of Americans the networks are the sole source of national and world news....

Now how is this network news determined? A small group of men, numbering perhaps no more than a dozen anchormen, commentators, and executive producers, settle upon the 20 minutes or so of film and commentary that's to reach the public. This selection is made from the 90 to 180 minutes that may be available. Their powers of choice are broad.

They decide what 40 to 50 million Americans will learn of the day's events in the nation and in the world. We cannot measure this power and influence by the traditional democratic standards, for these men can create national issues overnight. They can make or break by their coverage and commentary a moratorium on the war. They can elevate men from obscurity to national prominence within a week. They can reward some politicians with national exposure and ignore others....

It must be recognized that the networks have made important contributions to the national knowledge – through news, documentaries, and specials. They have often used their power constructively and creatively to awaken the public conscience to critical problems. The networks made hunger and black lung disease national issues overnight. The TV networks have done what no other medium could have done in terms of dramatizing the horrors of war. The networks have tackled our most difficult social problems with a directness and an immediacy that's the gift of their medium. They focus the nation's attention on its environmental abuses – on pollution in the Great Lakes and the threatened ecology of the Everglades. But it was also the networks that elevated Stokely Carmichael and George Lincoln Rockwell from obscurity to national prominence.

Nor is their power confined to the substantive. A raised eyebrow, an inflection of the voice, a caustic remark dropped in the middle of a broadcast can raise doubts in a million minds about the veracity of a public official or the wisdom of a Government policy. One Federal Communications Commissioner considers the powers of the networks equal to that of local, state, and Federal Governments all combined. Certainly it represents a concentration of power over American public opinion unknown in history.

Now what do Americans know of the men who wield this power? Of the men who produce and direct the network news, the nation knows practically nothing. Of the commentators, most Americans know little other than that they reflect an urbane and assured presence seemingly well-informed on every important matter. We do know that to a man these commentators and producers live and work in the geographical and intellectual confines of Washington, D.C., or New York City, the latter of which James Reston terms the most unrepresentative community in the entire United States.

Both communities bask in their own provincialism, their own parochialism. We can deduce that these men read the same newspapers. They draw their political and social views from the same sources. Worse, they talk constantly to one another, thereby providing artificial reinforcement to their shared viewpoints....

The American people would rightly not tolerate this concentration of power in Government. Is it not fair and relevant to question its concentration in the hands of a tiny, enclosed fraternity of privileged men elected by no one and enjoying a monopoly sanctioned and licensed by Government?

The views of the majority of this fraternity do *not* – and I repeat, not – represent the views of America. That is why such a great gulf existed between how the nation received the President's address and how the networks reviewed it. Not only did the country receive the President's speech more warmly than the networks, but so also did the Congress of the United States.

Yesterday, the President was notified that 300 individual Congressmen and 50 Senators of both parties had endorsed his efforts for peace. As with other American institutions, perhaps it is time that the networks were made more responsive to the views of the nation and more responsible to the people they serve.

Now I want to make myself perfectly clear. I'm not asking for Government censorship or any other kind of censorship. I am asking whether a form of censorship already exists when the news that 40 million Americans receive each night is determined by a handful of men responsible only to their corporate employers and is filtered through a handful of commentators who admit to their own set of biases....

Bad news drives out good news. The irrational is more controversial than the rational. Concurrence can no longer compete with dissent. One minute of Eldridge Cleaver is worth 10 minutes of Roy Wilkins. The labor crisis settled at the negotiating table is *nothing* compared to the confrontation that results in a strike – or better yet, violence along the picket lines. Normality has become the nemesis of the network news.

Now the upshot of all this controversy is that a narrow and distorted picture of America often emerges from the televised news. A single, dramatic piece of the mosaic becomes in the minds of millions the entire picture. The American who relies upon television for his news might conclude that the majority of American students are embittered radicals; that the majority of black Americans feel no regard for their country; that violence and lawlessness are the rule rather than the exception on the American campus.

We know that none of these conclusions is true.

Perhaps the place to start looking for a credibility gap is not in the offices of the Government in Washington but in the studios of the networks in New York! Television may have destroyed the old stereotypes, but has it not created new ones in their places? What has this "passionate" pursuit of controversy done to the politics of progress through logical compromise essential to the functioning of a democratic society?

The members of Congress or the Senate who follow their principles and philosophy quietly in a spirit of compromise are unknown to many Americans, while the loudest and most extreme dissenters on every issue are known to every man in the street. How many marches and demonstrations would we have if the marchers did not know that the ever-faithful TV cameras would be there to record their antics for the next news show?....
In this search for excitement and controversy, has more than equal time

gone to the minority of Americans who specialize in attacking the United States – its institutions and its citizens? ...

Now, my friends, we'd never trust such power, as I've described, over public opinion in the hands of an elected Government. It's time we questioned it in the hands of a small unelected elite. The great networks have dominated America's airwaves for decades. The people are entitled a full accounting their stewardship.

Source: Halford Ross Ryan (ed.), *American Rhetoric from Roosevelt to Reagan* (Prospect Heights, IL: Waveland Press, 2nd edn, 1987) pp. 212–19.

Discussion Questions

1. Compare the tone and content of Billy Graham's call for a renewal of "national purpose" with John Kennedy's inaugural address, delivered just seven months later.
2. According to sources such as the Sharon Statement and the speeches by Ronald Reagan, Richard Nixon and Spiro Agnew what did conservatives see as the main failings of 1960s liberalism?
3. What do the documents in this chapter reveal about the importance of race, religion, and anti-communism in the rise of the New Right?

Chapter 9   Science, Technology, and the Environment

1. John F. Kennedy, "The Nation's Space Effort," 1962

*In 1958 Congress created the National Aeronautics and Space Administration
(NASA), an ostensibly civilian agency designed to find a response to Soviet
advances in rocket and satellite technology. By the early 1960s, the "space
race" had captured the American imagination. Initially, NASA lagged
behind the Soviets, particularly in manned flight, but in 1961 President
John F. Kennedy had announced the Apollo program, explicitly designed
to send astronauts to the moon and return them safely to earth. His speech
at Rice University in September 1962 was one of several devoted to the
Apollo project, justifying the need to explore space in terms of Cold War
rivalry with the Soviet Union, the imperatives of scientific progress, and,
perhaps most revealingly, America's historic destiny. For Kennedy space
was another New Frontier: a challenging test of American ingenuity and
resolve that would help revitalize a shared sense of national unity, purpose,
and accomplishment.*

We meet at a college noted for knowledge, in a city noted for progress, in a
State noted for strength, and we stand in need of all three, for we meet in an
hour of change and challenge, in a decade of hope and fear, in an age of both
knowledge and ignorance. The greater our knowledge increases, the greater
our ignorance unfolds.

Despite the striking fact that most of the scientists that the world has ever
known are alive and working today, despite the fact that this Nation's own
scientific manpower is doubling every 12 years in a rate of growth more
than three times that of our population as a whole, despite that, the vast

stretches of the unknown and the unanswered and the unfinished still far outstrip our collective comprehension.

No man can fully grasp how far and how fast we have come, but condense, if you will, the 50,000 years of man's recorded history in a time span of but a half a century. Stated in these terms, we know very little about the first 40 years, except at the end of them advanced man had learned to use the skins of animals to cover them. Then about 10 years ago, under this standard, man emerged from his caves to construct other kinds of shelter. Only five years ago man learned to write and use a cart with wheels. Christianity began less than two years ago. The printing press came this year, and then less than two months ago, during this whole 50-year span of human history, the steam engine provided a new source of power.

Newton explored the meaning of gravity. Last month electric lights and telephones and automobiles and airplanes became available. Only last week did we develop penicillin and television and nuclear power, and now if America's new spacecraft succeeds in reaching Venus, we will have literally reached the stars before midnight tonight.

This is a breathtaking pace, and such a pace cannot help but create new ills as it dispels old, new ignorance, new problems, new dangers. Surely the opening vistas of space promise high costs and hardships, as well as high reward.

So it is not surprising that some would have us stay where we are a little longer to rest, to wait. But this city of Houston, this State of Texas, this country of the United States was not built by those who waited and rested and wished to look behind them. This country was conquered by those who moved forward – and so will space.

William Bradford, speaking in 1630 of the founding of the Plymouth Bay Colony, said that all great and honorable actions are accompanied with great difficulties, and both must be enterprised and overcome with answerable courage.

If this capsule history of our progress teaches us anything, it is that man, in his quest for knowledge and progress, is determined and cannot be deterred. The exploration of space will go ahead, whether we join in it or not, and it is one of the great adventures of all time, and no nation which expects to be the leader of other nations can expect to stay behind in the race for space.

Those who came before us made certain that this country rode the first waves of the industrial revolutions, the first waves of modern invention, and the first wave of nuclear power, and this generation does not intend to founder in the backwash of the coming age of space. We mean to be a part of it – we mean to lead it. For the eyes of the world now look into space, to the moon and to the planets beyond, and we have vowed that we shall not see it governed by a hostile flag of conquest, but by a banner of freedom and peace. We have vowed that we shall not see space filled with weapons of mass destruction, but with instruments of knowledge and understanding.

Yet the vows of this Nation can only be fulfilled if we in this Nation are first, and, therefore, we intend to be first. In short, our leadership in science and in industry, our hopes for peace and security, our obligations to ourselves as well as others, all require us to make this effort, to solve these mysteries, to solve them for the good of all men, and to become the world's leading space-faring nation....

There is no strife, no prejudice, no national conflict in outer space as yet. Its hazards are hostile to us all. Its conquest deserves the best of all mankind, and its opportunity for peaceful cooperation many never come again. But why, some say, the moon? Why choose this as our goal? And they may well ask why climb the highest mountain? Why, 35 years ago, fly the Atlantic? Why does Rice play Texas?

We choose to go to the moon. We choose to go to the moon in this decade and do the other things, not because they are easy, but because they are hard, because that goal will serve to organize and measure the best of our energies and skills, because that challenge is one that we are willing to accept, one we are unwilling to postpone, and one which we intend to win, and the others, too.

It is for these reasons that I regard the decision last year to shift our efforts in space from low to high gear as among the most important decisions that will be made during my incumbency in the office of the Presidency.

In the last 24 hours we have seen facilities now being created for the greatest and most complex exploration in man's history. We have felt the ground shake and the air shattered by the testing of a Saturn C-1 booster rocket, many times as powerful as the Atlas which launched John Glenn, generating power equivalent to 10,000 automobiles with their accelerators on the floor. We have seen the site where five F-1 rocket engines, each one as powerful as all eight engines of the Saturn combined, will be clustered together to make the advanced Saturn missile, assembled in a new building to be built at Cape Canaveral as tall as a 48 story structure, as wide as a city block, and as long as two lengths of this field.

Within these last 19 months at least 45 satellites have circled the earth. Some 40 of them were "made in the United States of America" and they were far more sophisticated and supplied far more knowledge to the people of the world than those of the Soviet Union.

The Mariner spacecraft now on its way to Venus is the most intricate instrument in the history of space science. The accuracy of that shot is comparable to firing a missile from Cape Canaveral and dropping it in this stadium between the 40-yard lines.

Transit satellites are helping our ships at sea to steer a safer course. Tiros satellites have given us unprecedented warnings of hurricanes and storms, and will do the same for forest fires and icebergs.

We have had our failures, but so have others, even if they do not admit them. And they may be less public.

To be sure, we are behind, and will be behind for some time in manned flight. But we do not intend to stay behind, and in this decade, we shall make up and move ahead.

The growth of our science and education will be enriched by new knowledge of our universe and environment, by new techniques of learning and mapping and observation, by new tools and computers for industry, medicine, the home as well as the school. Technical institutions, such as Rice, will reap the harvest of these gains.

And finally, the space effort itself, while still in its infancy, has already created a great number of new companies, and tens of thousands of new jobs. Space and related industries are generating new demands in investment and skilled personnel, and this city and this State, and this region, will share greatly in this growth. What was once the furthest outpost on the old frontier of the West will be the furthest outpost on the new frontier of science and space. Houston, your City of Houston, with its Manned Spacecraft Center, will become the heart of a large scientific and engineering community. During the next 5 years the National Aeronautics and Space Administration expects to double the number of scientists and engineers in this area, to increase its outlays for salaries and expenses to $60 million a year; to invest some $200 million in plant and laboratory facilities; and to direct or contract for new space efforts over $1 billion from this Center in this City.

To be sure, all this costs us all a good deal of money. This year's space budget is three times what it was in January 1961, and it is greater than the space budget of the previous eight years combined. That budget now stands at $5,400 million a year – a staggering sum, though somewhat less than we pay for cigarettes and cigars every year. Space expenditures will soon rise some more, from 40 cents per person per week to more than 50 cents a week for every man, woman and child in the United States, for we have given this program a high national priority – even though I realize that this is in some measure an act of faith and vision, for we do not now know what benefits await us. But if I were to say, my fellow citizens, that we shall send to the moon, 240,000 miles away from the control station in Houston, a giant rocket more than 300 feet tall, the length of this football field, made of new metal alloys, some of which have not yet been invented, capable of standing heat and stresses several times more than have ever been experienced, fitted together with a precision better than the finest watch, carrying all the equipment needed for propulsion, guidance, control, communications, food and survival, on an untried mission, to an unknown celestial body, and then return it safely to earth, re-entering the atmosphere at speeds of over 25,000 miles per hour, causing heat about half that of the temperature of the sun – almost as hot as it is here today – and do all this, and do it right, and do it first before this decade is out – then we must be bold....

However, I think we're going to do it, and I think that we must pay what needs to be paid. I don't think we ought to waste any money, but I think we ought to do the job. And this will be done in the decade of the sixties. It may be done while some of you are still here at school at this college and university. It will be done during the term of office of some of the people who sit here on this platform. But it will be done. And it will be done before the end of this decade....

Source: President John F. Kennedy, "Address at Rice University in Houston on the Nation's Space Effort," September 12, 1962, *Public Papers of the Presidents of the United States: John F. Kennedy, 1962* (Washington, DC: United States Government Printing Office, 1963), pp. 668–71.

2. Sony, Advertisement for Micro-TV, 1962

The 1960s saw tremendous advances in many fields of science and technology, not least in the world of telecommunications where the demands of the space race, the military, and the mass media created a dynamic, well-funded climate for research and development. By the end of the decade, scientists working for the military at Stanford had already sketched out the basic structure of ARPANET, which would become the internet. More immediately relevant to the general public was the steady refinement of the silicon chip – a tiny sliver of silicon capable of replacing thousands of individual transistors. The chip and integrated circuitry revolutionized consumer electronics, providing the basis for ever more powerful yet often smaller consumer products such as televisions, radios, audio systems and, eventually VCRs, personal computers, and mobile phones.

The Sony Corporation's 1962 advertisement for its new Micro-TV predated the widespread use of microchip technology but nevertheless offered the well-to-do a tantalizing taste of the lightweight, miniaturized future of telecommunications and home entertainment. The advertisement mobilized ideas of affluence and exclusivity in the copy, pointing out both the cutting-edge science involved and the flexibility of the product. Meanwhile, the use of an enraptured and impeccably groomed female model suggests that maybe Sony felt middle-class women would find this new, portable product most appealing – for use in the kitchen, perhaps?

Figure 9.1   Sony Corporation of America, "Micro-TV" Advertisement, 1962.

Source: Courtesy of The Advertising Archives.

3. Rachel Carson, *Silent Spring*, 1962

Marine biologist Rachel Carson's best-selling Silent Spring *is often seen as the starting point for the modern environmental movement in the US. There were precedents for some of Carson's basic arguments and rhetorical strategies, including a 1946* New Republic *article on the dangers of the pesticide DDT, which used the absence of birdsong as evidence of environmental malaise, and Eugene P. Odum's* The Fundamentals of Ecology *in 1953. Nevertheless, her passionate prose revealed the shocking and irresponsible use of toxic pesticides in US agriculture much more broadly, stimulating new levels of anxiety about the potentially devastating ecological consequences of human activities. President Kennedy was sufficiently moved by Carson's work – which was serialized in the* New Yorker *– to order his Science Advisory Committee to probe the perils of pesticides. Congressional Hearings on pollution, at which Carson testified, and the later creation of the Environmental Protection Agency were also attributable in part to the influence of Carson's work.*

Carson was not without her critics: some quibbled with the core science and conclusions of Silent Spring; *others were suspicious of the deliberately sensationalist, often highly sentimental, prose style that she uses to convey to the general public her grim scientific conclusions about the health of the planet; still other critics seemed unable to come to terms with the fact that as both a successful environmental activist and a scientist Carson was challenging conventional notions about gender roles and the key sites of authority and expertise in American life. Nevertheless, Carson, who died of breast cancer in 1964, was largely responsible for shifting the focus of environmental concerns away from Sierra Club-style celebrations of the wonders of nature and human mastery over it towards a more sophisticated appreciation of ecology, which stressed a complex, interdependent, and increasingly perilous relationship between humankind and the environment.*

The Obligation to Endure

The history of life on earth has been a history of interaction between living things and their surroundings. To a large extent, the physical form and the habits of the earth's vegetation and its animal life have been molded by the environment. Considering the whole span of earthly time, the opposite effect, in which life actually modifies its surroundings, has been relatively slight. Only within the moment of time represented by the present century has one species – man – acquired significant power to alter the nature of his world.

During the past quarter-century this power has not only increased to one of disturbing magnitude but it has changed in character. The most alarming of all man's assaults upon the environment is the contamination of air, earth, rivers, and sea with dangerous and even lethal materials. This pollution is for the most part irrecoverable; the chain of evil it initiates not only in the world that must support life but in living tissues is for the most part irreversible. In this now universal contamination of the environment, chemicals are the sinister and little-recognized partners of radiation in changing the very nature of the world – the very nature of its life. Strontium 90, released through nuclear explosions into the air, comes to earth in rain or drifts down as fallout, lodges in soil, enters into the grass or corn or wheat grown there, and in time takes up its abode in the bones of a human being, there to remain until his death. Similarly, chemicals sprayed on croplands or forests or gardens lie long in soil, entering into living organisms, passing from one to another in a chain of poisoning and death. Or they pass mysteriously by underground streams until they emerge and, through the alchemy of air and sunlight, combine into new forms that kill vegetation, sicken cattle, and work unknown harm on those who drink from once-pure wells. As Albert Schweitzer has said, "Man can hardly even recognize the devils of his own creation."

It took hundreds of millions of years to produce the life that now inhabits the earth – aeons of time in which that developing and evolving and diversifying life reached a state of adjustment and balance with its surroundings. The environment, rigorously shaping and directing the life it supported, contained elements that were hostile as well as supporting. Certain rocks gave out dangerous radiation; even within the light of the sun, from which all life draws its energy, there were short-wave radiations with power to injure. Given time – time not in years but in millennia – life adjusts, and a balance has been reached. For time is the essential ingredient; but in the modern world there is no time.

The rapidity of change and the speed with which new situations are created follow the impetuous and heedless pace of man rather than the deliberate pace of nature. Radiation is no longer merely the background radiation of rocks, the bombardment of cosmic rays, the ultra-violet of the sun that have existed before there was any life on earth; radiation is now the unnatural creation of man's tampering with the atom. The chemicals to which life is asked to make its adjustment are no longer merely the calcium and silica and copper and all the rest of the minerals washed out of the rocks and carried in rivers to the sea; they are the synthetic creations of man's inventive mind, brewed in his laboratories, and having no counterpart in nature.

To adjust to these chemicals would require time on the scale that is nature's; it would require not merely the years of a man's life but the life of generations. And even this, were it by some miracle possible, would be futile, for the new chemicals come from our laboratories in an endless stream; almost five hundred annually find their way into actual use in the United States alone. The figure is staggering and its implications are not easily grasped – five hundred new chemicals to which the bodies of men and animals are required somehow to adapt each year, chemicals totally outside the limits of biologic experience.

Among them are many that are used in man's war against nature. Since the mid 1940s over two hundred basic chemicals have been created for use in killing insects, weeds, rodents, and other organisms described in the modern vernacular as "pests"; and they are sold under several thousand different brand names.

These sprays, dusts and aerosols are now applied almost universally to farms, gardens forests, and homes – non-selective chemicals that have the power to kill every insect, the "good" and the "bad", to still the song of birds and the leaping of fish in the streams, to coat the leaves with a deadly film, and to linger on in soil – all this though the intended target may be only a few weeds or insects. Can anyone believe it is possible to lay down such a barrage of poisons on the surface of the earth without making it unfit for all life? They should not be called "insecticides", but "biocides".

The whole process of spraying seems caught up in an endless spiral. Since DDT was released for civilian use, a process of escalation has been going on in which ever more toxic materials must be found. This has happened because insects, in a triumphant vindication of Darwin's principle of the survival of the fittest, have evolved super races immune to the particular insecticide used, hence a deadlier one has always to be developed – and then a deadlier one than that. It has happened also because, for reasons to be described later, destructive insects often undergo a "flareback", or resurgence, after spraying, in numbers greater than before. Thus the chemical war is never won, and all life is caught in its violent crossfire.

Along with the possibility of the extinction of mankind by nuclear war, the central problem of our age has therefore become the contamination of man's total environment with such substances of incredible potential for harm – substances that accumulate in the tissues of plants and animals and even penetrate the germ cells to shatter or alter the very material of heredity upon which the shape of the future depends.

Some would-be architects of our future look towards a time when it will be possible to alter the human germ plasm by design. But we may easily be doing so now by inadvertence, for many chemicals, like radiation, bring about gene mutations. It is ironic to think that man might determine his own future by something so seemingly trivial as the choice of an insect spray.

Source: Rachel Carson, *Silent Spring* (New York: Houghton Mifflin, 1962), pp. 23–5.

4. US Congress, the Wilderness Act, 1964

After nearly eight years of lobbying and 66 re-writes, the Wilderness Act was finally signed into law by President Johnson on September 3, 1964. The Act was hailed as an important victory for a new environmental consciousness in the United States. Dedicated to preserving the sanctity of American lands that were, according to the Act, still "untrammeled by man," the legislation placed some 9.1 million acres of unspoiled forest into a new National Wilderness Preservation System (NWPS) and prohibited most forms of building or other commercial development on those lands. Some environmentalists pointed out that the wilderness lands initially included in the NWPS scheme had already been identified – and were to some extent also protected – by the Forest Service. What was really needed, they argued, was a wholesale re-evaluation of America's wilderness sites. Fortunately, the Act required the Secretary of the Interior to review all the roadless areas over 5,000 acres in size located within the national parks, the forests, and the wildlife refuge system and recommend further additions to the NWPS. By 1976, when the passage of the Federal Land Policy and Management Act allowed for the inclusion of territory controlled by the Bureau of Land Management, around 623 million acres or 26 percent of US land was under the purview of the NWPS.

An Act To establish a National Wilderness Preservation System for the permanent good of the whole people, and for other purposes

Be it enacted by the Senate and House of Representatives of the United States of America in Congress assembled, . . .

Short Title

Section 1. This Act may be cited as the "Wilderness Act".

Wilderness System Established Statement of Policy

Sec. 2. (a) In order to assure that an increasing population, accompanied by expanding settlement and growing mechanization, does not occupy and modify all areas within the United States and its possessions, leaving no lands designated for preservation and protection in their natural condition, it is hereby declared to be the policy of the Congress to secure for the American people of present and future generations the benefits of an enduring resource of wilderness. For this purpose there is hereby established a National Wilderness Preservation System to be composed of federally owned areas designated by Congress as "wilderness areas", and these shall be administered for the use and enjoyment of the American people in such manner as will leave them unimpaired for future use as wilderness, and so as to provide for the protection of these areas, the preservation of their wilderness character, and for the gathering and dissemination of information regarding their use and enjoyment as wilderness; and no Federal lands shall be designated as "wilderness areas" except as provided for in this chapter or by a subsequent Act....

Definition of Wilderness

(c) A wilderness, in contrast with those areas where man and his own works dominate the landscape, is hereby recognized as an area where the earth and its community of life are untrammeled by man, where man himself is a visitor who does not remain. An area of wilderness is further defined to mean in this chapter an area of undeveloped Federal land retaining its primeval character and influence, without permanent improvements or human habitation, which is protected and managed so as to preserve its natural conditions and which (1) generally appears to have been affected primarily by the forces of nature, with the imprint of man's work substantially unnoticeable; (2) has outstanding opportunities for solitude or a primitive and unconfined type of recreation; (3) has at least five thousand acres of land or is of sufficient size as to make practicable its preservation and use in an unimpaired condition; and (4) may also contain ecological, geological, or other features of scientific, educational, scenic, or historical value....

Use of Wilderness Areas

Sec. 4.

Prohibition of Certain Uses

(c) Except as specifically provided for in this chapter, and subject to existing private rights, there shall be no commercial enterprise and no permanent road within any wilderness area designated by this Act and, except as necessary to meet minimum requirements for the administration of the area for the purpose of this Act (including measures required in emergencies involving the health and safety of persons within the area), there shall be no temporary road, no use of motor vehicles, motorized equipment or motorboats, no landing of aircraft, no other form of mechanical transport, and no structure or installation within any such area.

Special Provisions

(d) The following special provisions are hereby made:

(1)   Within wilderness areas designated by this chapter the use of aircraft or motorboats, where these uses have already become established, may be permitted to continue subject to such restrictions as the Secretary of Agriculture deems desirable. In addition, such measures may be taken as may be necessary in the control of fire, insects, and diseases, subject to such conditions as the Secretary deems desirable.

(2)   Nothing in this chapter shall prevent within national forest wilderness areas any activity, including prospecting, for the purpose of gathering information about mineral or other resources, if such activity is carried on in a manner compatible with the preservation of the wilderness environment. Furthermore, in accordance with such program as the Secretary of the Interior shall develop and conduct in consultation with the Secretary of Agriculture, such areas shall be surveyed on a planned, recurring basis consistent with the concept of wilderness preservation by the Geological Survey and the Bureau of Mines to determine the mineral values, if any, that

may be present; and the results of such surveys shall be made available to the public and submitted to the President and Congress.

(3) Not withstanding any other provisions of this chapter, until midnight December 31, 1983, the United States mining laws and all laws pertaining to mineral leasing shall, to the extent as applicable prior to September 3, 1964, extend to those national forest lands designated by this chapter as "wilderness areas"; subject, however, to such reasonable regulations governing ingress and egress as may be prescribed by the Secretary of Agriculture consistent with the use of the land for mineral location and development and exploration, drilling, and production, and use of land for transmission lines, waterlines, telephone lines, or facilities necessary in exploring, drilling, producing, mining, and processing operations, including where essential the use of mechanized ground or air equipment and restoration as near as practicable of the surface of the land disturbed in performing prospecting, location, and , in oil and gas leasing, discovery work, exploration, drilling, and production, as soon as they have served their purpose...

(4) Within wilderness areas in the national forests designated by this chapter, (1) the President may, within a specific area and in accordance with such regulations as he may deem desirable, authorize prospecting for water resources, the establishment and maintenance of reservoirs, water-conservation works, power projects, transmission lines, and other facilities needed in the public interest, including the road construction and maintenance essential to development and use thereof, upon his determination that such use or uses in the specific area will better serve the interests of the United States and the people thereof than will its denial; and (2) the grazing of livestock, where established prior to September 3, 1964, shall be permitted to continue subject to such reasonable regulations as are deemed necessary by the Secretary of Agriculture.

(5) Other provisions of this chapter to the contrary notwithstanding, the management of the Boundary Waters Canoe Area, formerly designated as the Superior, Little Indian Sioux, and Caribou Roadless Areas, in the Superior National Forest, Minnesota, shall be in accordance with the general purpose of maintaining, without unnecessary restrictions on other uses, including that of timber, the primitive character of the area, particularly in the vicinity of lakes, streams, and portages: Provided, That nothing in this Act shall preclude the continuance within the area of any already established use of motorboats.

(6)   Commercial services may be performed within the wilderness areas designated by this Act to the extent necessary for activities which are proper for realizing the recreational or other wilderness purposes of the areas.

(7)   Nothing in this chapter shall constitute an express or implied claim or denial on the part of the Federal Government as to exemption from State water laws.

(8)   Nothing in this chapter shall be construed as affecting the jurisdiction or responsibilities of the several States with respect to wildlife and fish in the national forests.

Source: US Congress, Wilderness Act of 1964 (16 U.S.C. 1131–1136, 78 Stat. 890) – Public Law 88–577, approved September 3, 1964, 88th Congress, S. 4.

5. Stewart Brand, *Whole Earth Catalog*, 1968

The first edition of Stewart Brand's Whole Earth Catalog *appeared in 1968. Selling at $5 and subtitled "access to tools," this hefty compendium of self-help advice on how to develop ethically sound modes of independent living represented a fascinating synthesis of countercultural philosophy, environmentalism, conventional and alternative science, and commercial acumen. Brand was a Stanford-educated biologist who had served in the US Army for a couple of years on a ROTC commission before becoming a confederate of author Ken Kesey and his Merry Pranksters, a group of hippies and artists who organized the celebrated "acid tests" in San Francisco and later took a gaudily painted bus around the US, all to promote the power of the hallucinogenic drug LSD to unlock the mind and liberate society from its myriad hang-ups. On what would be his last LSD experiment, Brand imagined himself floating high above the ground and pondered why, with the space race in full gear, nobody had yet seen an image of the whole earth. Thus he began to stimulate interest in his projected* Catalog *with a "why have we not seen the earth?" campaign of buttons and advertisements. When NASA finally released a picture of the earth from space, Brand gleefully stuck this powerful image on the front and back covers of the first* Catalog, *where it expressed both the hippie turn towards "cosmic consciousness" – a meditation on humanity's place in creation – and the growing awareness of global interdependence that animated the environmental movement and spawned the first "Earth Day" celebrations in 1970. The* Catalog, *with its advice on everything from pig-rearing to yoga, organic gardening to shoe repair, and windmills to welding, subsequently became an oft-updated best seller. It was "sort of like Google in paperback form," remembered Apple founder and fan, Steve Jobs. "It was idealistic and overflowing with neat tools and great notions." Brand,* *ever an innovator and original thinker, went on to pioneer early efforts to develop the internet as well as writing critically acclaimed books on architecture.*

Whole Earth Catalog

Figure 9.2   Whole Earth Catalog.

Source: Courtesy of Department of Special Collections and University Archives, Stanford University Libraries, Whole Earth Catalog Records, 1969–1986, M1045.

Discussion Questions

1. From the evidence of his speech in Houston, how did John Kennedy justify the enormous expenditure of public money on space exploration?
2. What particular insights into the nature of 1960s environmentalism can historians get from sources as disparate as *Silent Spring*, The Wilderness Act and the *Whole Earth Catalog*?
3. How do the documents in this chapter reveal the relationships among commerce, science, and technical innovation?

Chapter 10   Racial and Ethnic Identity: Pride and Politics

1. Black Panther Party, "What We Want, What We Believe," 1966

Formed by Huey Newton and Bobby Seale in Oakland, California, in 1966, the Black Panther Party for Self-Defense (BPP) was among the most dynamic and influential of the Black Nationalist groups of the late 1960s and early 1970s. Initially the BPP focused on offering local blacks protection from police harassment, but as chapters sprung up around the inner cities of America it quickly expanded its remit to include a variety of social, political, economic, educational, and cultural initiatives, all designed to empower the black community psychologically as well as materially.

The BPP's insistence on the right of self-defense and conspicuous carrying of weapons in public, coupled with sensational media coverage of its activities, guaranteed that it became synonymous in many white minds with the violence that seemed to replace nonviolence at the heart of the African American freedom struggle in the late 1960s. The Panthers' guns and inflammatory rhetoric ensured that the BPP drew the attention of federal, as well as local, law enforcement agencies. Several dozen Panthers were killed by police and many more were jailed on charges with varying degrees of validity. The FBI's illegal COINTELPRO operation also did much to hasten the demise of an organization that was already struggling to cope with fierce personal rivalries and intense ideological disputes within its own ranks.

Despite the popular emphasis on the BPP's paramilitary aspects and its ongoing battles with law enforcement agencies, the organization's ten-point program, and a matching statement of beliefs that echoed the Declaration of Independence, linked America's enduring racial problems to the country's dominant economic, social, and political structures. Although occasionally subject to minor amendments, this platform formed the foundation of Panther beliefs and appeared in every issue of the Black Panther *newspaper.*

1. We want freedom. We want power to determine the destiny of our Black Community.
2. We want full employment for our people.
3. We want an end to the robbery by the white man of our Black Community.
4. We want decent housing, fit for shelter of human beings.
5. We want education for our people that exposes the true nature of this decadent American society. We want education that teaches us our true history and our role in the present-day society.
6. We want all black men to be exempt from military service.
7. We want an immediate end to police brutality and murder of black people.
8. We want freedom for all black men held in federal, state, county and city prisons and jails.
9. We want all black people when brought to trial to be tried in court by a jury of their peer group or people from their black communities, as defined by the Constitution of the United States.
10. We want land, bread, housing, education, clothing, justice and peace. And as our major political objective, a United Nations-supervised plebiscite to be held throughout the black colony in which only black colonial subjects will be allowed to participate for the purpose of determining the will of black people as to their national destiny.

What We Believe

1. We believe that black people will not be free until we are able to determine our destiny.
2. We believe that the federal government is responsible and obligated to give every man employment or a guaranteed income. We believe that if the white American businessmen will not give full employment, then the means of production should be taken from the businessmen and placed in the community so that the people of the community can organize and employ all of its people and give a high standard of living.
3. We believe that this racist government has robbed us and now we are demanding the overdue debt of forty acres and two mules. Forty acres and two mules was promised 100 years ago as restitution for slave labor and mass murder of black people. We will accept the payment as currency which will be distributed to our many communities.

The Germans are now aiding the Jews in Israel for the genocide of the Jewish people. The Germans murdered six million Jews. The American racist has taken part in the slaughter of over twenty million black people; therefore, we feel that this is a modest demand that we make.

4. We believe that if the white landlords will not give decent housing to our black community, then the housing and the land should be made into cooperatives so that our community, with government aid, can build and make decent housing for its people.

5. We believe in an educational system that will give to our people a knowledge of self. If a man does not have knowledge of himself and his position in society and the world, then he has little chance to relate to anything else.

6. We believe that Black people should not be forced to fight in the military service to defend a racist government that does not protect us. We will not fight and kill other people of color in the world who, like black people, are being victimized by the white racist government of America. We will protect ourselves from the force and violence of the racist police and the racist military, by whatever means necessary.

7. We believe we can end police brutality in our black community by organizing black self-defense groups that are dedicated to defending our black community from racist police oppression and brutality. The Second Amendment to the Constitution of the United States gives a right to bear arms. We therefore believe that all black people should arm themselves for self defense.

8. We believe that all black people should be released from the many jails and prisons because they have not received a fair and impartial trial.

9. We believe that the courts should follow the United States Constitution so that black people will receive fair trials. The 14th Amendment of the U.S. Constitution gives a man a right to be tried by his peer group. A peer is a person from a similar economic, social, religious, geographical, environmental, historical and racial background. To do this the court will be forced to select a jury from the black community from which the black defendant came. We have been, and are being tried by all-white juries that have no understanding of the "average reasoning man" of the black community.

10. When in the course of human events, it becomes necessary for one people to dissolve the political bands which have connected them with another, and to assume, among the powers of the earth, the separate and equal station to which the laws of nature and nature's God entitle them, a decent respect to the opinions of mankind requires that they should declare the causes which impel them to the separation.

We hold these truths to be self evident, that all men are created equal; that they are endowed by their Creator with certain unalienable rights; that among these are life, liberty, and the pursuit of happiness. That, to secure these rights, governments are instituted among men, deriving their just powers from the consent of the governed; that, whenever any form of government becomes destructive of these ends, it is the right of the people to alter or to abolish it, and to institute a new government, laying its foundation on such principles, and organizing its powers in such form, as to them shall seem most likely to effect their safety and happiness. Prudence, indeed, will dictate that governments long established should not be changed for light and transient causes; and accordingly, all experience hath shown, that mankind are more disposed to suffer, while evils are sufferable, than to right themselves by abolishing the forms to which they are accustomed. But, when a long train of abuses and usurpations, pursuing invariable the same object, evinces a design to reduce them under absolute despotism, it is their right, it is their duty, to throw off such government, and to provide new guards for their future security.

Source: *Black Panther*, December 20, 1969. Reprinted by permission of It's About Time (www.itsabouttimebpp.com) Black Panther Alumni Committee.

2. Associated Press, Black Power Salute at the Mexico Olympics, 1968

At the 1968 Mexico Olympic Games African American sprinters Tommie Smith and John Carlos won gold and bronze medals respectively in the 200 meters, with Smith setting a new world record. On the medal podium, as the national anthem played and the stars and stripes was raised on high, the two San José State University athletes thrust black-gloved fists into the air in black power salutes and bowed their heads in silent reflection, creating one of the decade's most enduring and dramatic visual images. Both men were shoeless, invoking black poverty, while Smith wore a black scarf round his neck to affirm his racial pride and Carlos donned a necklace of beads to honor those of African descent killed during the Middle Passage or lynched in America. As a show of solidarity the silver medallist, Australian Peter Norman, joined the two African Americans in wearing an Olympic Project for Human Rights badge on the podium – an act for which he was pilloried by the Australian media and ostracized by his own athletics board.

*   *As Smith later acknowledged, it was a "silent gesture heard around the world, and each individual had their own interpretation of what it meant." For many African Americans, this was a bold and exhilarating public display of heightened*

black consciousness that also reflected a determination to continue the fight against racial inequality. For others, the protest both sullied the supposedly apolitical idealism of the Olympics and represented an unacceptable insult to the American flag and all it stood for. In a typical example of the sensationalized reportage surrounding Black Power, influential Chicago columnist Brent Musburger condemned the athletes as "black-skinned storm troopers."

In the immediate aftermath of their protest, Smith and Carlos were expelled from the Olympic village for making a "violent breach of the fundamental principles of the Olympic spirit" and banned from future competition for the US national team. Both men were widely shunned and even received death threats. Although they continued to compete in track and field and had minor careers in pro-football, it was only in the 1980s that their reputations as fine athletes and principled social activists were rehabilitated, culminating in the erection of a statue in their honor on the San José State campus in 2005.

Figure 10.1   John Carlos and Tommie Smith Black Power Salute, Mexico Olympics, 1968.

Source: *Photo: Associated Press/AP/PA Photos.*

3. Indians of All Nations, "Alcatraz Proclamation," 1969

In 1963, members of the National Indian Youth Council (NIYC), an inter-tribal organization that had been fighting for Native American rights since 1961, issued a call for "Red Power," by which they meant power for American Indians to determine their own affairs and set their own cultural and educational agendas. This was some three years before Stokely Carmichael popularized the slogan "Black Power" to reflect a similar drive for African Americans to control the circumstances of their own lives. As the decade progressed, other groups joined the NIYC in a campaign to draw attention to the largely forgotten plight of Native Americans. Modelled on the Black Panther Party, the American Indian Movement (AIM) was the most important of the new groups. Founded in 1968 in Minneapolis (between a third and a half of the Native American population lived in cities by 1970), AIM quickly gathered a sizeable national membership and began a series of high profile protests.

Although it subsequently lent support to the action, AIM had no direct involvement with the planning and execution of the occupation of Alcatraz Island in San Francisco Bay on November 20, 1969 by a group called the Indians of All Nations who demanded the island should be returned to its original inhabitants. "The Alcatraz Proclamation" with its blend of bitter humor, Red Pride, and concrete proposals for reform, stands as eloquent testimony to Native American needs and aspirations.

The occupation of Alcatraz eventually ended in June 1971 when armed US coast guards removed the last 15 Indians from the island. By this time, the FBI's COINTELPRO had long since deemed AIM a "hate organization" and a threat to national security and targeted it for destruction. Ironically, however, the FBI inadvertently helped to promote public recognition of Native American grievances in 1973, when 300 FBI agents and federal marshals were involved in a stand-off with some 2,000 Native Americans, led by members of AIM, at Wounded Knee in South Dakota – the scene of an 1890 massacre of Sioux by the US Army. By the end of the dispute, which began over the issue of who should control the local Pine Ridge Reservation Tribal Council, two Indians were dead and a dozen wounded. The media coverage helped to increase sympathy for the Native American quest for civil rights and self-determination.

Fellow citizens, we are asking you to join with us in our attempt to better the lives of all Indian people.

We are on Alcatraz Island to make known to the world that we have a right to use our land for our own benefit.

In a proclamation of November 20, 1969, we told the government of the United States that we are here "to create a meaningful use for our Great Spirit's Land."

We, the native Americans, reclaim the land known as Alcatraz Island in the name of all American Indians by right of discovery.

We wish to be fair and honorable in our dealings with the Caucasian inhabitants of this land, and hereby offer the following treaty:

We will purchase said Alcatraz Island for twenty-four dollars in glass beads and red cloth, a precedent set by the white man's purchase of a similar island about 300 years ago. We know that $24 in trade goods for these 16 acres is more than was paid when Manhattan Island was sold, but we know that land values have risen over the years. Our offer of $1.24 per acres is greater than the $0.47 per acre the white men are now paying the California Indians for their lands.

We will give to the inhabitants of this island a portion of the land for their own to be held in trust ... by the Bureau of Caucasian Affairs ... in perpetuity – for as long as the sun shall rise and the rivers go down to the sea. We will further guide the inhabitants in the proper way of living. We will offer them our religion, our education, our life-ways in order to help them achieve our level of civilization and thus raise them and all their white brothers up from their savage and unhappy state. We offer this treaty in good faith and wish to be fair and honorable in our dealings with all white men.

We feel that this so-called Alcatraz Island is more than suitable for an Indian reservation, as determined by the white man's own standards. By this, we mean that this place resembles most Indian reservations in that:

1. It is isolated from modern facilities, and without adequate means of transportation.
2. It has no fresh running water.
3. It has inadequate sanitation facilities.
4. There are no oil or mineral rights.
5. There is no industry and so unemployment is very great.
6. There are no health-care facilities.
7. The soil is rocky and non-productive, and the land does not support game.
8. There are no educational facilities.
9. The population has always exceeded the land base.
10. The population has always been held as prisoners and kept dependent upon others.

Further, it would be fitting and symbolic that ships from all over the world, entering the Golden Gate, would first see Indian land, and thus be reminded of the true history of this nation.

This tiny island would be a symbol of the great lands once ruled by free and noble Indians.

What use will we make of this land?

Since the San Francisco Indian Center burned down, there is no place for Indians to assemble and carry on tribal life here in the white man's city. Therefore, we plan to develop on this island several Indian institutions:

1.   A Center for Native American Studies will be developed which will educate them to the skills and knowledge relevant to improve the lives and spirits of all Indian peoples. Attached to this center will be travelling universities, managed by Indians, which will go to the Indian Reservations, learning those necessary and relevant materials now about.

2.   An American Indian Spiritual Center, which will practice our ancient tribal religious and sacred healing ceremonies. Our cultural arts will be featured and our young people trained in music, dance, and healing rituals.

3.   An Indian Center of Ecology, which will train and support our young people in scientific research and practice to restore our lands and waters to their pure and natural state. We will work to de-pollute the air and waters of the Bay Area. We will seek to restore fish and animal life to the area and to revitalize sea-life which has been threatened by the white man's way. We will set up facilities to desalt sea water for human benefit.

4.   A Great Indian Training School will be developed to teach our people how to make a living in the world, improve our standard of living, and to end hunger and unemployment among all our people. This training school will include a center for Indian arts and crafts, and an Indian restaurant serving native foods, which will restore Indian culinary arts. This center will display Indian arts and offer Indian foods to the public, so that all may know of the beauty and spirit of the traditional Indian ways.

Some of the present buildings will be taken over to develop an American Indian Museum which will depict our native food and other cultural contributions we have given to the world. Another part of the museum will present some of the things the white man has given to the Indians in return for the land and life he took: disease, alcohol, poverty, and cultural decimation (as symbolized by old tin cans, barbed wire, rubber tires, plastic containers, etc.). Part of the museum will remain a dungeon to symbolize both those Indian captives who were incarcerated for challenging white authority and those who were imprisoned on reservations. The museum will show the noble and tragic events of Indian history, including the broken treaties, the documentary of the Trail of Tears, the Massacre of Wounded Knee, as well as the victory over Yellow-Hair Custer and his army.

In the name of all Indians, therefore, we reclaim this island for our Indian nations, for all these reasons. We feel this claim is just and proper, and that this land should rightfully be granted to us for as long as the rivers run and the sun shall shine.

We hold the rock!

Source: Indians of All Nations, "The Alcatraz Proclamation to the Great White Father and his People," November 1969. Reprinted by permission of the Center for World Indigenous Studies, Fourth World Documentation Project, Olympia, Washington, USA. Document at www.cwis.org/fwdp/Americas/alcatraz.htm.

4. Chicano National Conference, "El Plan de Aztlán," 1969

Presented at the first National Chicano Youth Liberation Conference in Denver in March 1969, "El Plan de Aztlán" attempted to harness a growing sense of Chicano pride to a radical political, economic, and cultural program that would lead to an independent Chicano nation called Aztlán – the colloquial name for the lands occupied by the US after the Mexican War of 1846–8. The manifesto was clearly influenced by some of the black nationalist rhetoric of the era, but it also drew on the specific historical experiences of La Raza – the "race" – as well as its distinctive social, religious, and cultural traditions. In championing Chicano nationalism as a means to unite La Raza and escape the racism and exploitation that had long characterized Chicano relationships with "gringo" America, "El Plan de Aztlán" was a powerful example of the kind of identity-based politics that flourished in the late 1960s and which some felt increasingly threatened the prospects for any consensus on America's future among its disparate populations.

El Plan Espiritual de Aztlán

In the spirit of a new people that is conscious not only of its proud historical heritage but also of the brutal "gringo" invasion of our territories, *we*, the Chicano inhabitants and civilizers of the northern land of Aztlán from whence came our forefathers, reclaiming the land of their birth and consecrating the determination of our people of the sun, *declare* that the call of our blood is our power, our responsibility, and our inevitable destiny.

We are free and sovereign to determine those tasks which are justly called for by our house, our land, the sweat of our brows, and by our hearts. Aztlán belongs to those who plant the seeds, water the fields, and gather the crops and not to the foreign Europeans. We do not recognize capricious frontiers on the bronze continent.

Brotherhood unites us, and love for our brothers makes us a people whose time has come and who struggle against the foreigner "gabacho" who exploits our riches and destroys our culture. With our hearts in our hands and our hands in the soil, we declare the independence of our mestizo nation. We are a bronze people with a bronze culture. Before the world, before all of North America, before all our brothers in the bronze continent, we are a nation, we are a union of free pueblos, we are *Aztlán*.

Por La Raza todo. Fuera de La Raza nada.

Program

El Plan Espiritual de Aztlán sets the theme that the Chicanos (La Raza de Bronze) must use their nationalism as the key or common denominator for mass mobilization and organization. Once we are committed to the idea and philosophy of El Plan de Aztlán, we can only conclude that social, economic, cultural, and political independence is the only road to total liberation from oppression, exploitation, and racism. Our struggle then must be for the control of our barrios, campos, pueblos, lands, our economy, our culture, and our political life. El Plan commits all levels of Chicano society – the barrio, the campo, the ranchero, the writer, the teacher, the worker, the professional – to La Causa.

Nationalism

Nationalism as the key to organization transcends all religious, political, class, and economic factions or boundaries. Nationalism is the common denominator that all members of La Raza can agree upon.

Organizational Goals

1.   UNITY in thinking of our people concerning the barrios, the pueblo, the campo, the land, the poor, the middle class, the professional – all committed to the liberation of La Raza.

2.   ECONOMY: economic control of our lives and our communities can only come about by driving the exploiter out of our communities, our pueblos, and our lands and by controlling and developing our own talents, sweat, and resources....

3.   EDUCATION must be relative to our people, i.e., history, culture, bilingual education, contributions, etc. Community control of our schools, our teachers, our administrators, our counselors, and our programs.

4.   INSTITUTIONS shall serve our people by providing the service necessary for a full life and their welfare on the basis of restitution, not handouts or beggar's crumbs. Restitution for past economic slavery, political exploitation, ethnic and cultural psychological destruction and denial of civil and human rights. Institutions in our community which do not serve the people have no place in the community. The institutions belong to the people.

5.   SELF-DEFENSE of the community must rely on the combined strength of the people. The front line defense will come from the barrios, the campos, the pueblos, and the ranchitos. Their involvement as protectors of their people will be given respect and dignity. They in turn offer their responsibility and their lives for their people. Those who place themselves in the front ranks for their people do so out of love and carnalismo....

6.   CULTURAL values of our people strengthen our identity and the moral backbone of the movement. Our culture unites and educates the family of La Raza toward liberation with one heart and one mind. We must insure that our writers, poets, musicians, and artists produce literature and art that is appealing to our people and relates to our revolutionary culture. Our cultural values of life, family, and home will serve as a powerful weapon to defeat the gringo dollar value system and encourage the process of love and brotherhood.

7.   POLITICAL LIBERATION can only come through independent action on our part, since the two-party system is the same animal with two heads that feed from the same trough. Where we are a majority, we will control; where we are a minority, we will represent a pressure group; nationally, we will represent one party: La Familia de La Raza!

Action

1.   Awareness and distribution of El Plan Espiritual de Aztlán. Presented at every meeting, demonstration, confrontation, courthouse, institution,

administration, church, school, tree, building, car, and every place of human existence.

2. September 16, on the birthdate of Mexican Independence, a national walk-out by all Chicanos of all colleges and schools to be sustained until the complete revision of the educational system: its policy makers, administration, its curriculum, and its personnel to meet the needs of our community.

3. Self-defense against the occupying forces of the oppressors at every school, every available man, woman, and child.

4. Community nationalization and organization of all Chicanos: El Plan Espiritual de Aztlán.

5. Economic program to drive the exploiters out of our community and a welding together of our people's combined resources to control their own production through cooperative effort.

6. Creation of an independent local, regional, and national political party.

A nation autonomous and free – culturally, socially, economically, and politically – will make its own decisions on the usage of our lands, the taxation of our goods, the utilization of our bodies for war, the determination of justice (reward and punishment), and the profit of our sweat.

El Plan de Aztlán is the plan of liberation!

Source: Alexander Bloom and Wini Breines (eds.), *"Takin' it to the Streets": A Sixties Reader* (New York and Oxford: Oxford University Press, 1995; 2nd edn, 2003), pp. 138–41.

Discussion Questions

1. Compare the manifestos issued by the Black Panthers, the Indians of All Tribes, and the Chicano National Conference and consider what these sources reveal about the various expressions of racial and ethnic pride in the 1960s.

2. How does the photograph of the Black Power salute at the Mexico Olympics help us to understand the importance of symbolic politics in the struggle for African American equality?

3. How do the various sources in this chapter express the complex relationship between national and group identity?

Chapter 11   Out of the 1960s: Alternative Endings

1. Robert F. Kennedy, Remarks on the Death of Martin Luther King, 1968

On April 4, 1968, Martin Luther King was assassinated while in Memphis to support a strike of sanitation workers for better pay and conditions. That evening New York Senator and former Attorney General Robert F. Kennedy flew into Indianapolis for a rally in support of his recently declared candidacy for the Democratic Party's presidential nomination. When he took to the stage to enthusiastic applause, Kennedy realised that nobody knew that King had been murdered and found himself breaking the news to a shocked and overwhelmingly African American crowd. In a brief impromptu speech that echoed many of the themes of his candidacy, Kennedy called for calm, racial reconciliation, and the rediscovery of a sense of common national purpose in the face of this tragedy. Over the next few days, however, virtually every urban center in the United States witnessed racial disturbances causing millions of dollars in damages and dozens of deaths. Barely two months later, Kennedy himself was assassinated in Los Angeles just minutes after claiming victory in the California Democratic primary.

Kennedy's death ended a campaign in which he had sought – with rather less success than many eulogies would later claim – to forge an ambitious interracial and multi-ethnic alliance of working-class Americans, the young, antiwar groups, and liberals who were interested in a greater degree of devolution of federal power and budgetary control to local authorities than was evident in many of Lyndon Johnson's Great Society programs. Yet Kennedy's death symbolized more than merely the tragic end of a promising campaign by a charismatic politician who inspired unusual levels of passion, hope, and commitment among his supporters. For some the double blows of the King and Kennedy assassinations marked the end of any faith in a genuinely progressive liberal politics that might transcend, let alone heal, deep fissures in American society along the lines of race, class, ethnicity, gender, and religion; for others, the twin murders confirmed the nation's descent into an ugly orgy of violence, whether exemplified in the brutal policing of the Chicago Democratic Party Convention, the My Lai massacre in Vietnam, the "Manson Family" slayings in Los Angeles, or the events at a free rock concert staged by the Rolling Stones at Altamont Speedway, where Hell's Angels handled security with lethal consequences; for others still, the unresolved questions surrounding the murders, coupled with widespread scepticism about the official version of events surrounding John F. Kennedy's assassination in 1963, fueled the kind of conspiracy theories that were one dark legacy of the 1960s.

Ladies and Gentlemen,

I'm only going to talk to you just for a minute or so this evening, because ... I have some very sad news for all of you, and, I think, sad news for all of our fellow citizens, and people who love peace all over the world; and that is that Martin Luther King was shot and was killed tonight in Memphis, Tennessee.

Martin Luther King dedicated his life to love and to justice between fellow human beings. He died in the cause of that effort. In this difficult day, in this difficult time for the United States, it's perhaps well to ask what kind of a nation we are and what direction we want to move in. For those of you who are black – considering the evidence evidently is that there were white people who were responsible – you can be filled with bitterness, and with hatred, and a desire for revenge.

We can move in that direction as a country, in greater polarization – black people amongst blacks, and white amongst whites, filled with hatred to-ward one another. Or we can make an effort, as Martin Luther King did, to understand, and to comprehend, and replace that violence, that stain of bloodshed that has spread across our land, with an effort to understand, compassion, and love.

For those of you who are black and are tempted to ... be filled with hatred and mistrust of the injustice of such an act, against all white people, I would only say that I can also feel in my own heart the same kind of feeling. I had a member of my family killed, but he was killed by a white man.

But we have to make an effort in the United States. We have to make an effort to understand, to get beyond, or go beyond these rather difficult times.

My favourite poem, my – – favorite poet ... was Aeschylus. And he once wrote:

> Even in our sleep, pain which cannot forget
> falls drop by drop upon the heart,

until, in our own despair,
against our will,
comes wisdom
through the awful grace of God.

What we need in the United States is not division; what we need in the United States is not hatred; what we need in the United States is not violence and lawlessness, but is love, and wisdom, and compassion toward one another, and a feeling of justice toward those who still suffer within our country, whether they be white or whether they be black.

So I ask you tonight to return home, to say a prayer for the family of Martin Luther King ... but more importantly to say a prayer for our own country, which all of us love – a prayer for understanding and that compassion of which I spoke.

We can do well in this country. We will have difficult times. We've had difficult times in the past ... and we will have difficult times in the future. It is not the end of violence; it is not the end of lawlessness; and it's not the end of disorder.

But the vast majority of white people and the vast majority of black people in this country want to live together, want to improve the quality of our life, and want justice for all human beings that abide in our land.

And let's dedicate ourselves to what the Greeks wrote so many years ago: to tame the savageness of man and make gentle the life of this world. Let us dedicate ourselves to that, and say a prayer for our country and for our people.

Thank you very much.

Source: www.americanrhetoric.com/speeches/rfkonmlkdeath.html.

2. Joni Mitchell, "Woodstock," 1969

In contrast to the murder and mayhem that seemed to cast a shadow over much of the late 1960s, Joni Mitchell's homage to the Woodstock Music and Arts Festival that took place on Max Yasgur's farm in upstate New York in August 1969 captured the Festival's status as emblematic of the best hopes and dreams of the counterculture. Despite appalling weather, poor organization, bad drugs, chronic food shortages, a dire lack of proper sanitary or medical facilities, and minimal security, the Festival passed off in a mood of remarkable unity with virtually no reports of personal crime or violence. For participants and some observers, the "Woodstock Nation" seemed to embody the triumph of nothing less than a new consciousness among the youth of America. As they listened to performances by many of the greatest musical acts of the era – among them Jimi Hendrix, Janis Joplin, Crosby Stills and Nash, The Who, Sly and the Family Stone – the enormous crowd conjured up a spirit of peace, love, brotherhood, personal freedom, and a return to a more simple, natural lifestyle that seemed a beguiling alternative to a contemporary world defined by war, myriad social and legal controls on individual behavior, acute racial, ethnic, religious, and gender tensions, and the fierce competitiveness and ecological damage associated with consumer culture.

Ironically, Mitchell, a Canadian-born folk singer, who had been seasoned in the folk club scene of mid-1960s New York, did not sing at Woodstock. She was due to appear on the last day of the Festival, but such was the traffic congestion caused by somewhere between 400,000 and half a million fans, she feared not being able to get away in time to perform on the prestigious Dick Cavett network television show the following evening. In 1970, the song appeared on Mitchell's Ladies of the Canyon *album while versions by Crosby Stills and Nash and Matthews Southern Comfort were major international hits. By this time, Woodstock's iconic status, bolstered by the release of a lucrative feature film and best selling triple album, was assured.*

I came upon a child of God
He was walking along the road
And I asked him, where are you going
And this he told me
I'm going on down to Yasgur's farm
I'm going to join in a rock 'n' roll band
I'm going to camp out on the land
I'm going to try an' get my soul free
We are stardust
We are golden
And we've got to get ourselves
Back to the garden

Then can I walk beside you
I have come here to lose the smog
And I feel to be a cog in something turning
Well maybe it is just the time of year
Or maybe it's the time of man
I don't know who I am
But you know life is for learning
We are stardust
We are golden
And we've got to get ourselves
Back to the garden

By the time we got to Woodstock
We were half a million strong
And everywhere there was song and celebration
And I dreamed I saw the bombers
Riding shotgun in the sky
And they were turning into butterflies
Above our nation
We are stardust
Billion year old carbon
We are golden
Caught in the devil's bargain
And we've got to get ourselves
Back to the garden

Source: Joni Mitchell, *Ladies of the Canyon*, 1970 (Siquomb Publishing Co., 1969).

3. John Filo, Kent State Killings, 1970

By the end of the 1960s, the antiwar movement was in full swing and some 80 per cent were "fed up and tired of the war." Popular disquiet mounted with the revelation that in Spring 1968 US troops had massacred hundreds of unarmed civilians, including many women and children, in the village of My Lai, only for the military and government to collude in a cover-up. Disillusionment with the war and distrust of the government's motivations further intensified in the spring of 1970 when Nixon announced that he had ordered US troops into Cambodia, ostensibly to protect US troops by destroying North Vietnamese sanctuaries and supply routes in that country. It later emerged that the US had been secretly bombing those sites for a year prior to the ground assault. The invasion itself was a disaster, fermenting civil war in Cambodia and leading to the rise to power of the ruthless, anti-American Khmer Rouge. Four years later, the US military action in Vietnam finally ended with the signing of the Paris Peace treaty and in late April 1975 the last American officials fled by helicopter from the rooftops of the US Embassy in Saigon as South Vietnam fell to the Vietcong. Since 1964 the war had cost the US $140 billion in direct costs, 45,941 combat fatalities, 10,420 noncombatant deaths, and left some 73,000 veterans classified as totally disabled.

The invasion of Cambodia triggered widespread protest on and off America's college campuses, including one at Kent State University in Ohio where the local Reserve Officers' Training Corp building was set ablaze. In response to the disturbances, Ohio governor James Rhodes sent in the National Guard. Facing a tough re-election campaign and sensing the desire of many Americans for a tougher stance on civil unrest and law and order issues, Rhodes urged a hard-line approach. On May 4, Guardsmen trying to

disperse a student rally responded to taunting and rock-throwing with live
ammunition, killing four people – only two of whom had actually been
involved in the protest – and injuring nine others.

   John Filo's photograph shows the body of slain student Jeffrey Miller at the feet
of Mary Ann Vecchio, a 14-year old runaway and antiwar protester from Florida.
Filo, a student himself, won the Pulitzer prize for his photo, a cropped version of
which, cut tighter to Vecchio's face, appeared on the cover of Newsweek alongside
the headline, "Nixon's Home Front." The Kent State killings intensified the anger
over the invasion of Cambodia and sparked protests on more than 1,200
campuses. Revealingly, however, in the immediate aftermath of the Kent State
tragedy, a survey showed that three-quarters of Americans felt it was wrong to
protest against the government and a large majority believed that in order to stop
antiwar protests continuing some of the basic freedoms secured by the Bill of
Rights should be suspended. At the dawn of the 1970s, as for much of the 1960s,
Vietnam and divergent attitudes towards the responsibilities and duties of
American citizens and government institutions continued to polarize American
society.

Photo © John Filo

Figure 11.1   Anti-War Protest at Kent State University, 1970.

Source: Photo: John Filo/Getty.

4. US Supreme Court, *Roe v. Wade*, 1973

In 1970, a single woman called Norma McCorvey, anonymized in the proceedings as Jane Roe, brought a class action suit to challenge the constitutionality of Texas criminal abortion laws. After a series of trials, in 1973 the Supreme Court agreed in Roe v. Wade *that the Texas laws violated Roe's privacy rights under the 14th Amendment, thereby affirming the constitutional right of American women to procure a first trimester abortion as a matter of choice, not medical necessity. For many,* Roe *marked the culmination of a long struggle to assert women's rights to control their own reproductive systems; for many others, the decision was a moral and social tragedy, the predictable and sordid nadir of the sexual revolution of the 1960s.*

Roe *was also a controversial moment in the Supreme Court's ongoing response to changing sexual mores and gender attitudes during this period. In an era characterized by unusual levels of judicial activism, the Court under Chief Justice Earl Warren had delivered a series of rulings that helped to solidify the idea of a new sexual permissiveness. In cases such as* Roth v. US *(1957) and* Memoirs v. Massachusetts *(1966), the Court steadily narrowed definitions of obscenity so as to allow much great sexual explicitness in American art, media, and culture without fear of criminal prosecution. Yet if the Court, as conservatives would often charge, was complicit in encouraging a dangerous new sexual license, its judgments invariably affirmed traditional heterosexual and marital "norms" and reflected a rather restricted concept of acceptable sexual preferences and behavior. For example, in the landmark* Griswold v. Connecticut *case of 1965, the Court may have declared unconstitutional a state law forbidding the sale of contraceptives to married couples, but it simultaneously upheld the constitutionality of other state laws against adultery, homosexuality, and fornication. Similarly, in 1967, the Court ruled unanimously in* Loving v. Virginia *that laws against interracial marriage were unconstitutional but based its decision in large measure on the argument that marriage was necessary for reproduction. In* Boutelier v. The Immigration and Naturalization Service *(1967) it allowed that under the provisions of the 1952 Immigration and Nationality Act homosexuals could be excluded or deported from the US because their sexual orientation constituted a "psychopathic" personality disorder. In 1968 Warren retired and the Court entered a more conservative period under the leadership of Warren Burger. In this context it is significant that the Court's decision in* Roe *turned as much on privacy issues as on any expanded concept of female sexuality and reproductive rights, and that it came the same year as the court's* Miller v. California *decision, which redefined the legal test of obscenity and restored to local jurisdiction power to apply local standards of decency to judge obscene materials.*

Held ...

3. State criminal abortion laws, like those involved here, that except from criminality only a life-saving procedure on the mother's behalf without regard to the stage of her pregnancy and other interests involved violate the Due Process Clause of the Fourteenth Amendment, which protects against state action the right to privacy, including a woman's qualified right to terminate her pregnancy.

I. The Texas statutes that concern us here are Arts. 1191–1194 and 1196 of the State's Penal Code. These make it a crime to "procure an abortion," as therein defined, or to attempt one, except with respect to "an abortion procured or attempted by medical advice for the purpose of saving the life of the mother." Similar statutes are in existence in a majority of the States.

XI

1. A state criminal abortion statute of the current Texas type, that excepts from criminality only a lifesaving procedure on behalf of the mother, without regard to pregnancy stage and without recognition of the other interests involved, is violative of the Due Process Clause of the Fourteenth Amendment.

   (a) For the stage prior to approximately the end of the first trimester, the abortion decision and its effectuation must be left to the medical judgment of the pregnant woman's attending physician.

   (b) For the stage subsequent to approximately the end of the first trimester, the State, in promoting its interest in the health of the mother, may, if it chooses, regulate the abortion procedure in ways that are reasonably related to maternal health.

   (c) For the stage subsequent to viability, the State in promoting its interest in the potentiality of human life may, if it chooses, regulate, and even proscribe, abortion except where it is necessary, in appropriate medical judgment, for the preservation of the life or health of the mother....

XII. Our conclusion that Art. 1196 is unconstitutional means, of course, that the Texas abortion statutes, as a unit, must fall.

Source: US Supreme Court, *Roe v. Wade*, 410 U.S. 113 (1973).

5. Watergate Special Prosecution Force, Memo on Prosecuting Richard M. Nixon, 1974

On August 9, 1974 Richard Nixon resigned the presidency of the United States to avoid Congressional impeachment and a likely conviction for obstruction of justice. Two years earlier during the 1972 presidential election campaign, members of Nixon's Committee to Re-elect the President (CREEP) had colluded with the "Plumbers" – a secret cadre of White House aides dedicated to neutralizing all of the president's enemies and political opponents – to bug the Democratic Party's National Committee headquarters in the Watergate apartment complex in Washington. When the Watergate break-in was discovered and the FBI began to investigate, Nixon moved to conceal the links between the Plumbers and his re-election team. He authorized hush-money payments to the Plumbers in return for their silence and instructed the CIA to inform the FBI that the break-in had been carried out for national security reasons so that the formal investigation was abruptly halted.

Two Washington Post *journalists, Carl Bernstein and Bob Woodward, continued to probe the story. Thanks largely to their efforts, the seedy and paranoid side of the Nixon administration, with its "dirty tricks" operations against the president's real and imagined enemies, gradually emerged. At the trial of the burglary team, it became clear that a cover-up, approved at the highest levels of government, had been attempted. From May to August 1973, a special Senate committee held dramatic televised hearings, which steadily eroded the plausibility of the Nixon administration's denials of wrong-doing. When it was revealed at those hearings that Nixon had secretly taped all his Oval Office conversations, he initially refused to hand the tapes over to the investigators until a Supreme Court decision ordered their release in July 1974. The tapes offered damning evidence of Nixon's complicity in the Watergate cover-up and exposed systemic abuses of executive power and clear disregard for the law and constitutional constraints.*

This memo, sent to Special Prosecutor Leon Jaworski on the day of Nixon's resignation, lays out the legal and political issues involved in pursuing criminal charges against the former president. Although Nixon's successor, Gerald Ford, issued a controversial pardon, the damage that the Watergate affair did to the prestige of the presidency and to the public's attitude towards the government and politics was enormous. Watergate, coupled with the stream of official disinformation about America's involvement in Southeast Asia meant that whereas in 1958 only 24 percent of all Americans complained that they did not trust their government, by the end of 1973 more than 57 percent felt that way.

SUBJECT: Factors to be Considered in Deciding Whether to Prosecute Richard M. Nixon for Obstruction of Justice

In our view there is clear evidence that Richard M. Nixon participated in a conspiracy to obstruct justice by concealing the identity of those responsible for the Watergate break-in and other criminal offenses. There is a presumption (which in the past we have operated upon) that Richard M. Nixon, like every citizen, is subject to the rule of law. Accordingly, one begins with the premise that if there is sufficient evidence, Mr. Nixon should be indicted and prosecuted. The question then becomes whether the presumption for proceeding is outweighed by the factors mandating against indictment and prosecution.

The factors which mandate against indictment and prosecution are:

1. His resignation has been sufficient punishment.
2. He has been subject to an impeachment inquiry with resulting articles of impeachment which the House Judiciary Committee unanimously endorsed as to Article I (the Watergate cover-up).
3. Prosecution might aggravate political divisions in the country.
4. As a political matter, the times call for conciliation rather than recrimination.
5. There would be considerable difficulty in achieving a fair trial because of massive pre-trial publicity.

The factors which mandate in favor of indictment and prosecution are:

1. The principle of equal justice under law requires that every person, no matter what his past position or office, answer to the criminal justice system for his past offenses. This is a particularly weighty factor if Mr. Nixon's aides and associates, who acted upon his orders and what they conceived to be his interests, are to be prosecuted for she same offenses.
2. The country will be further divided by Mr. Nixon unless there is a final disposition of charges of criminality outstanding against him so as to forestall the belief that he was driven from his office by erosion of his political base. This final disposition may be necessary to preserve the integrity of the criminal justice system and the legislative process, which together marshaled the substantial evidence of Mr. Nixon's guilt.
3. Article I, Section 3, clause 7 of the Constitution provides that a person removed from office by impeachment and conviction "shall nevertheless be liable and subject to Indictment, Trial, Judgment, and

Punishment, according to Law." The Framers contemplated that a person removed from office because of abuse of his public trust still would have to answer to the criminal justice system for criminal offenses.

4. It cannot be sufficient retribution for criminal offenses merely to surrender the public office and trust which has been demonstrably abused. A person should not be permitted to trade in the abused office in return for immunity.

5. The modern nature of the Presidency necessitates massive public exposure of the President's actions through the media. A bar to prosecution on the grounds of such publicity effectively would immunize all future Presidents for their actions, however criminal. Moreover, the courts may be the appropriate forum to resolve questions of pre-trial publicity in the context of an adversary proceeding.

Source: "Factors to be Considered in Deciding Whether to Prosecute Richard M. Nixon for Obstruction of Justice," Memo from Carl B. Feldbaum and Peter M. Kreindler to Special Prosecutor Leon Jaworski, August 9, 1974, Record Group 460, Records of the Watergate Special Prosecution Force, Department of Justice, National Archives and Records Administration, Washington, DC.

Discussion Questions

1. How can we try to reconcile the very different images of the 1960s and its legacies conjured up by the source materials in this chapter?
2. How do the sources in this chapter help to explain increasingly cynical public attitudes towards mainstream politics, the federal government and other expressions of state power at the start of the 1970s?
3. What does the *Roe* decision, read in conjunction with the other sources in the Reader relating to gender and sexuality, reveal about key changes in the lives of many American women after the 1950s?

Chapter 12   The 1960s in Myth and Memory

1. Dan Quayle, "Reflections on Urban America," 1992

In Spring 1992, Los Angeles witnessed the worst "race riot" in America since the long hot summers of the late 1960s. The immediate catalyst for the violence was the failure of a predominantly white jury to convict four white police officers who had been caught on video viciously beating Rodney King, an unarmed black man on parole who police believed to be driving under the influence of drugs and who had allegedly resisted arrest following a high-speed car chase. While the verdict provided the spark for six days of rioting that left more than 50 people dead and caused damage estimated at around a billion dollars, the underlying causes were complex and reflected the continuing economic and social problems faced by African Americans a quarter of a century after the major civil rights victories of the mid-1960s.

Speaking in the immediate aftermath of the riot, Vice-President Dan Quayle looked back over the previous twenty-five years in an attempt to understand its roots. In what became popularly known as the "Murphy Brown" speech because of Quayle's condemnation of the eponymous careerist heroine of a popular television sit-com who embraced the idea of being a single mother, he blamed the violence on what he saw as the disastrous erosion of traditional moral, religious, and family values among many inner-city blacks, and a growing culture of welfare dependency, all of which he traced to the personal excesses and political mistakes of the 1960s. Quayle prescribed a renewed commitment to family values, church-going, hard work, property rights, and sexual restraint as an antidote to riots, gang culture, dysfunctional families, welfare dependency, social fragmentation, and inner-city economic deprivation.

... When I have been asked during these last weeks who caused the riots and the killings in L.A., my answer has been direct and simple. Who is to blame for the riots? The rioters are to blame. Who is to blame for the killings? The killers are to blame. Yes, I can understand how people were shocked and outraged by the verdict in the Rodney King trial. But, my friends, there is simply no excuse for the mayhem that followed. To apologize or in any way to excuse what happened is wrong. It is a betrayal of all those people equally outraged and equally disadvantaged who did not loot, who did not riot, and who were, in many cases, victims of the rioting. No matter how much you may disagree with the verdict, the riots were wrong. If we as a society don't condemn what is wrong, how can we teach our children what is right? But after condemning the riots, we do need to try to understand the underlying situation.

In a nutshell, I believe the lawless social anarchy that we saw is directly related to the breakdown of the family structure, personal responsibility and social order in too many areas of our society. For the poor, the situation is compounded by a welfare ethos that impedes individual efforts to move ahead in society and hampers their ability to take advantage of the opportunities America offers. If we don't succeed in addressing these fundamental problems and in restoring basic values, any attempt to fix what's broken, will fail. One reason I believe we won't fail is that we have come so far in the last 25 years. There's no question that this country has had a terrible problem with race and racism. The evil of slavery has left a long and ugly legacy.

But we have faced racism squarely and we have made progress in the past quarter of a century. With landmark civil rights bills of the 1960s, we moved legal barriers to allow full participation by blacks in the economic, social and political life of the nation. By any measure, the America of 1992 is more egalitarian, more integrated and offers more opportunities to black Americans and all other minority members than the America of 1964. There is more to be done, but I think that all of us can be proud of our progress. And let's be specific about one aspect of this progress. The country now has a black middle class that barely existed a quarter-century ago. Since 1967, the median income of black two-parent families has risen by 60 percent in real terms. The number of black college graduates has skyrocketed. Black men and women have achieved real political power. Black mayors head 48 of our largest cities, including Los Angeles. These are real achievements, but as we all know, there's another side to that bright landscape.

During this period of progress, we have also developed a culture of poverty. Some call it the underclass that is far more violent and harder to escape than it was a generation ago. The poor you always have with you, scripture tells us, and in America we have always had poor people. But in this dynamic, prosperous nation, poverty has traditionally been a stage through which people pass on their way to joining the great middle class. And if one generation didn't get very far up the ladder, their ambitious, better-educated children would. But the underclass seems to be a new phenomenon. It is a group whose members are dependent on welfare for very long stretches and whose young men are often drawn into lives of crime. There is far too little upward mobility, because the underclass is disconnected from the rules of American society. And these problems have, unfortunately, been particularly acute for black Americans.

Let me share with you a few statistics on the difference between black poverty in the 1960s and now. In 1967, 68 percent of black families were headed by married couples. In 1991, only 48 percent of black families were headed by both a husband and a wife. In 1965, the illegitimacy rate among black families was 28 percent. In 1989, 65 percent, two-thirds of all black children were born with never-married mothers. In 1951, 9 percent of black youths between 16 and 19 were unemployed. In 1965, it was 23 percent. In 1980, it was 35 percent. By 1989, the number had declined slightly, but it was still 32 percent. The leading cause of death of young black males today is homicide.

It would be overly simplistic to blame this social breakdown on the programs of the Great Society alone. It would be absolutely wrong to blame it on the growth and success most Americans enjoyed during the 1980s. Rather, we are in large measure reaping the consequences of the decades of changes in social mores.

I was born in 1947, so I'm considered one of those baby boomers that we keep reading about. But let's look at one unfortunate legacy of the so-called boomer generation. When we were young, it was fashionable to declare war against traditional values. Indulgence and self-gratification seemed to have no consequences. Many of our generation glamorized casual sex and drug use, evaded responsibility and trashed authority. Today, the boomers are middle-aged and middle class. The responsibility of having families has helped many recover traditional values. And, of course, the great majority of those in the middle class survived the turbulent legacy of the '60s and '70s. But many of the poor, with less to fall back on, did not. The inter-generational poverty that troubles us so much today is predominantly a poverty of values.

Our inner cities are filled with children having children, with people who have not been able to take advantage of educational opportunities, with people who are dependent on drugs or the narcotic of welfare. To be sure, many people in the ghetto struggle very hard against these tides and some-times win. But too many people feel they have no hope and nothing to lose. This poverty is, again, fundamentally a poverty of values. Unless we change the basic rules of society in our inner cities, we cannot expect anything else to change. We will simply get more of what we saw three weeks ago. New thinking, new ideas, new strategies are needed. For the government, transforming underclass culture means that our policies and our programs must create a different incentive system. Our policy must be premised on and must reinforce values such as family, hard work, integrity, personal responsibility. I think we can all agree the government's first obligation is to maintain order. We are a nation of laws, not looting. It has become clear that the riots were fueled by the vicious gangs that terrorize the inner cities. We are committed to breaking those gangs and restoring law and order....

Our urban strategy is to empower the poor by giving them control over their lives. To do that, our urban agenda includes fully funding the Home Ownership and Opportunity for People Everywhere program. HOPE, as we call it, will help public housing residents become homeowners....

Empowering the poor will strengthen families, and right now the failure of our families is hurting America deeply. When family fails, society fails. The anarchy and lack of structure in our inner cities are a testament to how quickly civilization falls apart when the family foundation crashes. Children need love and discipline; they need mothers and fathers. A welfare check is not a husband, the state is not a father. It is from parents that children learn how to behave in society. It is from parents, above all, that children come to understand values and themselves as men and women, mothers and fathers. And for those who are concerned about children growing up in poverty, we should know this – marriage is probably the best anti-poverty program of all.

Among families headed by married couples today, there is a poverty rate of 5.7 percent. But 33.4 percent of the families headed by a single mother are in poverty. Nature abhors a vacuum. Where there are no mature, responsible men around to teach boys how to be good men, gangs serve in their place. In fact, gangs have become a surrogate family for much of a generation of inner-city boys. I recently visited with some former gang members in Albuquerque, New Mexico. In a private meeting, they told me why they had joined gangs. These teenage boys said that gangs gave them a sense of security. They made them feel wanted and useful. They got support from their friends and they said, "It was like having family." Like family? Unfortunately, that says it all.

The system perpetuates itself as these young men father children whom they have no intention of caring for, by women whose welfare checks support them. Teenage girls mired in the same hopelessness lack sufficient motive to say no to this trap. Answers to our problems won't be easy, my friends. We can start by dismantling a welfare system that encourages dependency and subsidizes broken families. We can attach conditions such as school attendance or work to welfare. We can limit the time a recipient gets benefits. We can stop penalizing marriage for welfare mothers. We can enforce child-support payments. Ultimately, however, marriage is a moral issue that requires cultural consensus and the use of social sanctions.

Bearing babies irresponsibly is simply wrong. Failing to support children one has fathered is wrong and we must be unequivocal about this. It doesn't help matters when primetime TV has Murphy Brown, a character who supposedly epitomizes today's intelligent, highly paid professional woman, mocking the importance of fathers by bearing a child alone and calling it just another lifestyle choice. I know it's not fashionable to talk about moral values, but we need to do it! Even though our cultural leaders in Hollywood, network TV and the national newspapers routinely jeer at them, I think most of us in this room know that some things are good and other things are wrong. And now, it's time to make the discussion public. It's time to talk again about the family, hard work, integrity and personal responsibility. We cannot be embarrassed out of our belief that two parents married to each other are better, in most cases, for children than one. That honest work is better than handouts or crime. That we are our brother's keepers. That is worth making an effort, even when the rewards aren't immediate.

So, I think the time has come to renew our public commitment to our Judeo-Christian values in our churches and synagogues, our civic organizations and our schools. We are, as our children recite each morning, one nation under God. That's a useful framework for acknowledging a duty and an authority higher than our own pleasures and personal ambition. If we live more thoroughly by these values, we would live in a better society. For the poor, renewing these values will give the people the strength to help themselves by acquiring the tools to achieve self-sufficiency, a good education, job training, and property. Then they will move from permanent dependence to dignified independence....

Source: Dan Quayle, "Reflections on Urban America," Speech to the Commonwealth Club of California, May 19, 1992, Program 19920519, Commonwealth Club Radio Program Collection, Hoover Institution Archives, Stanford University.

2. Stephen Holden, "Seeing the 60s Through a 90s Corrective Lens," 1999

American film-makers and television directors have long helped to shape popular conceptions and misconceptions about the 1960s. Whether perpetuating or debunking some of the most tenacious myths, films as diverse as

American Graffiti, The Big Chill, Apocalypse Now, and JFK as well as hit television shows like The Wonder Years and Mad Men have reflected and molded popular understandings of the era. Stephen Holden's perceptive review of Hideous Kinky and A Walk on the Moon – two 1999 feature films set in the 1960s – reminds us of the extent to which contemporary political, economic, and artistic agendas have always influenced the ways in which the 1960s are remembered and rendered in American culture. At the same time his review, which merges into a bittersweet memoir of his own 1960s experiences, describes how Hollywood has tended to reduce a tremendously complex era to a rather narrow set of stock themes and stylistic gestures, rarely grappling with the more genuinely radical personal and collective politics of the decade in favor of the hackneyed trinity of sex, drugs, and rock and roll.

A whiff of incense mixed with marijuana smoke drifts though two recent movies, *Hideous Kinky* and *A Walk on the Moon*, both of which conjure an era that Hollywood, in its devotion to snugly happy endings, has largely avoided. In the countercultural dream that has so intimidated Hollywood, a dippie Pied Piper with stingy shoulder-length hair, a fringed jacket and reeking of patchouli oil is banging a tambourine on his knee with one hand and flashing a peace sign with the other. Beside him are a trio of spaced-out go-go girls shimmying and gazing groggily into the purple haze.

Although that signature scent, blown across three decades of shifting winds, isn't overpowering in these films, it is just pungent enough to suggest that what we think of as "the 60s" – the years (1964–1972) bracketed musically by Beatlemania and "American Pie" – were not a hallucination but a messy, uncomfortable reality. In their hesitantly nostalgic ways, both films remind us that in the days of turning on, tuning in and dropping out, people actually followed Timothy Leary's notorious prescription for personal enlightenment.

But in remaining true to Hollywood's tidy, late-90's formulas, they also suggest that dropping back in was just as easy and that all that dope smoking, acid tripping, searching, protesting and free love was an adolescent prank, a temporary lapse of judgment.

The notion that this heady ethos was really just an episode in a cultural mini-series whose happy ending finds the Dow Jones industrials hovering around 10,000 and garish $1 million houses sprouting all over the American landscape is a quintessential revisionist view of what the 60's were about. These films insinuate that thousands of ex-hippies, now in their late 40's and 50's and presiding in executive suites, emulated Bill Clinton's experiment with marijuana and never inhaled. And if they did inhale, God forbid their children should follow suit.

Both films focus on young, attractive women who break the rules to pursue sexual and spiritual transcendence, then return to the middle-class lives they renounced. In the smart, beautifully acted *Hideous Kinky*, set in Morocco in 1972, Kate Winslett is Julia, a young Englishwoman drifting around North Africa with two young daughters in tow and no money. In Marrakech she meets a Moroccan street acrobat (Said Taghmaoui) who is also penniless. The two make love, smoke hashish and drag the girls along on a risky trek into the Moroccan countryside. Now and then, Julia, who aspires to learn Sufi dancing, makes noises about wanting to experience pure joy by obliterating her ego.

In reimagining an era of hippies, dropouts and seekers after a higher consciousness, *Hideous Kinky* is accurate as far as it goes. But that isn't very far. The movie conveys only the flavor of the time. Julia's quest is portrayed as muddled and vague, and the movie nudges us again and again to recognize what a terrible, irresponsible parent she is. When one daughter insists she wants to return to England and have a proper education, her mother is dumbfounded. True, Julia radiates a certain defiant charm. But in the film's overall judgment, she is also a silly spaced-out fool who must come to her senses. And in the end she does.

A Walk on the Moon follows its protagonist Pearl Kantrowitz (Diane Lane) to a working-class Jewish resort in the Catskills in the summer of 1969. Pearl, who married her husband, Marty (Liev Schreiber), when she became pregnant at 17, is now the mother of a 14-year-old daughter, Alison (Anna Paquin), who is just entering adolescence. On weekdays, while Marty is back in New York City repairing televisions, Pearl plunges into an affair with Walker (Viggo Mortensen), a smolderingly handsome peddler of blouses that he sells to the summer colony out of his van.

Pearl momentarily loses her head and slips off with Walker to the nearby Woodstock festival, where her daughter accidentally witnesses Pearl, body-painted and ecstatic, being whirled in her lover's arms. Alison is understandably upset. When Pearl finally must choose between Marty and Walker, the small, finely acted film caves in to 90's movie values. In the final scene, Pearl and her husband begin a tentative slow dance to music on the radio: a soupy version of Dean Martin's "When You're Smiling." Marty, realizing that his wife has almost left him behind in the 50s, switches to a station playing Jimi Hendrix's "Purple Haze." Signaling that he'll try to get with the times, he relaxes and swings out.

A Walk on the Moon is a decent little film, but in reducing a wrenching life decision to a matter of switching radio stations, it blithely denies the enormous power of the forces that have tugged Pearl into an affair. An earlier scene in the film juxtaposes images of Pearl and Walker making love at the exact moment Neil Armstrong first sets foot on the moon. The implication is clear. For Pearl, this is not just a dalliance but an earth-shaking, life-changing sexual awakening. Had *A Walk on the Moon* been made in the 70s, there is little doubt that the character would have forsaken her family to go on the road with her sexual savior. Today, that's just not permitted.

In what they show and don't show of the 60s, both films raise disturbing questions: When did it become embarrassing for the mass media to portray the counterculture as a movement driven by passionate idealism and a reckless insistence on crashing through barriers? Could it be that the movies are too scared of the era and the freedoms it represented to confront it head-on?

Every now and then, Hollywood has tried. *Easy Rider*, which came out of left field in 1969 and was made for a dime, proved to be a one-of-a-kind, a fluke. While other films of the period, like *Midnight Cowboy* and *Five Easy Pieces*, and later, *Shampoo* and *Coming Home*, expressed a combative, rebellious spirit, they didn't dive in to the thick of things. Hollywood was very late in addressing the Vietnam War. It had to be safely behind us before we could begin to watch movies about it. Among Hollywood's leading filmmakers, only Oliver Stone, in films like *Born on the Fourth of July*, *Platoon* and *The Doors*, has taken the passions of the 60s seriously enough to portray the full impact of the generational and political fissures that ripped open the American psyche.

Outside of Mr. Stone's films, vintage rock music and rock documentaries, from *Monterey Pop* to *Gimme Shelter*, seem to do a much better job than most feature films of capturing the era.

One could list a hundred reasons why Hollywood has never given the 60's their due. High on that list would be the problem of 60s fashions. Even at the time, the hordes who donned the more extravagant hippie regalia often looked ridiculous. How could anyone take such weirdly dressed characters seriously? Another problem is the stoned-out argot adopted by millions of young people in the late 60s and early 70s (with its "right ons"; "like, mans" and "heavies"). Today it sounds quaint and surprisingly conformist.

Post baby-boomers may find it hard to envision block after city block of shaggy-haired youth clad in exotic robes and finery milling in the streets. But such scenes were commonplace in San Francisco, in college communities and in the East Village of New York City in the late 60s. On Sunday afternoons, the area around the Bethesda Fountain in Central Park became a stoned soul picnic in which hundreds of artists, pot-smoking hippies, drug dealers and musicians congregated for fragrant, dreamy communal love-ins.

As one who embarked on the same pharmaceutical, sexual and political consciousness-raising adventures that millions of others did, I can remember a day when I was so convinced that the world had changed forever that I tossed all my neckties into the trash. In the antimaterialistic spirit of the times, I gave away treasured possessions, which amounted to almost nothing in those days: a collection of cherished 45 rpm records donated to a friend's jukebox. Determined to "rip off" the system, one day I bravely pilfered a can of tuna fish from a supermarket shelf.

Visiting some friends in Key West, Fla., in the Spring of 1969, I descended on a town crawling with drugged-out hippies, including a self-proclaimed white-robed Jesus. During that sojourn, I met a skinny, acid-tripping girl who solemnly informed me that *Any Day Now*, the title of Joan Baez's new album of Bob Dylan songs, referred to Mr. Dylan's imminent suicide. "He's just going to trip right out," she said with that special hushed "Wow!" in her voice that seriously hip people attached to all things mystical.

As much as that counterculture was mobilized by antiwar sentiment, its driving force was really drugs, and not only psychedelics. In the quest to "break on through to the other side," as Jim Morrison bellowed, any and every stimulant was enlisted for the cause. Amphetamines, which were widely available back then and carried little stigma, contributed immeasurably to the collective paranoia that was rapidly building up. And, or course, there was always booze to smooth the transitions.

Two other random flashbacks. In one, I am hounded out of a Chinese restaurant by a radical feminist and her poet husband after I describe my extremely liberal political views. But they and their revolutionary comrades have big plans to sabotage the 1968 Presidential elections by, among other tactics, vomiting on the voting machines. Liberals were their worst enemies. "When the revolution comes, you'll be one of the first to go!" they scream, and I'm out of there. Fast.

In the other, I am living in New York and supplying lyrics for a revolutionary rock band no one has ever heard of in another city. Asked to donate $300 – a third of my life savings at the time – for sound equipment, I gladly obliged, only to discover that the money has gone up the leader's nose in crystal methedrine. So much for the new Beatles!

Recalling such crazy 60's moments, I wonder if what we call the 60s was a mass psychosis that is either best forgotten or swept under the rug. But I don't think so. For all the smashed lives and insanity that such excesses brought, the root of that frenzied exploration still strikes me as an honest, if naïve, effort to improve the human condition by storming the barricades of consciousness. That idealism is distilled in the best music of the era, which combines a majestic rage with an exhilarating eroticism.

Today's social climate is in many ways antithetical to that of 30 years ago when the notion of capitalism itself was under siege. The power of today's American economy combined with the country's conservative, conformist values, make joining the system irresistible to all but a few. Rebellion is reduced to a matter of fashion statement.

If the AIDS epidemic ended the sexual revolution, sexual allure has increasingly become the major marketing tool fueling the economy. Rock may have been superseded by rap, but the history of rock-and-roll is probably the one with which more Americans are familiar than any other. As for drugs, the new miracle elixirs, Prozac and the other serotonin boosters are tools to help people become happier, more efficient producers in the great American money machine.

Movies may never get the 60s right. For one thing, those days are fading fast, and many of the Hollywood studio executives calling the shots are Wunderkinds in their 20s and 30s whose closest contact with the 60s are VH1 flashbacks or their parents' (censored) anecdotes.

In his sweetly prescient 60s ballad, "Younger Generation," John Sebastian, a quintessential Woodstock-era songwriter, contemplated impending fatherhood and the raising of an adolescent son. "And then I'll know that all I've learned my kid assumes/ And all my deepest worries must be his cartoons," he mused.

In a way he was right. But the lessons taught by the 60s are not the ones that those who lived through them imagined they would be.

3. David Greenberg, "Saigon and Saddam: The Use and Abuse of Vietnam Analogies," 2004

In Spring 2003, President George W. Bush committed US troops to Iraq, justifying his decision in terms of the need to rid the Middle East of a brutal, expansionist dictator who harbored weapons of mass destruction and gave succor to the kind of Islamic extremists who had perpetrated the 9/11 terrorist attacks on the US. American public opinion on the rationale, legality, and strategic wisdom of the invasion was immediately split, raising echoes of the divisions caused by Vietnam forty years previously.

For opponents of the war there were clear analogies in the way that the official justification for invasion soon rang false. Saddam Hussein's weapons of mass destruction failed to materialize and the links between Iraq and the Islamic terrorists of Al-Qaida were exposed as somewhere between tenuous and non-existent. Despite attempts by sections of the conservative media and some government forces to brand all dissenting voices on the war "unpatriotic," antiwar sentiment increased with revelations of how lucrative contracts for servicing the military effort and rebuilding post-invasion Iraq had been awarded to US companies with close ties to the Republican Party. Moreover, it soon became apparent that nobody in the US military or the government had any viable strategy for how to manage the "peace" in Iraq so as to allow for an orderly US withdrawal once Hussein's regime had been toppled. Years after Bush had declared "Mission Accomplished," thousands of US troops were still fighting an elusive and highly committed enemy, embroiled in an escalating civil conflict from which there seemed to be no easy or honorable retreat.

Bush carefully avoided any comparisons with Vietnam until late August 2007 when, with his approval ratings at an all-time low and his Iraq policy largely discredited, he boldly announced that there would be no US exit from the country during his presidency. Putting a rather idiosyncratic spin on the historical record, the president insisted that it was the premature US withdrawal from Indochina that had plunged the area into years of bloody oppression typified by the Khmer Rouge's reign of terror in Cambodia.

Ultimately, the temptation to draw on Vietnam for analogy and guidance, or as a cautionary tale, has proved irresistible for supporters and opponents of the war alike. In this 2004 article for the on-line journal The Slate, *Rutgers historian David Greenberg reminded readers that there were perils, as well as potential benefits, of drawing too close a comparison between the situations in Iraq and Vietnam.*

The Vietnam War is again dividing the country, this time by analogy. Doves liken the Iraqi occupation to the Indochina debacle. Hawks tick off the obvious differences. All this comparing and contrasting shouldn't be surprising. A law of rhetorical entropy seems to decree that every American war since 1975 – Grenada, El Salvador, Nicaragua, Panama, Bosnia, Kosovo, Kuwait, Afghanistan – tends toward comparison with Vietnam.

Indeed, for more than a year, hardly a month has passed without some new invocation of the Vietnam parallel. Even before the Iraq invasion, critics of the rush to war pointed to Vietnam as a cautionary reminder about the arrogance of power. The ground war had lasted barely a week before skeptics and hacks began whispering the dreaded word "quagmire."

The Vietnam parallel returned with a vengeance during last fall's controversy over Saddam's missing weapons cache. The dawning recognition that the Bush team's zeal for war had led it to misread data – and consequently to misrepresent the Iraqi threat to the world – stirred memories of another phony *casus belli*, the Gulf of Tonkin attacks of August 1964. Meanwhile, the administration's relentlessly upbeat forecasts and its withholding of key information opened a credibility gap reminiscent of Lyndon Johnson's.

In the past few weeks, the occupation has inspired still more Vietnam comparisons – this time to the ill-fated "pacification" program. Violent uprisings have shown far greater Iraqi anger toward the American presence than was assumed. The enemy of our enemy, it turned out, wasn't our friend: Many Iraqis thrilled about Saddam's ouster nonetheless had little love for their occupiers. But the Vietnam experience suggested that the odds against winning the "hearts and minds" of the Iraqi populace were long. Pacification failed in Vietnam, after all, both because the Army always focused mainly on its military goals, and, more important, because most Vietnamese didn't wish to be pacified. Discouraged and sour, U.S. troops put stock in an officer's memorable line: "Grab 'em by the balls and their hearts and mind will follow." That approach failed, too.

For all the resemblances, however, even most occupation critics agree that history isn't repeating itself. The Vietnam parallel, like all historical analogies, admits as many differences as similarities. Each time Vietnam is invoked, some administration booster effortlessly reels off the countless contrasts: the relative brevity of the American term in Iraq; the lighter casualty toll; the wholly different nature of the enemy. Most significantly, in Iraq the main battlefield victories have already been won. And so the Vietnam parallels and contrasts degenerate into partisan claims and counterclaims.

(What *does* genuinely echo Vietnam, however, is the barrage of scurrilous attacks against those who question the occupation. Richard Nixon used to argue, in a textbook case of black-is-white newspeak, that protesters who demanded an immediate end to the war were actually prolonging it – rather like saying that Martin Luther King Jr. was prolonging segregation. Now, sadly, that twisted logic is being revived to try to disparage administration critics.)

But if Vietnam offers little in the way of usable lessons today, it remains relevant as history and as a large part of the explanation of how we got into Iraq at all. Among the American public, especially on the left, Vietnam conferred a deep wariness – "the Vietnam Syndrome" – about military intervention. The war chastened many Cold Warriors, teaching them the wisdom of humility in foreign affairs. It demolished the domino-theory logic that had transformed the moderate policy of containment into an untenable duty to police the world for Communist influence.

But the Vietnam Syndrome had harmful consequences, too. If it rightly showed many liberals that the Nicaraguan Sandinistas posed no threat to the United States, it also blinded them to the wisdom of such interventions as the first Gulf War, which stopped a regional menace from taking over its neighbors, or the Balkan interventions, which saved thousands of Muslims. And the Vietnam Syndrome also saddled the Democratic party with a reputation as soft on defense, which Republicans have regularly exploited at the polls.

Along with the Vietnam Syndrome on the left, however, the Indochina war also bequeathed a different neurotic complex to the right. The Vietnam humiliation naturally spawned the sorts of "stabbed in the back" myths that accompany most lost wars: wishful claims that even more American troops and firepower could have, somehow, prevailed; that only a lack of will led to defeat.

Such thinking influenced conservative policymakers disenchanted with the realpolitik of Nixon and Henry Kissinger. In the 1970s, most leading diplomatic thinkers shared Nixon and Kissinger's view that America was declining as a hegemony and had to share global power with the Soviet Union, China, Europe, and Japan. Many on the right, however, including Dick Cheney and other key Bush advisers today, concluded otherwise.

Vietnam helped convince them that America had to deploy armed force around the world more often and with fewer qualms. The exercise of American might could not only achieve diplomatic ends but also dispel the debilitating shame of Vietnam.

This outlook gained strength in the 1980s. The movie *Rambo: First Blood*, with its narrative of avenging the Vietnam defeat, embodied the spirit of the age. Ronald Reagan's invasion of Grenada didn't much affect the long-term security of the United States, but it did induce waves of patriotic pride. George Bush Sr.'s 1989 invasion of Panama similarly did little militarily but remove a thorn in the president's side. Symbolically, though, it showed that the American armed forces were back and ready for action. Two years later, after the successful expulsion of Saddam's army from Kuwait, Bush could claim he had kicked the Vietnam Syndrome once and for all.

But the claim was premature, and not just because Saddam remained in power. The Vietnam Syndrome endures because Americans remain profoundly ambivalent about the use of military force to work our will. As well we should.

Source: *The Slate*, April 19, 2004; www.slate.com/id/2099168/.

4. Thomas J. Sugrue, "The End of the '60s," 2008

Following the 2008 election of Barack Obama as the first black president in US history, the Boston Globe *invited several leading historians of American race relations and the civil rights movement to "project themselves ahead to the middle of the century and gaze back, following the long threads of American politics and society; to report on how the emotionally charged event might appear from a cool distance." Most of those historians agreed that Obama's win represented the fulfilment of social and political developments that were set in motion, or accelerated, during the 1960s. Obama "is the culmination of the political aspirations of the civil rights movement," explained Steven Lawson. In his memoir-cum-manifesto,* The Audacity of Hope *(2006), Obama had said much the same thing, explaining his own "curious relationship to the sixties. In a sense, I'm a pure product of that era: As the child of a mixed marriage, my life would have been impossible, my opportunities entirely foreclosed, without the social upheavals that were then taking place."*

In the Boston Globe *symposium, historian Thomas Sugrue also linked Obama's victory to the 1960s. But Sugrue's point of reference was not the civil rights struggles of a previous generation, but rather the vicious culture wars and intense political partisanship that were unleashed during the 1960s and which dominated American political, social, and cultural life for the next forty years. While only time will tell if Sugrue was right to suggest that Obama's campaign and ultimate victory really heralded the demise of a politics of division, his remarks remind us that contemporary US history continues to be played out – and continues to be interpreted – in the long shadow of the 1960s.*

On election night, Barack Obama addressed nearly 200,000 supporters in Chicago's Grant Park – the place where, just 40 years earlier, antiwar protesters, hippies, yippies and black radicals clashed with police during the 1968 Democratic National Convention. Alternative visions of America had collided on Chicago's streets: dissent versus "America love it or leave it" patriotism, militancy versus law and order, sexual libertinism versus family values. Obama's Grant Park celebration – just like the election of 2008 – exorcized the ghosts of 1968, perhaps forever.

Campaigns in the 40-year period leading up to the election of Barack Obama hinged on the great question that Americans, both left and right, raised in the aftermath of the 1960s protests: "What side are you on?" Post-1960s politics fostered polarization: the "silent majority" versus raucous minorities, the Christian nation versus its libertine detractors, hard-working middle Americans versus welfare cheats, small-town gun owners versus latte-sipping urbanites, red states versus blue states. This year, John McCain attempted once again to turn the election into a plebiscite on the 1960s, from his first general election ad on the "Summer of Love," which contrasted McCain's military service and love of country with beaded and bearded protesters on the home front, to his campaign's attempt to brand Obama a socialist and pal of 60s fringe radicals like Bill Ayers of the Weathermen.

In 2008, however, the return to cultural warfare failed. Barack Obama distanced himself from the 1960s, reminding voters that he was but a child in Hawaii when America exploded in conflict. The activists who protested in the streets in the 1960s and the "silent majority" who railed against them are aging out. Their passions are mostly irrelevant to many younger people who grew up, like Obama, in the world that the 1960s made, a place where cultural differences were a source of pride, not conflict. Obama – and the voters who propelled him to victory (a majority of whom are his age or younger) – inhabit an ethnically and racially diverse America. Hippies and yippies are a thing of the past, but the values of sexual freedom and liberty have entered the mainstream; they even touched Sarah Palin's family.

Generation Obama has its own issues: global warming, worldwide epidemics, the threat of terrorism, and the collapse of the financial markets, to name a few. McCain's evocations of small-town values, of dissent and the silent majority and campus radicalism, left those problems unaddressed. Obama's rhetoric of unity – of common purpose and common cause – threw the dated politics of division and resentment into the dustbin of history. The cultural warriors, fighting over law and order, God, guns, and family values, will not be silent during the Obama administration, but they are increasingly relics of the past.

Source: *Boston Globe*, November 9, 2008, K2–3.

Discussion Questions

1. What do Dan Quayle, Stephen Holden, David Greenberg, and Thomas Sugrue contend were the most important legacies and lessons of the 1960s for contemporary America?
2. What do these sources tell us about the particular ways in which the 1960s have been remembered in US political and popular culture?
3. Thinking about all the evidence collected in this Reader, what would you rate as the major accomplishments and biggest failures of the 1960s?

Further Reading

General

John Blum, *Years of Discord: American Politics and Society, 1961–1974* (Norton, 1991).

David Chalmers, *And the Crooked Places Made Straight: The Struggle for Social Change in the 1960s* (Johns Hopkins University Press, 1991).

Gerard DeGroot, *The Sixties Unplugged: A Kaleidoscopic History of a Disorderly Decade* (Macmillan, 2008).

David Farber, *The Age of Great Dreams: America in the 1960s* (Hill & Wang, 1994).

David Farber (ed.), *The Sixties: From Memory to History* (UNC, 1994).

Maurice Isserman and Michael Kazin, *America Divided: The Civil War of the 1960s*, 3rd edn (Oxford University Press, 2007).

Mark Lytle, *America's Uncivil Wars: The Sixties Era from Elvis to the Fall of Richard Nixon* (Oxford University Press, 2006).

Douglas T. Miller, *On Our Own: Americans in the Sixties* (D. C. Heath, 1996).

Sharon Monteith, *American Culture in the 1960s* (Edinburgh University Press, 2008).

Milton Viorst, *Fire in the Street: America in the 1960s* (Simon & Schuster, 1979).

Chapter 1 Into the 1960s

Michael Bertrand, *Race, Rock and Elvis* (Illinois University Press, 2000).

Peter Biskind, *Seeing is Believing: How Hollywood Taught us to Stop Worrying and Love the Fifties* (Henry Holt and Company, 2000).

Thomas Doherty, *Cold War, Cool Medium: Television, McCarthyism and American Culture* (Columbia University Press, 2006).

James Gilbert, *A Cycle of Outrage: America's Reaction to the Juvenile Delinquent in the 1950s* (Oxford University Press, 1986).

David Johnson, *The Lavender Scare: The Cold War Persecution of Gays and Lesbians in the Federal Government* (University of Chicago Press, 2006).

Susan Lynn, *Progressive Women in Conservative Times: Racial Justice, Peace and Feminism, 1945 to the 1960s* (Rutgers University Press, 1993).

David Stebenne, *Modern Republican: Arthur Larson and the Eisenhower Years* (Indiana University Press, 2007).

Elaine May Tyler, *Homeward Bound: American Families in the Cold War* (Basic Books, 2000).

Michael Varhola, *Fire and Ice: The Korean War* (Savas Woodbury, 2000).

Steven Watson, *The Birth of the Beat Generation: Visionaries, Rebels and Hipsters, 1944–1960* (Pantheon, 1995).

Chapter 2 The Economy: Abundance, Consumerism, and Poverty

Warren Belasco, *Appetite for Change: How the Counterculture Took on the Food Industry* (Cornell University Press, 2006).

Lizbeth Cohen, *A Consumers' Republic: The Politics of Mass Consumption in Postwar America* (Knopf, 2003)

Thomas Frank, *The Conquest of the Cool: Business Culture, Counterculture, and the Rise of Hip Consumerism* (University of Chicago Press, 1997)

Robert Mayer, *The Consumer Movement: Guardians of the Marketplace* (Twayne, 1989).

Jill Quadango, *The Color of Welfare: How Racism Undermined the War on Poverty* (Oxford University Press, 1996).

Judith Russell, *Economics, Bureaucracy and Race: How Keynesians Misguided the War on Poverty* (Columbia University Press, 2004).

Gareth Davies, *From Opportunity to Entitlement: The Transformation and Decline of Great Society Liberalism* (Kansas University Press, 1999).

John Tropman, *Does America Hate the Poor? The Other American Dilemma – Lessons from the 1960s and 1970s for the Twenty-First Century* (Praeger, 1998).

Irwin Unger, *The Best of Intentions: The Triumph and Failure of the Great Society Under Kennedy, Johnson, and Nixon* (Brandywine, 1995).

Thomas Zieler, *American Trade and Power in the 1960s* (Columbia University Press, 1992).

Chapter 3 The Cold War Context

Michael Beschloss, *Crisis Years: Kennedy and Kruschev, 1960–63* (Edward Burlingame, 1991)

Mary Dudziak, *Cold War, Civil Rights: Race and the Image of American Democracy* (Princeton University Press, 2002)
Douglas Field, *American Cold War Culture* (Edinburgh University Press, 2005)
John Lewis Gaddis, *The Cold War: A New History* (Penguin, 2006)
Margot Henrikson, *Dr. Strangelove's America: Society and Culture in the Atomic Age* (California University Press, 1997)
Robert McMahon, *The Cold War: A Very Short Introduction* (Oxford University Press, 2003)
Andrew Preston, *The War Council: McGeorge Bundy, The NSC, and Vietnam* (Harvard University Press, 2006)
Frances Stonor Saunders, *The Cultural Cold War: The CIA and the World of Arts and Letters* (New Press, 2001)
Trumbell Higgins, *Perfect Failure: Kennedy, Eisenhower, and the Bay of Pigs* (Norton, 1991)
Stephen Whitfield, *The Culture of the Cold War*, 2nd rev. edn (Johns Hopkins University Press, 1996)

Chapter 4 The Civil Rights Movement

Raymond Arsenault, *Freedom Riders: 1961 and the Struggle for Racial Justice* (Oxford University Press, 2006)
James Cone, *Martin, Malcolm and America* (Orbis, 1991)
John Dittmer, *Local People: The Struggle for Civil Rights in Mississippi* (Illinois University Press, 1995)
Adam Fairclough, *To Redeem the Soul of America: The Southern Christian Leadership Conference and Martin Luther King, Jr.* (Georgia University Press, 1987)
Hugh Davis Graham, *The Civil Rights Era: Origins and Development of National Policy, 1960–1972* (Oxford University Press, 1990)
Wesley Hogan, *Many Minds, One Heart: SNCC's Dream for a New America* (University of North Carolina Press, 2007)
Gerald Horne, *Fire This Time: The Watts Uprising and the Meaning of the 1960s* (University of Virginia Press, 1995)
Mark Stern, *Calculating Visions: Kennedy, Johnson, and Civil Rights* (Rutgers University Press, 1992)
Timothy Tyson, *Radio Free Dixie: Robert F. Williams and the Roots of Black Power* (University of North Carolina Press, 1999)
Simon Wendt, *The Spirit and the Shotgun: Armed Resistance and the Struggle for Civil Rights* (University Press of Florida, 2007)

Chapter 5 The New Left and the Counterculture

Todd Gitlin, *The Whole World is Watching: Mass Media in the Making and Unmaking of the New Left*, 2nd edn (University of California Press, 2003)

Peter Levy, *The New Left and Labor in the 1960s* (Illinois University Press, 1994)

James Miller, *Democracy is in the Streets: From Port Huron to the Siege of Chicago* (Simon & Schuster, 1987)

Abe Peck, *Uncovering the Sixties: The Life and Times of the Underground Press* (Pantheon, 1985)

Charles Perry, *The Haight-Ashbury: A History*, rev. edn (Wenner, 2005)

Timothy Miller, *Hippies and American Values* (University of Tennessee Press, 1991)

William O'Neill, *The New Left: A History* (Harlan Davidson, 2001)

Doug Rossinow, *The Politics of Authenticity: Liberalism, Christianity, and the New Left in America* (Columbia University Press, 1998)

Julie Stephens, *Anti-Disciplinary Protest: Sixties Radicalism and Postmodernism* (Cambridge University Press, 1998)

Richie Unterberger, *Turn! Turn! Turn!: The 60s Folk-Rock Revolution* (Backbeat, 2002)

Chapter 6   Vietnam

Christian Appy, *Vietnam: The Definitive Oral History, Told By All Sides* (Ebury, 2006)

Larry Berman, *No Peace, No Honor: Nixon, Kissinger and Betrayal in Vietnam* (Free Press, 2002)

Michael Belnap, *The Vietnam War on Trial: The My Lai Massacre and the Court-Martial of Lieutenant Calley* (Kansas University Press, 2002)

Frederick Downs, Jr., *The Killing Zone: My Life in the Vietnam War* (Norton, 1993)

Simon Hall, *Peace and Freedom: The Civil Rights and Antiwar Movements in the 1960s* (Pennsylvania University Press, 2004)

Andrew Hunt, *The Turning: The History of Vietnam Veterans Against the War* (New York University Press, 1999)

Michael Hunt, *Lyndon Johnson's War: America's Cold War Crusade in Vietnam, 1945–1968* (Hill & Wang, 1997)

Stanley Karnow, *Vietnam: A History*, 2nd edn (Penguin, 1997)

Robert McNamara, *In Retrospect: The Tragedy and Lessons of Vietnam* (Vintage, 1996)

Clarence Wyatt, *Paper Soldiers: The American Press and the Vietnam War* (University of Chicago Press, 1995)

Chapter 7   Gender and Sexuality

Barry Adam, *The Rise of the Gay and Lesbian Movement*, rev. edn. (Twayne, 1997)

David Allyn, *Make Love, Not War: The Sexual Revolution – An Unfettered History* (Little, Brown, 2000)

Beth Bailey, *Sex in the Heartland* (Harvard University Press, 2002)

Patricia Bradley, *Mass Media and the Shaping of American Feminism* (University Press of Mississippi, 2003)

Winifred Breines, *The Trouble Between Us: An Uneasy History of Black and White Women in the Feminist Movement* (Oxford University Press, 2006)

John D'Emilio, *Sexual Politics, Sexual Communities: The Making of a Homosexual Minority in the United States* (University of Chicago Press, 1998)

Susan Douglas, *Where the Girls Are: Growing up Female with the Mass Media* (Three Rivers, 1995)

Sarah Evans, *Personal Politics: The Roots of Women's Liberation in the Civil Rights Movement and New Left* (Knopf, 1979)

Ruth Rosen, *World Split Open: How the Modern Women's Movement Changed America* (Penguin, 2001)

Amy Swerdlow, *Women's Strike for Peace: Traditional Motherhood and Radical Politics in the 1960s* (University of Chicago Press, 1993)

Chapter 8   Conservatism and the New Right

John Andrew, *The Other Side of the Sixties: Young Americans for Freedom and the Rise of Conservative Politics* (Rutgers University Press, 1997)

Mary Brennan, *Turning Right in the Sixties: The Conservative Capture of the GOP* (University of North Carolina Press, 1995)

Dan T. Carter, *Politics of Rage: George Wallace, the Origins of New Conservatism and the Transformation of American Politics* (Louisiana State University Press, 1996)

Donald Critchlow, *Phyllis Schlafly and Grassroots Conservatism* (Princeton University Press, 2005)

Thomas and Mary Edsall, *Chain Reaction: The Impact of Race, Rights and Taxes on American Politics* (Norton, 1992)

Matthew Lassiter, *The Silent Majority: Suburban Politics in the Sunbelt South* (Princeton University Press, 2005)

Robert Mason, *Richard Nixon and the Quest for a New Majority* (North Carolina University Press, 2004)

Lisa McGirr, *Suburban Warriors: The Origins of the New American Right* (Princeton University Press, 2002)

Rick Perlstein, *Before the Storm: Barry Goldwater and the Unmaking of an American Consensus* (Hill & Wang, 2001)

Jonathan Schoenwald, *A Time for Choosing: The Rise of Modern Conservatism* (Oxford University Press, 2001)

Chapter 9   Science, Technology, and the Environment

Nicholas Bloom, *Suburban Alchemy: 1960s New Towns and the Transformation of the American Dream* (Ohio State University Press, 2001)

Robert Gottleib, *Forcing the Spring: The Transformation of the American Environmental Movement*, rev. edn (Island, 2005)

Gene Kranz, *Failure is Not an Option: Mission Control from Mercury to Apollo 13 and Beyond* (Simon & Schuster, 2000)

Linda Lear, *Rachel Carson: Witness for Nature* (Penguin, 1997)

Martin Lee and Bruce Schlain, *Acid Dreams: The Complete Social History of LSD, the CIA, the Sixties and Beyond*, rev. edn. (Grove, 1994)

John Markoff, *What the Dormouse Said: How the Sixties Counterculture Shaped the Personal Computer Industry* (Viking, 2005)

Walter McDougall, *The Heavens and the Earth: A Political History of the Space Race* (Johns Hopkins University Press, 1997)

Fred Turner, *From Counterculture to Cyberculture: Stewart Brand, the Whole Earth Network and the Rise of Digital Utopianism* (University of Chicago Press, 2006)

Elizabeth Siegal Watkins, *On the Pill: A Social History of Oral Contraceptives, 1950–1970* (Johns Hopkins University Press, 2001)

Chapter 10   Racial and Ethnic Identity: Pride and Politics

Curtis Austin, *Up Against the Wall: Violence in the Making and Unmaking of the Black Panther Party* (Arkansas University Press, 2006)

Craig Jenkins, *The Politics of Insurgency: The Farm Workers Movement in the 1960s* (Columbia University Press, 1985)

Carlos Munez, *Youth, Identity, Power: The Chicano Movement*, rev. edn (Verso, 2000)

Jeffrey Ogbar, *Black Power: Radical Politics and African American Identity* (Johns Hopkins University Press, 2005)

Laura Pulido, *Black, Brown, Yellow and Left: Radical Activism in Los Angeles* (University of California Press, 2006)

James Smethurst, *The Black Arts Movement: Literary Nationalism in the 1960s and 1970s* (Johns Hopkins University Press, 2005)

Andres Torres, *The Puerto Rican Movement* (Temple, 1998)

William Van DeBurg, *New Day in Babylon: The Black Power Movement and American Culture, 1965–1975* (University of Chicago Press, 1993)

Brian Ward, *Just My Soul Responding: Rhythm and Blues, Black Consciousness and Race Relations* (University of California Press, 1998)

Robert Allen Warrior and Paul Chaat Smith, *Like A Hurricane: The Indian Movement from Alcatraz to Wounded Knee* (New Press, 1997)

Chapter 11   Out of the 1960s: Alternative Endings

Dan Berger, *Outlaws of America: The Weather Underground and the Politics of Solidarity* (AK Books, 2006)

Philip Caputo, *13 Seconds: A Look Back at the Kent State Shootings* (Chamberlain, 2005)

Robert Ellwood, *The Sixties Spiritual Awakening: American Religion Moving from Modern to Postmodern* (Rutgers University Press, 1994)

Amy Erdman, *Yours in Sisterhood: Ms. Magazine and the Promise of Popular Feminism* (University of North Carolina Press, 1998)

David Garrow, *Liberty and Sexuality: The Right to Privacy and the Making of Roe v. Wade* (Macmillan, 1994)

Philip Jenkins, *Decade of Nightmares: The End of the Sixties and the Making of Eighties America* (Oxford University Press, 2006)

Kendrick Oliver, *The My Lai Massacre in American History and Memory* (Manchester University Press, 2007)

Michael Schudson, *Watergate in American Memory: How We Remember, Forget, and Reconstruct the Past* (Basic Books, 1992)

Tommy Udo, *Charles Manson: Music, Mayhem, Murder* (Sanctuary Books, 2002)

Jules Witcover, *The Year the Dream Died* (Warner Books, 1997)

Chapter 12   The 1960s in Myth and Memory

Keith Beattie, *The Scars that Bind: American Culture and the Vietnam War* (New York University Press, 1998)

David Burner, *Making Peace with the 60s* (Princeton University Press, 1996)

Peter Collier and David Horowitz, *Destructive Generation: Second Thoughts about the Sixties*, rev. edn (Encounter, 2005)

Alice Echols, *Shaky Ground: The 60s and its Aftershocks* (Columbia University Press, 2002)

Lauren Kessler, *After All These Years: Sixties Ideals in a Different World* (Thunder's Mouth Press, 1990)

Peter Knight, *The Kennedy Assassination* (Edinburgh University Press, 2007)

Paul Lyons, *New Left, New Right, and the Legacy of the Sixties* (Temple University Press, 1996)

Stephen Macedo (ed.), *Reassessing the Sixties: Debating the Political and Cultural Legacy* (R. S. Means, 1997)

Daniel Marcus, *Happy Days and Wonder Years: The Fifties and Sixties in Contemporary Cultural Politics* (Rutgers University Press, 2003)

Jack Whalen and Robert Flacks, *Beyond the Barricades: The Sixties Generation Grows Up* (Temple, 1990)

Index